Employment Grievances

and Disputes Procedures in Britain

EMPLOYMENT GRIEVANCES AND DISPUTES PROCEDURES IN BRITAIN

By K. W. Wedderburn
and P. L. Davies

UNIVERSITY OF CALIFORNIA PRESS
BERKELEY AND LOS ANGELES 1969

University of California Press
Berkeley and Los Angeles, California

University of California Press, Ltd.
London, England

Printed in the United States of America

Foreword

Because this volume is the first of what, it is hoped, will be a series of works in the comparative labor law field, a few comments about that project are in order. Acting on a suggestion first made to me in 1962 by Professor Otto Kahn-Freund of the University of Oxford, I decided, in 1966, to undertake an analytical comparison of disputes procedures in the United States with those of selected European countries.

France, West Germany, and Sweden were obvious choices because each has a well-established labor court system with special features distinguishing it from the others. Italy was chosen because it has neither a labor court system nor a general private system for settling labor disputes, which are handled largely, at the present time, by the ordinary courts. Finally, Britain was included for two principal reasons: first, because it has the widest variety of institutional devices for settling labor disputes of any of the countries involved; and second, because a Royal Commission, which has since reported,[1] was then considering a number of different proposals, including the establishment of labor courts.

A most distinguished group of foreign scholars consented to work with me on this project. They included, in addition to Professor K. W. Wedderburn and his able collaborator, P. L. Davies, Professors Xavier Blanc-Jouvan of the University of Aix-en-Provence, France; Thilo Ramm of the University of Giessen, West Germany; Gino Giugni of the University of Bari, Italy; and Folke Schmidt of the University of Stockholm, Sweden. We held our initial meeting in Stockholm in the summer of 1966, and speedily agreed upon the general structure of the project. As first envisaged, our research was to result in the publication of two volumes: the first comprising "national reports" from each of the

---

[1] Royal Comm'n on Trade Unions and Employers' Ass'ns 1965–1968, Report, Cmnd. No. 3623 (1968).

FOREWORD

five European countries, and the second consisting of a monograph
seeking to relate the findings and conclusions of those reports to the
American experience and to current proposals in this country for rather
radical changes in existing federal labor laws.

During 1966-67, the European members of the research team worked
in their own countries, collecting data and preparing preliminary
drafts of their national reports. In the fall quarter of 1967, they came
to the University of California, Los Angeles, as visiting professors,
where they taught courses in law, political science, and business administration. Most of their time at UCLA, however, was spent in a
more or less continuous colloquium, in which the national reports and
the various problems of labor relations law and practice common to
all six countries were discussed. In November 1967, the UCLA Institute of Industrial Relations sponsored a comparative labor law conference on disputes procedures in the five European countries. The
proceedings of that conference have since been published.[2]

The decision to bring out *Employment Grievances and Disputes Procedures in Britain* as a separate volume, contrary to the original plan,
was made necessary by the scope and detail of the study. Although
Wedderburn and Davies purport to "write as lawyers" (p. xii), they
have given us a sociological as well as legal analysis of the complex
British industrial relations system. Their book is the most recent and
the most comprehensive exploration of the subject, and makes an important contribution to the current debate in Britain over proposed
changes in its system of industrial relations.

The significance of this volume, however, is not limited to British
institutions; it also raises fundamental issues of industrial relations
policy for many other countries, especially the United States. Consider, for example, the standard dichotomy in the classification of labor
disputes which, in the United States at least, has achieved the status
of an almost immutable principle. "Grievances," arising out of alleged
violations of *rights* established by law or contract, are sharply distinguished from *interest* disputes, that is, controversies involving new
terms and conditions of employment, which are normally determined
by economic bargaining power rather than by law. The typical collective agreement in the United States spells out those matters which
may be made the subject of grievances, as well as which grievances
may, as a matter of right, be submitted to final and binding arbitration. Arbitration itself, although existing in a variety of forms and

[2] *Dispute Settlement Procedures in Five Western European Countries* (Institute
of Industrial Relations, University of California, Los Angeles, University of California Printing Department, 1969).

styles, is essentially a quasi-judicial procedure; the arbitrator's jurisdiction is carefully circumscribed and his decision, if it does not exceed
the terms of submission, has the force of law.

In Britain, however, this tidy distinction between disputes over
rights and disputes over interests has never been observed in practice.
As Wedderburn and Davies demonstrate, every dispute, regardless of
its theoretical classification, is treated simply as a problem to be solved
by the most effective means at hand. Thus, a claim clearly outside the
scope of a collective agreement will not be rejected for that reason; it
may, indeed, be settled by adding a new provision to that agreement.
To horrified American traditionalists, this represents the improper
substitution of "negotiation" for "adjudication," the disposition of a
dispute over "interests" under a procedure that should be reserved
exclusively for disputes over "rights."

Criticisms of this sort reflect an inability to appreciate that particular
policies and practices must be considered in the total context of the
economic, political, and social life of a country. One of the principal
objectives of this series of studies is to dispel some of the widespread
ignorance about industrial relations systems in the six countries involved, and thereby to discourage institutional hubris or chauvinism
wherever it may exist.

The findings of Wedderburn and Davies fully support the statement
in the Royal Commission report that

> Britain has two systems of industrial relations. The one is the formal
> system embodied in the official institutions. The other is the informal
> system created by the actual behaviour of trade unions and employers'
> associations, of managers, shop stewards and workers.[3]

More importantly, the authors conclude that this state of affairs is, on
the whole, a satisfactory one which should not be drastically altered.
In addition, they make it clear that, in their view, informal methods
of disputes settlement work better than formal ones. Their comments
about the new industrial tribunals, or more particularly about those
established under the Redundancy Payments Act of 1965, suggest that
this move "toward rather than away from the judicial method in employment disputes" (p. 243) was a step in the wrong direction.

Formal and relatively legalistic arbitration, on the American model,
also is not favored by Wedderburn and Davies. Their informative and
often entertaining discussion and analysis of private machinery for

---

[3] Royal Comm'n on Trade Unions and Employers' Ass'ns 1965–1968, Report,
at 12.

vii

disputes settlement, as well as of public procedures of conciliation, arbitration, and inquiry, lead them to conclude that informality and flexibility work best. Their hero is Mr. Jack Scamp, an industrial relations specialist, who, despite his connection with big industry (he is currently personnel director of General Electric Co., Ltd.), achieved considerable success in settling difficult labor disputes. Scamp's personality and methods can best be described to American students and practitioners of industrial relations as an amalgam of Harry Shulman, Cyrus Ching, and George W. Taylor.

The authors note with approval the relatively small amount of participation by lawyers in dispute settlement; favor tripartite "committee meetings" rather than "hearings" or "courts" as the appropriate forum for airing controversies; express no concern because an arbitrator went beyond his "terms of reference" (submission agreement) in order to get to the heart of the dispute; and endorse a disputes procedure that permits the utmost freedom to employ conciliation and mediation. They also prefer arbitration awards without supporting opinions, on the grounds that the latter may exacerbate the dispute rather than settle it, and, in addition, may tend to create precedents, which they think should not be rigidly adhered to in industrial relations.

Doubtless, many American and British readers will disagree with some or all of the views expressed by Wedderburn and Davies. They cannot, however, ignore the tremendous amount of factual material, which the authors have presented with commendable objectivity. What we are shown in a panoramic view of the British industrial relations system at work, from the local plant level to the High Court. Considering the broad scope of the study, it is remarkable that it has also achieved so much depth.

Today, it is fashionable in the United States to characterize the British system of industrial relations as an unmitigated disaster, and to blame it for most of the economic problems which beset that country. The judgment of the British people on this indictment will be reflected, at least partially, in statutory changes in existing labor laws. Americans, however, would be better advised to reexamine their own disputes procedures in the light of the information and commentary presented in the Wedderburn-Davies study. We should be reminded, for example, that the techniques of Mr. Scamp resemble those employed by impartial umpires or chairmen in some of our older collective bargaining systems, and that the sharp theoretical line between disputes over rights and disputes over interests is often somewhat blurred in practice. And we should remember that these disparities between theory and practice result from the pragmatic judgment of the parties themselves that rigid adherance to formal distinctions sometimes prevent the resolution of urgent problems.

Of particular interest to Americans are the findings by Wedderburn and Davies on the operation to date of the British industrial tribunals established to adjudicate claims arising under the Redundancy Payments Act of 1965. Those findings and the authors' observations are recommended for study by advocates of the establishment of labor courts in the United States. It is true, of course, that the types of labor courts so far proposed for this country would differ markedly in structure and function from the British industrial tribunals; the point is that they would embody, to an even greater extent than do the British tribunals, the principle of formal, legalistic adjudication of employment disputes. Whether that system would be better than the one we now have is a debatable question; but we ought not to consider taking such a drastic step without first examining the experience in Britain and in the other countries included in these studies.

Several organizations and a number of persons have helped to make it possible for my colleagues and me to carry out our research and to publish the results. The project has been financed largely by the UCLA Committee on International and Comparative Studies, out of a Ford Foundation grant to the University of California, Los Angeles. Supplementary support for my own research in this country was provided by the Walter E. Meyer Research Institute of Law. Without this assistance, the project could not have been undertaken. I also acknowledge with thanks the generosity of the firm of Seyfarth, Shaw, Fairweather & Geraldson, of Chicago, Illinois, which kindly made available to my colleagues and me, in advance of publication, a series of comparative studies of labor law and related practices and procedures in selected European countries.[4] Finally, I should note that the UCLA Institute of Industrial Relations provided space, secretarial assistance, and some financial support for the project, and that our Institute editor, Felicitas Hinman, has been of invaluable assistance in preparing the manuscripts for publication.

BENJAMIN AARON
Professor of Law and Director,
Institute of Industrial Relations, UCLA

---

[4] Two of these studies have since been published: *Labor Relations and the Law in the United Kingdom and the United States* (Ann Arbor: University of Michigan, 1968), and *Labor Relations and the Law in Belgium and the United States* (Ann Arbor: University of Michigan, 1969).

Preface

T he study that follows forms part of an international research project organized by Professor Benjamin Aaron between 1965 and 1967, with the assistance of the UCLA Committee on International and Comparative Studies. To the committee, and especially to Professor Aaron, we owe a debt of gratitude. Professor Aaron has been a source of constant encouragement and assistance to us in the midst of many difficulties, and we have benefited greatly from his initiation and guidance of the whole project. We also owe much to the many discussions with our European colleagues in the project, Professors Xavier Blanc-Jouvan, Gino Giugni, Thilo Ramm, and Folke Schmidt.

It was not easy to describe the processing of employment disputes in Britain in a way that made sense by way of a comparison with "grievance arbitration" in the United States—and that was the starting point of the project. Initially we encountered two difficulties: (1) the irrelevance of law and legal thinking in Britain to many of the issues that arise in such arbitration; and (2) the paucity of factual material about what actually happens in regard to British employment grievances. We have tried to assess the first and, where possible, remedy the second. During 1967, we were fortunate in having access to the first results of research conducted for the Royal Commission on Trade Unions and Employers' Associations; and, wherever possible, we built on that firm base to describe the British position.

The text that follows was completed in January 1968 at the conclusion of the international seminar held in the Institute of Industrial Relations, University of California, Los Angeles. We have thought it right to add only two features to the study as it then stood. First, where they have introduced developments of primary importance, we have tried to incorporate major subsequent changes in, or decisions concerning, the law in the footnotes (usually in brackets) or on the relevant page of the text. Second, we have amended the final section summarizing our conclusions to present a short account of the Report of the Royal Commission which appeared in June 1968. In so doing, we have been able to compare our own suggestions with those reached by the commission and to offer to readers a brief commentary on the report in the light of our own research.

We write as lawyers. To the English reader, it may well seem odd that a subject which in practice has such little relationship with the law should be studied by academic lawyers. The American reader will be less surprised, though he will probably be startled by the picture revealed. We have been encouraged by the helpful contacts with our American and European colleagues (which have been for us one of the most beneficial fruits of this project) to believe that, whatever the relationship in any particular system between industrial relations and the law, the lawyer who fails to investigate not merely black letter labor law but also the dynamics of his own system of labor relations is likely not merely to be ignorant of reality but even to make interventions that have effects harmful both to that system and to the standing of the very law itself. The academic labor lawyer, we believe, owes to his subject the duty of avoiding that error. While we expect, therefore, that our colleagues in the fields of industrial sociology, industrial relations, and other social sciences will discover defects in what follows, we offer the study to them, as well as to our fellow lawyers on both sides of the Atlantic, as an attempt to look at a critical area of British social experience from a legal standpoint, and to relate it to the problems we have discussed with our American and European colleagues whose accompanying volume will form an integral part of the project. All the systems we discussed had at least this in common: the remedying of employees' grievances is an absorbing and growing problem of advanced industrial societies. We address ourselves, therefore, to the question: What part does and can the law play in that process?

We would like to thank warmly for their continuous assistance the officials of the Ministry of Labour without whose kind help parts of this study could not have been made. Similarly we are greatly in the debt of the President and the Central Office of the Industrial Tribunals, and of the Royal Commission on Trade Unions and Employers' Associations (especially its secretariat and research department). Others to whom we are deeply grateful for help, and for information unavailable elsewhere, are: the Railways Board; Trades Union Congress; General Post Office; Post Office Engineering Union; Post Office Workers Union; Transport and General Workers Union; National Joint Council for the Building Industry; Motor Industry Joint Labour Council; Ford Motor Company; Firestones, Ltd.; President and Secretary of the Industrial Court; British Transport Docks Board; various arbitrators who must remain anonymous; Mr. M. Plumridge; Mr. E. Fletcher; the chairmen of the Industrial Tribunals for England and Wales; and the National Coal Board. None of these persons, of course, bears any responsibility whatever for views or conclusions expressed in this study. Material based upon confidential disclosures has throughout been presented so as to preserve the anonymity of any parties involved.

We wish to add our gratitude to Miss G. Hurley, of the London School of Economics, and to all the staff of the Institute of Industrial Relations, Los Angeles, for their generous help with typing and assembling the manuscript. For defects that remain we are, of course, responsible. We repeat, however, that (except for the appendix and certain additional footnotes) the text represents the results of our research concluded in January 1968.

K. W. WEDDERBURN
P. L. DAVIES

The London School of Economics,
London University.

Contents

Introduction

Labor law[1] in Britain has to most observers an odd appearance. In particular, two factors complicate the explanation to a legal audience of the practices governing settlement of British employment disputes. Both relate to the paucity of legalism in the system—for there *is* a "system" whatever be the appearance.

First, law has played very little part at all in the ordering and regulation of modern collective labor relations in Britain. Collective bargaining has grown up into a nationwide institution; yet "it owes very little to the law and is often ignored by the law."[2] The system has been "voluntary." The law, as Professor O. Kahn-Freund has it, "abstains" from industrial relations as far as possible. "All statutory methods of fixing wages and other conditions of employment are by the law itself considered as a second best. All British labour legislation is, in a sense, a gloss or a footnote to collective bargaining—or at least was so until the Prices and Incomes Acts, 1966 to 1968."[3] It is indeed true that "when British industrial relations are compared with those of the other democracies they stand out because they are so little regulated by law."[4] There is not even a legal duty upon employers to bargain (apart from the loose and scarcely enforceable statutes of the nationalized industries). The collective agreement is generally understood not to be itself legally enforceable as a contract. There are no labor courts, no statutory works councils.

One result of this legal "absention" from collective questions which

---

[1] The law as stated is that which applies to England unless otherwise specified. The effective structure is usually similar in Scotland, the differences between the two systems in labor law being usually more linguistic than substantial.

[2] K. W. Wedderburn, *The Worker and the Law* (1965), p. 13.

[3] *The System of Industrial Relations in Great Britain*, ed. Flanders and Clegg (1954), p. 66. See too his valuable lecture on "Labour Law," in *Law and Opinion in England in the 20th Century*, ed. Ginsberg, p. 215.

[4] E. H. Phelps Brown, *The Growth of British Industrial Relations* (1959), p. 355.

1

is of great moment to our subject is the paradoxical importance in the system of British labor law of the *individual* contract of employment. As we shall see, it is through actions based upon that contract or complaints related to its breach that employment disputes could most often come before the ordinary courts. Grievances, however, are rarely pursued by use of legal machinery. Aggrieved workers seek their shop steward rather than a solicitor; and their cases will invariably be processed not by way of writs and lawyers but through the maze of varied voluntary "procedures" established by collective agreements, which serve for their solution in different ways in different industries. Only recently has information begun to be available about the use of those procedures; and an attempt is made later in chapter 7 to examine their use and their relationship to legal sanction.

This leads to the second factor. In most systems of labor law a sharp distinction is drawn between "conflicts of rights" and "conflicts of interest." In an Australian appeal to the Privy Council, Viscount Simonds approved of the "essential difference" between "the ascertainment, declaration and enforcement of the rights and liabilities of the parties as they exist," and the job of an arbitrator whose function "in relation to industrial disputes is to ascertain and declare, but not to enforce, what in the opinion of the arbitrator ought to be the respective rights and liabilities of the parties in relation to each other."[5] English law knows of this distinction at the individual level: a worker suing for wages due under his employment contract is not to be put in the same category as a worker claiming a wage increase. But when we turn to the realities of industrial life—that is to say, to the collective level— the modern practice of British industrial relations has largely ignored the distinction. Thus, we shall see the critical definition of a "trade dispute" pays no attention to this distinction. Furthermore, the all-important voluntary procedural agreements do not usually observe it. As Allan Flanders puts it:

> Most important perhaps is our lack of concern for the distinction between conflicts of interests and conflicts of right which is fundamental in European labour law or between negotiation and grievance procedure as in the United States. So long as the agreed disputes procedure is followed through its various stages we are not particularly interested in whether new substantive rules are being made or old ones applied; the main thing is to find an acceptable and, if possible, a durable compromise by means of direct negotiation between respresentatives of the two sides.[6]

---

[5] *Attorney General for Australia* v. *The Queen and the Boilermakers Society for Australia* [1957] A.C. 288, at p. 310, quoting Rich and Isaacs, JJ.
[6] *Industrial Relations—What is Wrong with the System?* (1965), p. 28.

In this the British system may show at once a great wisdom and a certain tension. Certainly one of the questions facing the Royal Commission on Trade Unions and Employers' Associations,[7] appointed in February 1965, under Lord Donovan, was whether to recommend the introduction of such a legal distinction into areas of British collective labor relations.

The reasons for these two factors can be understood only in the light of the history and context of British labor law. One consequence of them is that there is no neatly packaged system for the writer to describe. One can only describe the various ways in which an employment dispute in Britain *may* be processed. As a result, this work is divided into four parts: The General Legal Framework, Collective Bargaining and Procedure Clauses, Machinery Provided by Law to Assist in the Resolution of Disputes, and New Tribunals.

---

[7] The commission's report (CMND. 3623) appeared in June 1968 and is referred to in the revised Concluding Appendix.

Part One

THE GENERAL LEGAL FRAMEWORK

1.

COLLECTIVE LABOR LAW

THE BASIC LAW

T he basic statutes that make up collective labor law in Britain are still the Trade Union Act, 1871; Conspiracy and Protection of Property Act, 1875; and Trade Disputes Act, 1906 (now supplemented by a further Act of 1965).[1] These statutes share one characteristic in common: they reflect the gradual emergence of workers' collective organizations from illegality. But they establish no positive rights for the trade unions. They are all "negative" protections against illegalities that threatened the existence or activities of trade unions or their members. Thus, in 1870 the civil status of a trade union was of doubtful legality by reason of the doctrine of "restraint of trade." The Act of 1871 freed the trade union from this burden by declaring that its purposes should not be unlawful by reason of that doctrine in either the criminal or the civil law. This apparent "immunity" from a common law doctrine was the first victory gained by the newly strengthened trade union movement. Part of the price demanded and willingly paid, and enacted in section 4 of the 1871 Act, was a prohibition on the "direct enforcement" in the courts of certain domestic trade union contracts, including: "(4) Any agreement made between one trade union and another."

The trade union movement of the time, a wholly industrial move-

---

[1] See for details Wedderburn, *The Worker and the Law*, chaps. 1, 7, and 8; and Hedges and Winterbottom, *Legal History of Trade Unionism;* Grunfeld, *Modern Trade Union Law;* Citrine *Trade Union Law* (3d ed., M. A. Hickling).

7

ment with as yet no political arm, was to make its pressure felt increasingly with the extensions of the franchise in 1867 and 1885. It sought to meet the liabilities imposed by a largely hostile judiciary along the pattern established by the 1871 Act, that is to say by the exclusion of those liabilities through what were, in form at least, statutory immunities. Thus the conviction of gas strikers in 1872 for a conspiracy on the ground that it was a combination that was an "unjustifiable annoyance and interference" with the employer's right to carry on his trade eventually gave rise to the exclusion of such forms of "simple" criminal conspiracy from *trade disputes*. By section 3 of the Act of 1875, no combination was to be indictable as a conspiracy if it was a combination to do or procure any act "in contemplation or furtherance of a trade dispute . . . if such act committed by one person would not be punishable as a crime." This section is still the rock upon which the freedom to strike in Britain is built. In form it is an immunity granted in trade disputes. In substance it gave a liberty of action within the terms of the golden formula of acts done in furtherance of a trade dispute.

It was in 1875 also that the long-standing *criminal* liabilities under various Master and Servant Acts for breaches of employment contracts were abolished. Certain other crimes of general relevance (such as "intimidation" and "watching or besetting") were restricted for the first time by careful and clear definition.[2] But two forms of criminal liability relevant to employment disputes were created which are today still law. They can arise when a person *willfully* breaks a contract of service (i.e., employment). He may be convicted of an offense if either:

> *Section 4:* he is employed by a gas or water undertaking [or after the Electricity Act, 1919, an electricity undertaking] and knew or had reasonable cause to believe that the probable consequence of the breach would be to deprive the inhabitants wholly or to a great extent of the supply; or
> *Section 5:* he knows or has reasonable cause to believe that the probable consequence of the breach will be to endanger life or cause serious injury to persons or valuable property.

Neither of these criminal sections has been the ground of any major prosecution in the last fifty years.[3] A notice of section 4 is posted in the

---

[2] Conspiracy and Protection of Property Act, 1875, secs. 17 and 7, respectively.

[3] The Gas Council, in evidence to the Royal Commission, mentioned that "only one summons has been taken out and that by the Attorney General" (Royal Commission's Minutes of Evidence, hereafter cited as R.C.M.E. [H.M.S.O., 1966], vol. 11, para. 1774).

workplace of every such gas, water, or electricity enterprise; and the trade unions concerned undoubtedly advise their members to give notice to terminate employment contracts before striking in order to avoid the possibility of breach. Various trade unions have called for the repeal of section 4; some employers wish to see an extension; but the most that the public utility employers were able to say for it to the Royal Commission was that, although it might have some psychological effect in preventing strikes, they had no intention of using it for prosecutions.[4] Some other similar criminal liabilities remain in Britain for special groups, such as merchant seaman,[5] or the police. Such peripheral problems are not discussed in this chapter. Despite the sections discussed, the Act of 1875 saw the effective end of criminal sanctions in time of peace as a major factor in British employment disputes. The importance of the change may be judged from the fact that in 1872 (less than a century ago) over 10,400 convictions of workers had been secured under the Master and Servant Acts for "aggravated" breach of employment contracts.

The response of the judiciary after 1875 was to develop certain forms of civil liability. Most of these were established by provisions in the Trade Disputes Act of 1906, which is still the modern law. Four main areas must be mentioned, though no detailed account can be given here. First, the courts liberally granted both damages and injunctions against picketing on the ground that it was a common-law "nuisance" in tort (and therefore an illegal "watching or besetting").[6] The 1906 Act therefore declared in section 2 that "picketing is lawful at or near a place if conducted merely for the purpose of obtaining or communicating information or peacefully persuading any person to work or not to work."

Second, since section 3 of the 1875 Act protected only against charges of criminal conspiracy, courts granted remedies against trade unionists on the ground that they were indulging in a *civil* "conspiracy to injure" the employer or his customers.[7] Section 1 of the Trade Disputes Act, 1906, therefore declared:

---

[4] Electricity Council, R.C.M.E., vol. 21, paras. 3137–3158. For extension, London Transport Board, R.C.M.E., vol. 5 (but the proposal fared badly under cross-examination, paras. 893 *et seq.*). For abolition, National Association of Local Government Officers (memorandum published separately from R.C.M.E., vol. 26, paras. 109–115).

[5] See *Cunard S. S., Ltd.,* v. *Stacey* [1955] 2 Lloyd's Rep. 247, in K. W. Wedderburn, *Cases and Materials on Labour Law* (1967), hereafter cited as *Cases,* p. 522.

[6] *Lyons* v. *Wilkins* [1896] 1 Ch. 811; [1899] 1 Ch. 255; *Cases,* p. 424.

[7] As in *Quinn* v. *Leathem* [1901] A.C. 495; *Cases,* p. 443; where a strike and secondary boycott to enforce a closed shop were held to be unlawful.

> An act done in pursuance of an agreement or combination by two or more persons shall, if done in contemplation or furtherance of a trade dispute, not be actionable unless the act, if done without any such agreement or combination, would be actionable.

Third, after 1853 it was a clearly established tort knowingly and intentionally to induce a breach of contract. For reasons explained in chapter 2, withdrawals of labor by workers are often a breach of their individual employment contracts; therefore, trade union officials stood in constant peril of liability for tort in inducing workers to commit such breaches in taking industrial action. To meet this area of judge-made liability, section 3 of the 1906 Act provides:

> An act done by a person in contemplation or furtherance of a trade dispute shall not be actionable on the ground only that it induces some other person to break a contract of employment or that it is an interference with the trade, business, or employment of some other person, or with the right of some other person to dispose of his capital or his labour as he wills.

It will be noticed that all three of these sections protect not merely "official" trade union action but any person acting in contemplation or furtherance of a trade dispute. They all create "negative" protections clearing the way for freedom of industrial action by excluding the common law. It was this process of exclusion which was later rationalized into the view that the law "abstained" from controlling economic pressure in trade disputes.

In one respect the Act of 1906 went even further. To the surprise of most observers, the House of Lords had held in 1901 that actions in tort could be brought against a registered union (registration being voluntary under the 1871 Act, which did not make registered unions legal persons), thereby exposing them to damages and injunctions.[8] Section 4 therefore purported to prohibit any action in tort "in respect of any tortious act alleged to have been committed" by, or on behalf of, a trade union. The exemption extends beyond trade disputes; and it was once thought to provide the "British solution of the 'labour injunction,'"[9] although this view, as we shall see, was too sanguine.

But nothing in that section protected union officials. Their protections resided within the area of "trade dispute," defined in the 1906 Act as

---

[8] *Taff Vale Ry. Co.* v. *Amalgamated Soc'y of Ry. Servants* [1901], A.C. 426; *Cases,* p. 541.

[9] O. Kahn-Freund, *System of Industrial Relations in Great Britain,* p. 110.

any dispute between employers and workmen, or between workmen and workmen, which is connected with the employment or non-employment, or the terms of the employment, or with the conditions of labour, or any person, and the expression "workmen" means all persons employed in trade or industry, whether or not in the employment of the employer with whom a trade dispute arises.

Such a definition clearly covers a wide area of industrial action, including sympathetic and secondary strikes and boycotts. Nor does it rely in any way upon a distinction between disputes of "rights" and of "interests." A very similar definition is used in the Industrial Courts Act, 1919 (below, p. 165).

In many respects this basic structure not merely remained unaltered but was confirmed both by Parliament and the judiciary after World War I until the end of the 1950's. Parliament enacted the two types of legislation which had become traditional to the system: (1) positive regulation of certain incidents of working conditions (such as the Factories Acts from 1833 to 1961 dealing with safety, health, and welfare in factories) but not of hours and wages, etc., of ordinary adult male workers; (2) legislation designed to bolster voluntary collective bargaining, such as the Terms and Conditions of Employment Act, 1959, section 8, whereby the voluntarily bargained terms for an industry may be "extended" to cover an employer not party to the agreement. In a similar category came the Wages Councils Acts (now the Act of 1959) under which tripartite wages councils propose orders which, on ministerial approval, establish legal minimum wages and holidays for workers in an industry where collective bargaining is not adequately developed. About four million workers are currently covered by such machinery; but it is exceptional in the sense that the minister will abolish a wages council (and thereby the legal sanctions) if the parties in an industry establish an adequate pattern of *voluntary* collective bargaining. The supreme ambition of a statutory wages council is suicide. Into the same conceptual category come the Conciliation Act, 1896, and the Industrial Court Act, 1919, discussed in Part III.

Only in time of war was this tradition seriously broken. From 1940 to 1951 statutory regulation imposed compulsory arbitration in trade disputes and made lockouts and strikes illegal while that process took place. The prosecution of leaders of gas and dock workers on "unofficial" strikes in 1950 and 1951 showed the impossibility of enforcing this provision in time of peace. Both prosecutions failed and demonstrated that, "in peacetime the power to interfere with freedom to

11

strike was tolerated only as long as it was not used."[10] The exceptional wartime criminal liabilities, of little value during the war and shown to be useless in peacetime, confirmed the "voluntary" philosophy that had become conventional wisdom. In 1951 the sanctions against strikes were removed; but another order (1376) was made establishing a form of compulsory arbitration in respect of "issues" and "disputes." Order 1376 was itself repealed in 1958, but the decisions of this historical period are sufficiently interesting to merit analysis in chapter 9.

In other respects, too, Parliament displayed an anxiety not to interfere in the "voluntary" system of industrial relations. The legislation of the new "welfare state" in 1946 strove manfully to maintain neutrality, by attempting, for example, to ensure that unemployment benefits should not be used to finance strikes.

As for the judiciary, from the 1920's a new attitude was apparent in the judgments. Comprehensive union membership and the closed shop were accepted in 1921 and 1924 as legitimate union objectives for the purposes of furthering a "trade dispute" and for the common-law doctrine of conspiracy to injure, the latter being justified as a proper desire to secure and maintain the "advantages of collective bargaining."[11] It was perhaps remarkable that a liberal wave of judgments, so different from those of twenty years earlier, should accompany the bitter labor relations and high unemployment of this era, which included the general strike of 1926. The tendency toward judicial abstention, however, and the refusal to develop new common-law liabilities to evade the Trade Disputes Act, was maintained, and any remaining doubts were set at rest by the House of Lords in the *Crofter* decision of 1942.[12] Here the power of a large union to combine with big employers to force small manufacturers out of a market by arranging for men to "black" their supplies (without any acts unlawful as such) was validated. Such a combination was not an unlawful conspiracy at common law, and the union officials did not even need the protection of section 1 of the Trade Disputes Act, 1906. Lord Wright remarked that the law "has for better or worse adopted the test of self-interest or selfishness as being capable of justifying the deliberate doing of lawful

---

10 O. Kahn-Freund, *Law and Opinion in England*, p. 256. [The story of the famous prosecution of coal industry strikers in 1941 is told in Appendix 6 of the *Donovan Report* (CMND. 3623), recounting how a procession of miners led by bands marched to the courthouse in "festive" mood; how of about one thousand men fined only nine paid; and how, when eight years later their union asked that the fines be repaid, it "was told in appropriate official language to forget it."]

11 *Reynolds* v. *Shipping Federation* [1924] Ch. 28; *Cases*, p. 466.

12 *Crofter Handwoven Harris Tweed* v. *Veitch* [1942] A.C. 435; *Cases*, p. 453.

acts which inflict harm so long as the means employed are not wrong-ful. . . . If further principles of regulation or control are to be intro-duced that is a matter for the legislature." And he added, "the right of workmen to strike is an essential element in the principle of collective bargaining."

The attitude was maintained into the 1950's. In 1958 even union objectives that could not be translated into cash terms were accepted as legitimate (e.g., opposition to a color bar). Conspiracy to injure was restricted to cases such as those where the combiners pursued their grievance because of a personal grudge. In such a case the common law considers the object illegitimate and the conspiracy tortious, and the Act of 1906 cannot protect because the combiners are pursuing not a trade dispute but a grudge. In most of the modern cases, however, genuine belief in trade union objects acquits the combines of liability for common-law conspiracy.

Similarly, until recently the courts have shown a tendency to restrict liability for other economic torts unprotected by the Act of 1906. Take, for example, the procurement of a breach of commercial contracts. In a case in 1952 union officials were sued. An injunction was sought against various union officials who had called on members in various trades to "black" supplies to D. C. Thomson, Ltd., an employer well known for refusing to allow workers to belong to trade unions. The action was based upon an alleged procurement of breach and the commercial contract to supply materials (not therefore protected by the Act of 1906, section 3, which applies only to employment con-tracts). The court denied the action. At every point the judges con-strued the technical rule so as to restrict the plaintiff. The defendants, they held, did not have sufficient knowledge of the supply contract's terms to be liable. The breach, moreover, had to be a *necessary* conse-quence of this type of procurement and that had not been proved. Nor had it been shown that their *indirect* procurement of its breach had been effected by unlawful means.[13] By manipulating such technicalities the court upheld the abstentionist tradition; for, of course, it is fre-quently the objective of trade unionists to interfere with commercial contracts, and a wide liability on that account would affect the whole structure of British employment disputes.

---

[13] *Thomson, Ltd.,* v. *Deakin* [1952] Ch. 646; *Cases,* p. 472. The dispute was also the subject of a report by a Court of Inquiry (CMND. 8607; 1952); below, p. 224. [In 1968 the Court of Appeal materially developed this area of liability in *Torquay Hotel co. v. Cousins* (1968), [1969] 2 W.L.R. 289 (C.A.).]

MODERN JUDICIAL INNOVATION

In the 1960's, however, a new judicial attitude became apparent. Middle-class opinion swung toward the unions, and a period of union "ascendancy was maintained until 1956. It was then challenged by the employers."[14] Concern over inflation and "wage drift," associated with the high proportion of unofficial stoppages, affected the minds of many people including, no doubt, the judges. In the situation of full employment, union strength (especially at plant level), middle-class criticism of, and employers' resistance to, the unions, and growing anxiety over inflation, we can detect, with the time lag that attends the habitual translation of social moves into judgments, a sharp twist in judicial policy. This twist affected radically most labor law developments; seriously introduced prospects of a new system with, for example, labor courts; was one of the reasons for the appointment in 1965 of the Royal Commission itself; and can best be understood in relation to the five areas of law mentioned briefly below.

Inducing Breach of Commercial Contract

In *Stratford* v. *Lindley* (1965),[15] the House of Lords, without changing the overt legal rules, took a different view of their content. A dock workers union had called out its members and placed an embargo on barges operated and hired out by the plaintiff company, which was one of a group of companies controlled by an employer who refused to bargain with the union. The company successfully obtained an interlocutory injunction against the union officials. The Law Lords took the view that the officials had "sufficient knowledge . . . to know that they were inducing a breach of contract" (the contract to hire out barges). Furthermore, some of the judges regarded the procurement of breach as direct; others thought it was indirect but that the necessary element of independently illegal means was added (despite the 1906 Act) by inducing the workers to break their employment contracts. Again, the need to show that the breach of the hiring contracts was a "necessary" consequence was either ignored or replaced by the rule that it be only a "foreseeable" consequence. The action for inducing breach of commercial contract, looked on in this light, acquired a new breadth, and later cases have shown its importance in the legal ordering of collective

---

14 H. Clegg, *The Employer's Challenge*, p. 155.
15 [1965] A.C. 269; *Cases*, pp. 405, 478.

disputes. In 1966,[16] for example, an injunction was issued against union officials taking ordinary industrial action against the practice of "labour-only contracting" (i.e., contracts for the *supply* of workers, who are often nonunion). Lord Denning, M.R., remarked:

> Even if they did not know of the actual terms of the contract, but had the means of knowledge—which they deliberately disregarded—that would be enough. Like the man who turns a blind eye. So here, if the officers deliberately sought to get this contract terminated, heedless of its terms, regardless whether it was terminated by breach or not, they would do wrong.

Diplock, L.J., added:

> A defendant who acts with such intent runs the *risk* that, if the contract is broken as a result of the party acting in the manner in which he is procured to act by the defendant, the defendant will be liable in damages to the other party to the contract.

A Scots decision of 1966[17] has shown an equal readiness in that jurisdiction to grant interim orders against union activity that discloses a prima facie case of knowingly procuring breach of commercial contracts. Such labor injunctions are, of course, the most serious incursions ordinary courts can make into industrial relations, as American experience has shown. The revival of the labor injunction led the Trade Union Congress, in its Supplementary Evidence to the Royal Commission, to ask for further protection, for example, by the extension of section 3 of the 1906 Act to cover this form of liability.[18]

Intimidation

In *Rookes* v. *Barnard* the courts were faced with an action brought by a dismissed draughtsman who had resigned from his union at a place of work where 100 percent union membership had been agreed

---

[16] *Emerald Construction Co., Ltd.,* v. *Lowthian* [1966], 1 W.L.R. 691; *Cases,* p. 492. In this case and others there were also suggestions that there might be a liability (hitherto unknown) for interference with contract short of inducing a breach.

[17] *Square Grip Reinforcement Co., Ltd.,* v. *MacDonald* [1966] Scots. L.T.R. 232 (Court of Session, Outer House). [Confirmed by a second decision (1968) S.L.T. 65. Furthermore in *Torquay Hotels, Ltd.,* v. *Cousins* [1968] 3 All E.R. 43, an English judge held that liability could extend to a case where the interference with a commercial contract had not in law caused any *breach* as such because an exemption clause in the contract made that impossible in the case of performance being prevented by strikes.] The Court of Appeal took the matter further [1968] 2 W.L.R. 289 (C.A., where Lord Denning, M.R. and Winn, L.J., agreed).

[18] "Trade Unionism," T.U.C. Evidence (rev. ed.), para. 543.

on between union and employers. After long argument, the other employees threatened to strike if he were not removed from the office, and eventually, with due notice, he was dismissed. He sued two employees (one the local shop steward) and the divisional union official, alleging a conspiracy to "intimidate" the employers (BOAC) to his damage. Previously, civil intimidation in England had been known only in the form of threats of violence or the like; but Rookes argued that if the employees *had* struck they would have been acting in breach of their employment contracts (a point which was conceded) and that threats of breach of contract were equally illegal for the purposes of the tort of intimidation. The Court of Appeal rejected the contention at common law, refusing to put violence and breach of contract into the same category, and added that the Act of 1906 would provide a good defense anyway. The House of Lords[19] accepted the contention, holding that a threat to strike could be "expected to be certainly no less serious than a threat of violence" (Lord Hodson). Lord Devlin remarked: "I find . . . nothing to differentiate a threat of a breach of contract from a threat of physical violence or any other illegal threat." Furthermore, the union official was jointly liable with the employees, even though he had no employment contract that he could threaten to break, because he conspired with them to organize the threat of an intimidatory strike. Lastly, their Lordships found nothing in the Act of 1906 which expressly protected this form of intimidation. Clearly, no one in 1906 had dreamed of such a liability; but their Lordships refused to provide a defense, as the Court of Appeal would have done, by a liberal interpretation of the final words of section 3.

Professor O. Kahn-Freund called this decision "a frontal attack on the right to strike." So it was regarded certainly by the trade union movement. An outcry arose which compelled the Labour Government of 1964 to enact as one of its first measures the Trade Disputes Act, 1965. But this statute did not reverse the major novelty of their Lordships' decision: the equivalence of violence and breach of contract for the purposes of the law of tort. What was asked for and what was given was a statute in traditional form, enacting yet another "immunity" in trade disputes. It declares that no person shall be liable only for threatening to break a contract of employment, or to induce another

---

[19] *Rookes* v. *Barnard* [1964] A.C. 1129; *Cases*, p. 503. The decision prompted many articles and comments: See *Cases*, p. 520 n. for a full bibliography. The consequences of Rookes are described in Wedderburn, *The Worker and the Law*, chapter 8.

to break such a contract, so long as he acts in furtherance or contemplation of a trade dispute.

Residual Liabilities Based on Breach of Employment Contracts

If breach of an employment contract is truly in the same category of illegality as violence, then clearly the 1965 Act does not, in protecting threats made in trade disputes, protect against all the possible forms of new liability. For example, a combination to *act* in breach of contract must now presumably be seen as a conspiracy to use unlawful means in the same way as a combination to act in breach of a statute. The latter liability was foreseen and guarded against in the legislation of 1966 and 1967 giving the government powers to impose a "standstill" of up to seven months on specified awards or settlements increasing wages. Section 16 of the Prices and Incomes Act, 1966, sets out specific offenses during the standstill period but adds: "(5) This section shall not give rise to any criminal or tortious liability for conspiracy or any other liability in tort." Plainly, if a strike is in breach of individual employment contracts, the risk of a conspiracy action in tort remains until the law is altered, and the Trade Disputes Act, 1906, would be no defense. In this and similar ways, possibilities of residual tort liabilities were enormously widened by *Rookes* v. *Barnard*.

It must here be interpolated that strikes very often *are* in breach of individual employment contracts, and the employer can sue for the breach (see p. 27). The Trade Disputes Acts have always been concerned to protect against the higher damages and injunction remedies of tort law. English law knows of no doctrine of *unilateral suspension* of contracts.[20] Suspension is possible only by agreement. Therefore, a worker who engages in a small-scale or one-day stoppage is clearly in breach of his contract. So also if he engages in a "go-slow," or he is working more slowly than contractually he should. (More difficult questions on the borderline can arise if workers announce they will "work-to-rule," i.e., to an abnormally punctilious observance of work rules, or, as a group of draughtsmen did in November 1967, obtain a pay increase by four months "working without enthusiasm!")

But what of an indefinite stoppage? First, if no notice is given, clearly the employment contracts are broken. Second, if the employees give due notice to terminate their employment contracts, the contracts

---

[20] [But in *Morgan* v. *Fry* [1968] 3 W.L.R. 506 (C.A.), Lord Denning, M.R., has said there *is* such a doctrine in the modern law of employment, contracts of employment being suspended in a trade dispute so long as notice of the strike was given equivalent in length to notice to quit.]

17

end when the strike begins so no question of breach arises. (This is the practice in some industries, for example, when official union stoppages occur in coal mining, cinematograph work, or the public utilities when the residual criminal risk remains; see above, p. 8.) But, third, men giving a strike notice do not normally intend to terminate their employment and the judges have recognized this. Reviewing the cases in 1967, Widgery, J., in *Morgan* v. *Fry*,[21] remarked that nothing in the authorities supported the view that "strike action, whether after notice or not, is other than a breach of contract." As Lord Denning, M.R., put it:

> Suppose that a trade union officer . . . says to an employer: "We are going to call a strike on Monday week . . . unless you dismiss yonder man who is not a member of the union . . . ." Such a notice is not to be construed as if it were a week's notice on behalf of the men to terminate their employment; for that is the last thing any of the men would desire. . . . The strike notice is nothing more nor less than a notice that the men will not come to work. In short that they will break their contracts.[22]

In that situation, Donovan, L.J., must have been right when he remarked, "There can be few strikes which do not involve a breach of contract by the strikers."[23] Lacking a doctrine of suspension, English law has created new risks of tort liability based on breach of contract.

"Trade Disputes"

Two other areas of judicial innovation will be very briefly noted. First, the judges have in some cases shown a tendency to construe the "golden formula" of acts done *in furtherance or contemplation of a*

---

[21] [1967] 2 All E.R. 386 a case imposing liability for intimidation on two union officials on the law as it stood before the Act of 1965.

[22] In *Stratford* v. *Lindley* [1965] A.C., at p. 285 (C.A.). See this whole question discussed in *Cases*, chap. 4, Excursus A, p. 525.

[23] [In 1968 the Court of Appeal expressed three different views about the nature of the strike notice in *Morgan* v. *Fry* [1968] 3 W.L.R. 506, where union officials gave notice that their members would not work with nonunionists after a certain date. By that date the men *could* have ended their employment by due notice to terminate. Russell, L.J., held that this was a notice of impending breach, but not "intimidation" of the plaintiff (a nonunionist who was dismissed) because the pressure could have been effected as well or better by a threat of (lawful) termination. Davies, L.J., held that it amounted to an offer to work on new terms which the employer accepted. Denning, L.J., thought that in a modern contract of employment, both sides accepted that it could be suspended during a strike so long as men gave notice of equivalent length to due notice to terminate—a finding of novel and pregnant significance.]

trade dispute with a new strictness. For example, in *Stratford* v. *Lindley,* the embargo, which the Court of Appeal held to be "clearly" an act done in furtherance of such a dispute (i.e., about recognition of the union and therefore "connected with" terms of employment) was held by the Law Lords not to be within the formula, largely because there was no dispute *about* terms of employment and because rivalry between two unions involved ousted all other elements to such an extent as to prevent the contest from being a trade dispute.[24] Such novel limitations upon the formula could, if continued, have a devastating effect upon British labor law. As early as 1921 the Court of Appeal had treated an essentially interunion quarrel as clearly within the formula.

Trade Union Immunity

Lastly, the judges have recently taken a new look at the immunity from actions in tort granted by the 1906 Act, section 4. Contrary to previous interpretations, a majority of them since 1963 have taken the view that the words "any tortious act alleged to have been committed" protect the union only in respect to past acts. An injunction will therefore lie for future or threatened torts.[25] Strangely, this would mean that the section had not accomplished the one objective it set out to achieve, namely the reversal of the Taff Vale case and the prohibition of labor injunctions against trade unions as such. Although there is something to be said for the new view on semantic grounds, the change of policy inherent in the changed interpretation of a section that touches raw nerves in the British trade union movement illustrates nicely the type of development which has led in the last ten years to a renewal of distrust of judges and courts by trade unionists. The atmosphere of the 1960's has been of the kind which caused Winston Churchill to remark in 1911: "It is not good for trade unions that they should be brought in contact with the courts and it is not good for the courts." The trade unions believed that they had seen the last of new common-law liabilities in 1906. After *Rookes* v. *Barnard, Stratford* v. *Lindley,* and the new interpretations of Section 4, they felt that the courts had regressed to an earlier age. The Trades Union Congress General Secretary, George Woodcock, said in 1964: "Really we cannot . . . be responsible to courts unless those courts are operat-

---

24 This decision is critically examined in detail in (1965) 28 M.L.R. 205.

25 For a general discussion, see *Boulting* v. *Assoc. of Cinamatograph, Television and Allied Technicians* [1963] 2 Q.B. 606; *Cases,* pp. 530, 532 n.

ing the minimum of reasonable sensible laws, related to the circumstances and functions of trade unions." This renewed hostility is one of the contextual facts that should be borne in mind in interpreting the remainder of this study.[26]

---

[26] [The new view was, however, rejected by the C.A. and the full protection of s. 4 restored in *Torquay Hotel Co.* v. *Cousins* [1969] 2 W.L.R. 289.]

2.

INDIVIDUAL EMPLOYMENT LAW

THE FORMATION OF EMPLOYMENT CONTRACTS

L egal processing of individual employment disputes in the English system rests naturally upon the enforcement of the individual contract of employment. It will be assumed that the worker under discussion is, unless otherwise specified, employed under such a contract of employment (i.e., one the common law still terms a "contract of service," as opposed to a "contract for services"). This is the normal situation though in some industries, such as building, firms supplying labor increasingly provide "employers" with workers on the basis that the latter are to be "independent contractors" or "self-employed" persons. These practices are of great concern to the trade unions, as we have already seen.[1] Furthermore, some legislation applies only to employees under a contract of "service," as in the Contracts of Employment Act, 1963, and Redundancy Payments Act, 1965, discussed below. In such instances, translation of the worker into "self-employed" status can be an easy means of evading the legislation. The vast majority of the 24 million workers in Britain are, however, employed under individual employment contracts.

---

[1] On the distinction see Wedderburn, *The Worker and the Law*, p. 32; *Cases* pp. 2–31. On the legal and social problems to which "self-employment" and "labour-only contracts" give rise, see G. de N. Clark (1967) 30 M.L.R. 6. As to directors of companies as "employees," see *Cases*, p. 21; and *Brocklebank & Co., Ltd.* v. *Construction Industry* (1968) 3 I.T.R. 147.

The ordinary "contract of service" is governed largely by the common law. As to its formation, the white-collar worker usually expects and has some document explaining the terms of his contract; but traditionally for the ordinary manual workers very little formality has attended the formation of the contract of employment in Britain, except in a few rare instances where the law demanded writing.[2] The most common document for the worker to receive has been a booklet containing the "work rules" or Employees' Handbook, drawn up (often without bargaining with a union) by the employer. In many places of work today the works rules are acknowledged by the worker to form part of his contract, the employer obtaining his signature to some such clause (to quote an actual example) as: "I hereby acknowledge receipt of a copy of the book containing Works Rules governing my employment. I have read these Rules, I understand them and as a condition of my employment I undertake to observe them."

The works rules can be of great importance to the employer, for they frequently form the basis of his contractual disciplinary rights over the worker. Most works rules, for example, contain provisions concerning smoking, timekeeping, negligent work, pilfering, safety, and the right to search employees. As we shall see, one of the most important of such rules relates to the right to "suspend" a worker without pay. Moreover, penalties will be set out in the rules. Litigation in 1964 involved an employment relationship in which the employer took the power summarily to dismiss any employee who drank intoxicating liquor or took drugs to excess or committed any conduct "likely to be prejudicial to the interests of the employers." Railway employees have been held to be bound by a clause in the regulations providing that: "All employees must reside at whatever places may be appointed, attend at such hours as may be required, promptly obey persons placed in authority over them and conform to all the Rules and Regulations of the Railway Executive."[3] In one confectionery firm, "the works rule book contained phrases informing the worker that if caught smoking or arriving late or found guilty of 'insubordination' he was liable to 'instant dismissal.'"[4] The research worker who quoted this instance pointed out that no mention was made of the shop steward's role in any disciplinary process. In most factories, the shop steward

---

[2] Including, it seems, contracts of apprenticeship. Batt, *Law of Master and Servant* (5th. ed.), p. 603. The same is true in Scotland: *Douglas* v. *Melville, Ltd.* [1967] 2 I.T.R. 100.

[3] [*Miller* v. *British Railways Workshops* (1968) 3 I.T.R. 89, at pp. 90–91.]

[4] W. E. J. McCarthy, *The Role of Shop Stewards in British Industrial Relations*, Research Paper No. 1 for the Royal Commission on Trade Unions and Employers' Associations, hereafter cited as McCarthy, *Shop Stewards*, p. 13.

would normally expect to play a part in that process in the three ways described: (1) communicating to members management concern over breaches of rules and warning of any intention to tighten up; (2) providing information as to the extent of breaches of rules; and (3) acting as spokesman for members who are disciplined. In most works with trade union organization, serious penalties would not frequently be imposed without the worker having some chance to contact his shop steward or union official and have the matter taken higher than first level supervisors; but such practices appear, as McCarthy put it in his survey of current practice in a number of firms, "to run contrary to the intention of most of the works' rule books."[5] In the very formation of most British workers' contracts of employment, therefore, a tension is created between the employer's legal rights and the institutions of collective labor relations, which are described in Part II.

The Contracts of Employment Act, 1963, section 4, made new legal demands for writing. The statute does not demand written *contracts* but obliges an employer to "give to the employee" (unless he be in a few excepted categories such as dock worker, seaman, or parent, spouse, or child of the employer) a written statement of particulars within thirteen weeks of the commencement of employment. The period of thirteen weeks means that some workers engaged upon short, casual employment (e.g., on construction work) never receive the "particulars" at all. Further, the employer need inform the worker of changes in the terms only within a period of one month. The 1963 Act demands that the "particulars" specify the terms concerning date of commencement; remuneration; hours of work; holidays and holiday pay; incapacity for work through sickness or injury, including payments; pension plans; and length of notice required to terminate the contract. Where no terms are agreed on any of these matters, that fact is to be stated. (It will be noticed that none of these mandatory particulars concern grievances or disciplinary questions.) It is uncertain what the effect of these provisions has been since they came into effect in July 1964. Some observers considered that they would tend to tougher plant bargaining on such matters as pensions, the attention of workers being drawn to them; but it is doubtful if this has happened. Indeed, there are indications that many smaller employers have not given any (or any adequate) written particulars to their employees.[6]

---

[5] *Ibid.* p. 13. This study is of the highest value in explaining British industrial practices and the place of shop stewards in them. For example of works rules, see Wedderburn, *Cases,* pp. 62–66.

[6] Research has not as yet established the point; but the writers have seen many statements that either do not satisfy the act, or are vague and self-contradictory.

Three other features of the legislation demand attention. First, the written particulars are not themselves the contract. Indeed the act does not apply to an employee who has a written contract which covers the ground of the mandatory particulars and of which he has a copy available to him. Rather the position is that, "The contract is the agreement reached between the employer on the one hand and the employee (whether acting personally or through his authorized trade union) on the other. If that contract is later varied, the particulars should be amended to include the variation. Failure so to vary the particulars cannot vitiate the agreed variation."[7] The particulars have only an evidential value; and as we have seen, a party to the contract might claim that they are out of date. Second, the act provides that the written particulars satisfy the act if they merely *refer* the employee to another document he has a "reasonable opportunity of reading in the course of his employment or what is made reasonably accessible to him." The reference will, of course, very often be to a collective agreement made between the employers and the relevant trade union. Evidence is mounting that increasing numbers of particulars make use of this method of "reference."[8] As we shall see, this does not solve all the difficulties of discovering with certainty the contractual terms; but the act usefully permits the employer to give his workers these standardized particulars after which he need not notify them individually of changes in terms so long as the changes are recorded so as to be available for the workers' information.

Third, since 1965, the enforcement of the employer's obligation has been taken out of normal civil and criminal legal procedures. Today, the worker aggrieved at failure to receive his proper particulars either at all or within the proper time has the right to apply to one of the new Industrial Tribunals (described in Part IV). An employer may also apply to the tribunal to adjudicate on any "question" that arises concerning the particulars. The tribunal may confirm particulars already issued; or amend them to record the proper terms; or, where none exist, determine what are the proper particulars (Redundancy Payments Act, 1965, sec. 38). The proceedings of the tribunals are similar to those described later in the matter of redundancy payments.[9]

---

[7] The Industrial Tribunal in *Chant* v. *Turriff Construction, Ltd.* (1967) 2 I.T.R. 380, 383. On the place of these tribunals, see below, pp. 39, 243.

[8] For example, very many of the cases in volumes 1 and 2 of the Industrial Tribunal Reports (I.T.R.) for 1966 and 1967 disclose such a practice. [For such a case, see *Hanson* v. *Wood* (1968) 3 I.T.R. 46 (High Court).]

[9] The procedure is governed by *Industrial Tribunals Regulations,* 1967, S.I. 361, which allows for considerable flexibility and informality. Between 1964 and 1966 the sanction for employer's failure to give particulars was a criminal prosecution.

Many of the applications made to the tribunals under this section appear to have been contested on the ground that ex-employees have no right to apply, a view that now seems to be erroneous.[10] It can be very important for an ex-employee to have his particulars adjusted, as it were retroactively, to amend the evidence of his contractual terms, if he is suing the ex-employer on that contract after the relationship has terminated. An analysis of the conduct of 187 such cases (in the survey described below, p. 252) heard between December 1965 and January 1967, revealed that 30 were successful, 85 unsuccessful, and 72 were withdrawn or not proceeded with by the employee.

THE EMPLOYER'S RIGHTS UNDER THE CONTRACT

The common law had a clear concept of fundamental duties which, in the absence of contrary agreement, are still implied into the employment contract. The employee is under obligations as to "faithful service"; as to skill and care; and as to obedience.[11] The first duty has been applied not merely to restrict an employee's use of the employer's resources or confidential information, but also to prevent him from gaining more from the employment relationship than his wages. Thus he has been made to hold on trust for the employer any inventions or discoveries made by him (even in his own time) where they relate to the course of his employment duties. The second set of duties was rigorously upheld by a majority of judges in the House of Lords in 1957 in a case in which a lorry driver had caused his employer to be liable in damages to a third party whom he had negligently injured. The employer was entitled, the court held, to recover damages over against his careless servant irrespective of the fact (as was the case) that he was insured against such liability. In technical terms, no term could be "implied" into the modern employment contract ensuring that the employee should always have the benefit of his employer's insurance contracts; for, as one Law Lord put it: "To grant the servant immunity from such an action would tend to create a feeling of irresponsibility in a class of persons from whom, perhaps more than any other, constant vigilance is owed to the community."[12]

More important to our discussion is the third heading. The employer has the right to expect obedience from the employee to his "reasonable

---

[10] See the decision cited in *Cases*, p. 68, especially *Mackay* v. *Henderson, Ltd.* (1967) 2 I.T.R. 98.

[11] See *The Worker and the Law*, chap. 3, for details.

[12] *Lister* v. *Romford Ice and Cold Storage* [1957] A.C. 555, at p. 579; *Cases*, p. 75.

lawful orders." The right to give such orders is not affected by the employer's knowledge that the employee's trade union has already ordered its members not to do the act in question. Recent decisions have clearly rejected the notion that the latter is at all relevant. Even in a case where there were daily hirings and the employer knew of the union's orders, the court rejected the contention that employment was continued on the condition that the employer gave no inconsistent instructions.[13] A number of modern legal disputes have involved the employer's rights to order the worker to work elsewhere than at his normal place of work or in a different capacity. Such disputes usually involve an examination of the terms under which the employee was engaged. If he was engaged as a "chargeman," then to order him to work as a "fitter" may be, in law, to dismiss him (e.g., for the purposes of the Redundancy Payments Act, 1965).[14] But if the worker is employed as a "traveling man," or as a general production worker who can be switched from workshop to workshop, an order to move may be legitimate.[15] But the employer must take care. Even when it was arguable (though not proved) that the worker's employment contract included a condition of the collectively agreed working rules stating: "At the discretion of the employer an operative may be transferred at any time during the period of his employment from one job to another," an employer was held to have *dismissed* an operator to whom he sent a notice saying: "We regret . . . we shall have no further work in the Sussex area [where he worked]. But we can offer you continuation of employment with similar conditions in [other areas] . . . ." This was, the court held, a dismissal and offer of reengagement because the employer had not sought even to invoke the working rule condition.[16]

If it be asked what is the sanction whereby the employer can enforce his right to the performance of these obligations, the answer discloses a dichotomy between law and practice which will be encountered again and again in the British system. In practice, one recent study of the auto industry reported the

---

13 *Stratford* v. *Lindley* [1965] A.C. 269; *Cases*, p. 478. [But in *Morgan* v. *Fry* [1968] 3 W.L.R. 506, Davies, L.J., seemed prepared to apply this analysis to a notice threatening withdrawal of labor unless the employer refrained from employing nonunion men.]

14 *Adsett* v. *C. H. Bailey, Ltd.* (1967) 2 I.T.R. 273.

15 *Bounds* v. *Smith* (1966) 1 I.T.R. 53; *Stannard* v. *Dexion, Ltd.* (1966) 1 I.T.R. 274; See *Cases*, p. 223 *et seq.* for such decisions of the tribunals. [See too now *McCaffrey* v. *Jeavons* (1967) 2 I.T.R. 636 (High Court).]

16 *McCulloch, Ltd.,* v. *Moore* (1967) 2 I.T.R. 289 (High Court appeal from Industrial Tribunal; see below, p. 258).

"most common sanctions" are "verbal admonitions"—or "bollickings" —*in situ,* and there is normally no record of these . . . . But continued incompetence or breaches of regulations may land a worker "in the office"; he reports to the departmental manager, who warns him in the presence of the foreman and his own shop steward, while the warning is recorded. These records are essential evidence where the final sanction of dismissal may be resorted to, or where a case may be appealed to the Personnel Office.[17]

Some rules will be rigidly enforced; others not; and sometimes management will "tighten up." The authors comment "discipline generally—although real—is often handled superficially and cynically as a kind of game by both sides." Another recent study emphasizes the gradations of sanctions that can be applied in *practice* by both sides on the factory floor, within the framework of, but without reference to, the legal position. For example, in one firm "overtime restrictions among one group of workers were met by the cancellation of all overtime in the plant until the group concerned gave an undertaking that 'reasonable amounts of overtime would be forthcoming.' "[18]

The employer's legal remedies are rather different. He retains, it is true, the right to dismiss the worker, either summarily for certain breaches, or always on giving due notice, without vouchsafing any reason at all, which is, after all, the final remedy in an employment relationship. But he cannot ordinarily obtain any order from the court for performance of the contract. Common-law courts refuse to turn a contract of service into a contract of slavery by way of specific performance, and judges have regularly refused to grant "an injunction compelling an employer to continue a workman in his employment or to oblige a workman to work for an employer."[19] Two rare quasi-exceptions may be noted. First the statute book still includes sections 3 to 5 of the Employers and Workmen Act, 1875, which gives a special jurisdiction to magistrates' courts in cases between employers and workmen involving amounts up to £10 ($24) or in apprenticeship matters, and to the County Courts (whose normal limit of jurisdiction since January 1, 1966, is a money claim of £500). The power is given here to order performance if a defendant is willing to give a security in the form of a pledge to pay a penalty if he defaults. But this remedy has scarcely ever been used in practice; and a few cases today

---

[17] H. A. Turner, G. Clack, and G. Roberts, *Labour Relations in the Motor Industry* (1967), hereafter cited as Turner, *Motor Industry*, pp. 43–44.

[18] McCarthy, *Shop Stewards*, p. 24.

[19] R. v. *National Arbitration Tribunal, ex parte Horatio Crowther, Ltd.* [1948] 1 K. B. 424, p. 431.

appear in the magistrates' courts, since inflation has altered the meaning of the £10 limit and legal aid is available to workers who wish to sue in the County Courts. The 1875 Act is, in truth, virtually a dead letter in respect of this jurisdiction.

The second exception arises in the case of the servant who has given an independent "negative" promise (e.g., *not* to do something during his period of service). In such a case the ordinary civil courts (County Court or High Court) will grant an injunction enforcing that promise *so long as* to do so does not amount in the result as specific performance of the whole contract. Thus, when in 1937, Bette Davis had agreed to act exclusively for a certain period for one company and not for any other, the company obtained an injunction preventing her from breaking the latter part of the agreement since this would not compel her to perform the contract: "She will not be driven although she may be tempted," said the court, "to perform the contract."

Neither of these exceptions is likely to be of great relevance today in an employment dispute. Where, for example, workers have engaged in a limited or indefinite withdrawal of labor, the employer can usually treat this as a breach entitling him to discharge, as we shall see. But usually he "waives" his right to do so because, as Lord Donovan once put it, "he does not want to lose his labour force; he simply wants to resist the claim"; and once having waived his right to terminate the contract, he cannot normally go back on it. He will be left with a claim for damages. How much can he recover? The matter was tested in the Court of Appeal (to which appeals from both the High Court in London and the local County Courts go) in *National Coal Board v. Galley* (1958).[20] A group of safety deputies in the coal mines had refused to work Saturday shifts. The employers alleged that this broke an agreement to "work such days . . . as may reasonably be required by management." The court held that this phrase was not too ambiguous to enforce (all contractual terms must satisfy minimum requirements as to their clarity) and the court could say whether management was being reasonable in demanding Saturday shifts, deciding that here it was reasonable. The absence of the deputies meant that the whole mine had to close, until substitutes were brought in at a cost of £3 18s 2d per man. The loss of production was very great. But the court held that in an action for breach of contract (as opposed to tort) the damages against each of the defendants could not include loss of profits (as the trial judge had held), but must be limited to £3 18s 2d, the cost of the substitute. If they had been productive

---

[20] [1958] 1 W.L.R. 16; *Cases*, p. 184.

workers, the measure of damages against each would have been the actual output lost by his *personal* absence less the expenses that would have been incurred in obtaining it. Thus the employer's damages will be limited against each striker, and he will not be able to pick out the ringleaders and sue them for large sums for breach of their employment contracts. In this respect, the old common-law rules on measure of damages, confirmed in *N.C.B.* v. *Galley,* operate in England with a function similar to that of the Swedish rules limiting damages against individual workers.

The low amount recoverable has not, however, been the only reason employers have been slow to sue workers in the courts. The paucity of such actions in England is so well known as to need no statistical proof. Indeed, employers who have appeared before the Royal Commission asking for new rights to claim monetary penalties against strikers have been reminded that, since the Trade Disputes Act does not protect the breach of employment contract itself, they already have the right to sue workers in this way. For example, the London Transport Board representative said:

> I do not think that we have ever summoned anybody in this particular way [*Professor Kahn-Freund*]: This is of course not the criminal law but it is the law of contract and you have not in fact used this weapon: Why not?—It is rare that it does affect fewer than two or three or four hundred people. You are getting the difficulty that taking proceedings against three or four hundred people of that sort may not be valuable.[21]

Oddly, the one industry in Britain in which for decades writs were issued in the County Court for breach of employment contracts was the coal industry. The practice survived nationalization in 1946 and the National Coal Board regularly issued such writs until about 1960 when a change of policy took place. The evidence of the board to the Royal Commission swung behind the orthodox employers' view that this is not the weapon to use; for example, in reply to the question:

> 810.   [Mr. Wigham]: You said a little while ago that the Board has on occasion taken action against a man for breach of contract. I think it is very seldom now that happens, if at all. Does that mean you regard recourse to law in the individual case as not worth the trouble?

The board's representative answered:[22]

---

21 *R.C.M.E.* vol. 5, p. 198.
22 *R.C.M.E.* vol. 4, p. 170.

All our responsible people are against any suggestion that legal action should be taken. If you do take legal action, you might get an award of damages which you may not be able to recover anyway. The proceedings may be protracted and it may affect agreements which are to be made with the trade unions in future. All kinds of things can happen after that. The whole basis of our conciliation in this country has been its voluntary nature, and when we see that any policy means that there has to be recourse to law, my reaction to that would be that it would be far better to pursue a different line, and that different line would be to get the ordinary person covered by the agreements seized as to what they really mean.

In fact, George Woodcock said to the Motor Industry Employers that, if the employee has broken his contract, "he is at your mercy . . . . You can do almost anything. If he is a member of a superannuation fund you can treat him as having lost his superannuation entitlement. If he is subject to a holiday with pay agreement you can treat him as having lost his entitlement." One representative of the employers answered by remarking, "It is true that we are in a position to penalize employees but in the system that we have, we have also got to pay regard to general industrial relationships."[23] These relationships involve the collective bargaining realities. Before we can turn to them, however, we must complete our account of the employee's legal situation.

THE EMPLOYEE'S PROTECTION UNDER THE CONTRACT

In matters of discipline, then, the individual employee is, under the law of contract, usually lacking in protection against his employer. It is true that in the absence of express terms the employer cannot "suspend" him without wages;[24] but we have seen that the express employment contract usually gives such rights. Even then, however, certain statutes purport to protect the manual workman from abuses by the employer involving deductions from wages. The Truck Act, 1831, still demands that an employer pay to his manual workers (other than domestic servants) their full agreed wage in cash, not in kind, and without deduction or restriction as to where it shall be spent,[25]

---

23 *R.C.M.E.* vol. 23, p. 902.

24 *Hanley* v. *Pease & Partners, Ltd.* [1915] 1 K.B. 698; *Cases,* p. 143.

25 After an amending act in 1887, the statute applied to all "workmen" as defined in Employers and Workmen Act, 1875, sec. 10. See generally Wedderburn, *The Worker and the Law,* chap. 5, and for details Fridman, *Modern Employment Law,* chap. 25. The limitation has never applied to white-collar workers. Only since a statute of 1960 has it been possible to arrange payment to manual workers by check.

unless statute expressly authorizes an exception. The courts held as early as 1894, however, that the statutes did not prohibit payment of part of the wages to a third person other than the worker. Thus it is possible in law for employers to require employees to agree to deductions (e.g., for social funds or pension schemes) so long as these are to be paid to third parties, for example, trustees of such funds. Still on the statute book is the Shop Clubs Act (1902), which purports to regulate severely the conditions under which an employer can compel workers to join the employer's own "thrift fund." The conditions include certification of the scheme and the approval of 75 percent of the workers involved. This obscurely drafted statute has been largely ignored, and the evidence to a Departmental Committee in 1960 indicated that there may be occupational pension schemes covering some seven and three quarter million workers which ought to be certified under it but are not.

More important is the Truck Act, 1896. This statute prohibits deductions from wages, or enforced repayments by the employee, by way (1) of disciplinary fines; (2) of compensation for damaged goods; or (3) of sums charged for use of materials, unless the conditions laid down are observed. These are, broadly, in the first case (when shop assistants, as well as manual workers, are protected) that the terms of the contract for the deduction be written and signed by the workman, or a copy of it be posted where it may be easily seen; that the contract specify the offenses and fines; that the offenses be likely to cause loss or damage to the employer; that the fine be "fair and reasonable" to the offense; and that written notice of each offense and fine be given to the workman. Similar provisions limit deductions for negligent work damaging goods and for sums charged for materials supplied. If the employer contravenes the act, he commits a crime and the employee can recover the illegal deductions (within the short limitation period of six months). But this protection against disciplinary fines turns out on inspection to be more apparent than real. The act prohibits only deductions from the wages the employer has agreed to pay. It does not prevent the employment contract from containing a "suspension" clause whereby wages cease to be payable in certain events, for example, disciplinary offenses or bad workmanship. Such clauses may be looked upon as clauses governing the calculation of the agreed wage. While at the stage of calculating the wage, the Court of Appeal has held, you cannot have reached the stage of deductions "because you cannot deduct something from nothing. . . . Under the suspense clause the right to wages ceases and the wages are not earned; no deduction can be made from wages which are not payable."

And "it follows . . . that such a contract is not a contract for any deduction from the sum contracted to be paid since no sum was ever contracted to be paid during the suspension."[26] This type of interpretation has rendered the act scant protection, and has increased the importance of suspension clauses in works rules. It is part of the context in which the employee's reliance in Britain upon his shop steward and trade union for extralegal protection becomes so important.

A similar point affects the employee's tenure in his job. It has been suggested that there is "strong evidence of the development of a deep seated notion among workers that jobs belong to them and that they are not to be deprived of them arbitrarily, nor are the jobs themselves to be destroyed without regard to their established equities. As is so often the case in Britain, one must look behind the formal institutions to find expressions of these attitudes and evidences of practices which effectuate them."[27] Certainly the formal law gives little evidence of them. The employee may be subject to dismissal either summarily or with due notice; but in neither case does the law give him a right to have a hearing or a reason ascribed.

As regards summary dismissal, the employer is entitled to dismiss the employee for any breach "going to the root" of the employment contract. For example, intoxication will be enough only if it is habitual and gross, and directly interferes with the business of the employer or with the ability of the servant to render due service.[28] Negligence in the employment will be judged sufficiently serious to merit instant dismissal only when it is measured against the nature of the employment and the probable, not the actual, consequences of the mistake. Thus, an ordinary worker would not be properly dismissed *summarily* except for gross or continued negligence that threatened serious loss. Further, whereas the older cases had suggested that a single act of direct disobedience would always give the employer the right to dismiss on the spot, the Court of Appeal in 1959 reconsidered the application of the principle in modern conditions,[29] and concluded that "one act of disobedience or misconduct can justify dismissal only if it is of a nature which goes to show (in effect) that the servant is repudiating the contract or one of its essential conditions. . . ." On the other hand, acts of dishonesty such as pilfering, or even the

---

[26] Scott, L.J., and Lawrence, L.J., in *Bird* v. *British Celanese, Ltd.* [1945] K.B. 336; *Cases,* p. 130.

[27] F. Meyers, *Ownership of Jobs,* Institute of Industrial Relations, University of California, Los Angeles (1964), p. 42.

[28] *Clouston* v. *Corry* [1906] A.C. 122; *Cases,* p. 142.

[29] *Laws* v. *London Chronicle, Ltd.* [1959] 1 W.L.R. 698; *Cases,* p. 147.

temporary taking of money with an intention to replace it, are still regarded by the courts as sufficient to merit summary firing.[30]

The right of the employer to dismiss summarily without giving a reason is reinforced by the peculiar rule that he need not even *know* of the reason justifying the dismissal at the time. As Lord Reid has said:

> So the question in a pure case of master and servant does not at all depend on whether the master has heard the servant in his own defence; it depends on whether the facts emerging *at the trial* prove breach of contract.[31]

This right of the employer to dismiss for serious breach, even where proof of it is made only long after the dismissal, has been remarkably little challenged even in the practice of British collective bargaining. Indeed, the basic National Agreement in Engineering between the Engineering Employers Federation and the Confederation of Shipbuilding and Engineering Unions explicitly states in its procedure section: "(g) Nothing in the foregoing shall affect the usual practice in connection with the termination of employment of individual work people." Company agreements are sometimes more explicit. Thus the agreement of 1958 between Ford Motor Co., Ltd., and twenty-two trade unions of employees states in clause 10(v): "The company shall have the right, for any reason, to suspend any employee without pay for a day or shift or days or shifts. . . . Furthermore an employee's services may be terminated without notice for serious misconduct." The Civil Engineering Construction Conciliation Board Agreement for that industry provides that "in cases of misconduct, an operative may be summarily discharged at any time." However, even such apparent ratifications in collective agreements of the managerial prerogatives which are legally secured by way of the common law of the employment contract do not normally prevent disputes and differences about dismissals, whether summary or not, from being processed through the disputes "procedures" (discussed in chapter 7).

Whether or not there has been a serious breach of the contract, either side may normally terminate the contract of employment by giving due notice (or the employer may give wages in lieu of notice).

---

[30] *Sinclair* v. *Neighbour* [1966] 3 All E.R. 988. The Industrial Tribunals take a similar view, and such "misconduct" can deprive an employee of his redundancy payment, or reduce its amount if committed during a period of notice: *Jarmain* v. *Pollard, Ltd.* (1967) 2 I.T.R. 406. [See too now as to "misconduct" *Statham* v. *Hadlow's Garage, Ltd.* (1967) 2 I.T.R. 656.]

[31] *Ridge* v. *Baldwin* [1964] A.C. 40; *Cases*, p. 153.

Contracts of employment which are not so terminable are highly unusual and need not be discussed here. The length of notice required is that which is expressly set out in the contract, or, where none is specified, that which is to be implied either from custom or as a "reasonable" period of notice. Where there are neither relevant customs nor express terms in the contract, the court may have to decide what is "reasonable." The decisions have shown that "the higher the position held by the servant and the larger his salary, the longer is the notice which will be required to put an end to his contract of service, whilst the humbler servant receives much shorter shrift; and the longer the periods between payment of wages (week, month, quarter, etc.) the longer the notice required."[32] Thus a hairdresser's assistant was held to be entitled to receive one week; a senior clerk, three months; a ship's chief officer, one year. The Engineering Agreement made in 1946 provided for no more notice than "the equivalent to the nonovertime weekly hours operating in the establishment for the time being" (in cases "other than misconduct"), or "payment in lieu" for those hours. The Civil Engineering Agreement previously quoted provided for "termination of employment . . . upon the tendering of 2 hours' notice by either Employer or Operative" during the first six days of employment; and the employer could give two hours' notice when work was not available for any reason other than inclement weather, and in other cases two hours' notice ending with the end of work on a Friday. Before 1964, the typical period of notice for a worker in manufacturing industry was about one week, especially in the case of workers paid at weekly intervals.[33]

After July 1964, the Contracts of Employment Act, 1963, introduced an entirely new floor of rights in regard to notice. Section 1 of this act states that (1) the employee must give his employer at least one week's notice after serving 26 weeks of continuous employment; (2) the employer must give the employee at least one week's notice after 26 weeks of continuous employment; two weeks after two years; and four weeks after five years. These minima may, of course, be increased by express agreement. Further, the act does not apply to fixed-term contracts of five weeks or above (although if the term falls below five weeks subsequently such periods if continuous count toward the continuity of employment). "Continuity of employment" is an important concept under the statute. Any week of work counts in which

---

[32] Batt, *Law of Master and Servant,* 58.
[33] See for example *Security and Change,* Ministry of Labour (H.M.S.O., 1961), p. 9.

the employee is employed for 21 hours or more or is employed under a contract involving at least 21 hours of normal work. Absence through sickness or injury (up to 26 weeks) or temporary layoffs do not break continuity;[34] nor do weeks where any "custom or arrangement" with the employer provides that the week shall count. In the 1963 Act provision was made for strikes to *break* continuity if they were in breach of employment contracts. This enactment gave rise to so many difficulties and problems[35] that a change was made in 1965. By the Redundancy Payments Act, 1965, section 37, it is now provided that weeks spent on strike do not count toward an employee's continuity of service; but the strike does not rupture that continuity whether or not it is a breach of any contract. Thus, statute has here introduced a doctrine similar to that of "suspension" as it is known in European systems. Time does not run during the strike — nor, indeed, during a lockout — but the employee's rights to the minimum notice provided by the act are not otherwise affected.

The Act of 1963 further expressly reserved the right of an employee to waive his notice, and to accept payment in lieu of notice; and the right of an employer to dismiss in cases of misconduct (section 1(3) (6)). Also, in section 2 it provided what were the minimum sums to be paid during the periods of notice made obligatory. The employee is usually entitled to his normal pay (without overtime) if there are normal working hours, even if he is sick or absent on a proper holiday. Where the pay varies with work done, the employer is to pay the average of the previous four weeks. If there are no normal working

TABLE 1

Reason	Estimated dismissals per year
Redundancy	750,000–1,000,000
Misconduct	333,000– 500,000
Sickness (including those reengaged)	Nearly 1,000,000
Involuntary retirement	50,000– 100,000
Unsuitability, etc.	500,000– 750,000

SOURCE: *Dismissals Procedures* (1967).[36]

---

[34] [The High Court has now held that whether a gap in employment amounts to a "temporary cessation" within the statute must be looked at with hindsight, and not with reference to the intention of the parties at the *time* of the layoff: *Hunter* v. *Smith's Dock, Ltd.* [1968] 1 All E.R. 81 (High Court). See too *Cann* v. *Co-operative Retail Service, Ltd.* (1967) 2 I.T.R. 649.]

[35] Discussed in Wedderburn, *The Worker and the Law*, p. 85.

[36] *Dismissals Procedures*, Report of Committee of the National Joint Advisory Council to the Minister of Labour (H.M.S.O., 1967), para. 7; method of calculation explained in Appendix 1.

hours, and the worker is willing and ready to work, the pay is to be the average of the previous twelve weeks (schedule 2 of the 1963 Act, amended by Redundancy Payments Act, 1965, sec. 39).

It has been estimated that there are annually some three million "dismissals" in British industry, made up as shown in Table 1. Not unnaturally some of these dismissals are bound to be made without proper notice, or as summary dismissals where the facts subsequently disclose no sufficiently serious breach to merit that extreme step. In such instances what are the remedies in law for the employee?

First, the law provides no remedy of reinstatement. This is regarded as axiomatic by courts that see such a remedy as a form of specific performance of a personal contract, an unthinkable combination to the common-law mind. There has even been a reluctance to grant the dismissed employee a "declaration" that he has been improperly dismissed, and the correct legal proposition still seems to be that a declaration is not an available remedy.[37] Exceptionally in some cases, employment has had imposed upon it a statutory status. For example, a dock worker is not merely employed by his dock employer; he and the employer are registered under the statutory scheme for dock work which regulates many of the incidents of the relationship. If he is improperly removed by the National Dock Labour Board or a local board from the statutory register of dock workers, he can obtain a declaration to prevent this infringment of the statutory arrangements, for the act is a nullity in law.[38] As was said in such a case. "This is not a straight-forward relationship of master and servant. Normally, and apart from the intervention of statute, there would never be a nullity in terminating an ordinary contract of master and servant. Dismissal might be in breach of contract and so unlawful but could only sound in damages. Here we are concerned with a statutory scheme of employment" (Lord Keith). This legal reluctance even to approach the shadows of a remedy of reinstatement contrasts starkly with the reality of its use in British industrial practice, both in negotiating procedures and in the awards of arbitrators, none of which have any legal sanction (below, pp. 135, 177).

The remedy for the employee wrongfully dismissed then is damages. What is the measure of those damages? In the absence of special cir-

---

[37] See *Taylor* v. *National Union of Seamen* [1967] 1 All E.R. 767, for a careful discussion of the point.

[38] *Vine* v. *National Dock Labour Board* [1957] A.C. 488; *Cases*, p. 41; then the Dock Workers (Regulation of Employment) Act, 1946, and the Order of 1947; now the Dock Workers (Regulation of Employment) (Amendment) Order of 1967, S.I. 1252.

cumstances foreseen by the parties (such as the special damage to an actor's chance of publicity if he is wrongfully dismissed from a play), damages are limited to the loss arising "naturally in the ordinary course of things" from the breach of contract. For the ordinary worker this will be merely the wages of those few weeks' notice he should have received. No damages for injured feelings or the like are recoverable in England for breach of contract. In a few cases, the worker may be able to show that he would have earned something more than the mere wages (e.g., if he can prove loss of an obligatory bonus, or where the wrongful dismissal deprives him of a chance to obtain a pension he might have received[39]). But that will be exceptional.

Second, the amount of compensation will now be reduced still further by two other newly developed rules of law. The plaintiff is in the first place under a duty reasonably to "mitigate" his loss. Whereas he will not be expected to take another job with materially less pay (or, probably, less status)[40], he will be expected to accept and seek reasonable alternative employment; and his damages will be reduced by the amount he does earn, or he could have earned, thereby. If the employee lives, therefore, in an area of high employment, this duty to mitigate will more or less wipe out his remedy of damages for wrongful dismissal. On the other hand, even if he retains a right to damages, the courts have recently held that the weeks' wages to which he is entitled must be computed rather differently from the way thought right before 1955. The principle is that the plaintiff must be compensated but not make a profit; therefore, if the earnings would have come to him subject to tax, the amount of the tax must be deducted (even though the sum now remains with the wrongdoing defendant instead of going to the Revenue). Again, if the plaintiff has exercised his right under the State National Insurance scheme to draw "unemployment benefit" during the period when he is without work, the amount of that benefit too is to be deducted from the total when assessing the liability of the wrongdoing employer.[41] This mystifying new line of decisions by the courts has reduced the significance of the remedy of

---

[39] See the division of opinion in the Court of Appeal in *Lavarack* v. *Woods of Colchester, Ltd.* [1966] 3 All E.R. 683; *Cases*, p. 179. The prevailing view is that "the assumption to be made is that the defendant . . . will perform his legal obligation under his contract with the plaintiff and nothing more" (Diplock, L.J.).

[40] See the discussion in *Yetton* v. *Eastwoods Froy, Ltd.* [1966] 3 All E.R. 353; *Cases*, p. 170.

[41] See on both points: *Parsons* v. *B. N. M. Laboratories, Ltd.* [1963] 1 Q.B. 95. This problem cannot be explored further here, but see: *Cases*, p. 191; for a criticism, Wedderburn, *The Worker and the Law*, pp. 80–81; and details, Mayne and McGregor on *Damages*, p. 251 *et seq.*

damages for the wrongfully dismissed employee even more than for the wronged employer.

The employee who wishes to bring an action for wrongful dismissal would probably be assisted by either his trade union or the state legal aid scheme (to which, however, he might have to make a contribution unless really very poor). It has been estimated by the Law Society that the simplest contested action of, say, a claim by a worker for £40 damages would run into costs of about £30.[42] It is true that if successful the plaintiff would recover most of those costs from his defendant; but it is readily understandable that an employee wrongly dismissed from his job would rather put £30 of his own money into looking for other work than risk it in litigation. Such actions as are brought, therefore, are either, it is thought, supported by trade union financial help or are unusual cases where the prize of high damages is a possibility.

It is certainly the general impression of practitioners that very few actions for wrongful dismissal are brought in the County Courts. (It is clear that they are rare in the High Court.) Unfortunately the published *Civil Judicial Statistics* do not disclose the types of action brought, though they do show that of the 1,553,587 actions launched in the County Courts in 1966, 1,397,538 were for claims not exceeding £100. Happily the Lord Chancellor's Department has been kind enough to collect figures (see Table 2) for the months of October to December 1967 in twelve County Courts carefully selected to represent a variety of regions and districts in England. The plaints issued annually in these courts are, on the average, 7½ percent of the total for England and Wales.

Two final points may be made concerning the employee's legal

TABLE 2

Employment actions in county courts	Number of plaints in size, per year	Nationally adjusted (percentage of total)
1. For wrongful dismissal..............	40	(4)
2. Other sums due under employment contracts*	67	(7)
3. Industrial accidents claims	867	(88)
4. Other employment actions	13	(1)
		(100)

*Mostly actions for wages due or sums such as holiday pay, usually for less than £200.

SOURCE: Based on figures collected by the Lord Chancellor's Department.

[42] We are grateful to the Law Society for this estimate. An action might, of course, cost less or, certainly, more.

rights. Some of the recent actions for money due under employment contracts have been brought about by reason of the Prices and Incomes Acts, 1966 and 1967. These are the statutes by virtue of which the government *inter alia* (1) has taken reserve powers to impose a standstill of up to seven months on collectively agreed awards and settlements increasing pay; (2) has provided employers with limited protection in actions for breach of contract of employment where they fail to pay certain agreed increases; (3) took, for 12 months prior to August 1967, powers for the minister to ban individual increases of remuneration above that paid before a date in July 1966.[43] The legislation is extremely complicated and cannot be fully explored here. What matters to our present purpose is that a group of trade unions, in particular a number of militant white-collar trade unions, have waged a determined struggle against what they see as an illegitimate interference with free collective bargaining. One method these unions have employed has been to encourage a member to sue his employer in the County Court for wages allegedly due with the object of showing that the relevant sections of the acts did not, on some technical ground, apply. In a number of cases the members have been successful. The employers, in such cases, have usually defended reluctantly, and on losing the action have treated their defeat as a test case, usually paying all the other employees in the same position as the plaintiff without further demur.[44] A new use has thus been found for the simple action for wages due to the employee.

Lastly, a statute has already been mentioned which has in certain respects transformed the situation of some dismissed British employees, the Redundancy Payments Act, 1965. The act will be only very briefly described here;[45] its working in the new Industrial Tribunals is discussed in Part IV. As of October 6, 1965, any employee (with the exception of certain groups such as dock workers, spouses, and domestic servants who are close relatives) who has completed two years of continuous service and is then dismissed by an employer "by reason of redundancy" is entitled to a redundancy payment from his employer. The amount to be paid varies according to age and length of service, between the ages of 18 and 65. The employer recovers most, usually about two thirds, of his payment from a national fund financed

---

[43] [The Prices and Incomes Act, 1968, extends the standstill powers for up to eleven months.]

[44] This happened, for example, after *Brand* v. *Greater London Council, The Times,* October 28, 1967. For an earlier action that went to the Court of Appeal see *Allen* v. *Thorn Electrical Industries, Ltd.* [1967] 2 All E.R. 1137.

[45] A full account of the act is given in (1966) 29 M.L.R., pp. 55–67.

by contributions from all employers. In this way the act crosses the wires of employment and social security law. "Redundancy" is said to exist when the employer ceases or intends to cease to carry on the business (either altogether or in that place of employment) or when the requirements of the business for "work of a particular kind" have ceased or diminished or are expected so to do. The responsibility for proving that a dismissal is *not* caused wholly or mainly by redundancy rests with the employer (sec. 9). Furthermore, the employer must give his reason for the dismissal when claiming his rebate (*Redundancy Payment Rebates Regulations*, para. 4). These two factors have gone some way toward eroding, though indirectly, the common law principle that an employer need give no reason for a dismissal.

Even if the dismissal arises from redundancy, the employee is not entitled to a payment in three situations under section 2. First, if the employer is entitled to dismiss summarily by reason of the worker's misconduct. Second, where the employer offers, before his notice to terminate has run out, to reengage the employee on the old terms. Third, and most important, where before termination, the employer offers in writing to reengage the worker on terms that differ but offer employment "suitable in relation to the employee" to take effect within four weeks after the termination, and the worker has "unreasonably refused" that offer. Not unnaturally a very large jurisprudence has emerged in recent years in decisions of the Industrial Tribunals, to which bodies is entrusted the adjudication of disputes under these and other provisions of the act. The statute is, in truth, so complex that it would have been hard to avoid a rapid growth of a jungle of decisions. Moreover, another part of the act, in order to avoid easy evasion by employers, entitles employees to claim redundancy payments where they have been "laid off" or put on "short time" (so that their earnings are reduced to half their normal week's pay) for certain periods (basically four continuous weeks or six broken weeks in thirteen). The complexities of making a claim under these sections are even greater; and one of the present writers has elsewhere expressed the view that it would have been "comforting to think that the Ministry of Labour was holding intensive courses" for the union officials and employers who have had to operate the scheme.

For the present, what matters is that the act laid a new floor of rights to the individual employment relationship. Employees can claim payments from employers not because they have been "wrongfully" dismissed, but simply because of their severance from the job. One government spokesman described the philosophy behind the bill as being "the proposition that service with a particular employer is in itself a valuable thing and something for which a man is entitled to receive a measure of compensation when the service is brought to an end by reasons of redundancy." Such a concept of "property" in *the* job, and in *a particular* job, has become widespread. At other times, ministers defended the act as a statute aimed at the relief of hardship in order to promote mobility of labor. To the eyes of some observers, the two objectives, protection of "job property" and promotion of mobility, were in conflict rather than harmony, and the act has probably done more to achieve the first rather than the second. However that may be, the 1965 Act, together with the Contracts of Employment Act, 1962, broke new ground in Britain in setting minimum statutory terms to employment relationships which hitherto it had been thought right to regard as the prerogative of the individual contract of employment supplemented by collective bargaining.[46]

---

[46] It may be noted that the vast amount of statutory regulation of employment conditions (e.g., of safety health and welfare in the Factories Acts, 1833 to 1961) has never been thought in Britain, as in France, to create legal norms that enter the realm of the employment contract. The enforcement of such statutes has traditionally been accomplished by either criminal prosecution, civil actions for damages in tort, or administrative action by the Factory Inspectorate.

3.

COLLECTIVE BARGAINING
AND EMPLOYMENT LAW

THE COLLECTIVE BARGAIN

B ritish collective agreements present an infinite and almost bewildering variety. Despite this, it has become a well-known proposition that the collective agreements in Britain are not normally enforceable by legal sanction as contracts. There is no statute nor even any legal decision establishing such a general proposition; but the writers accept this as the proper view.[1] Two points need to be distinguished in the discussion: (1) the status of the collective arrangements between collective parties; (2) their relationship to the individual employment contract, or "normative" effect, if any.

There are two distinct reasons for believing that collective agreements are not enforceable contracts as between the collective parties in English law. First, there is the Trade Union Act, 1871, section 4 (4), which states:

> Nothing in this Act shall enable any court to entertain any legal proceeding instituted with the object of directly enforcing or recovering damages for the breach of any of the following agreements, namely, . . .
> (4) Any agreement made between one trade union and another;

Enacted with the quite different purpose of keeping workers' trade

---

[1] [The *Donovan Report* in 1968 unanimously adopted this interpretation as the normal status of British collective bargains. See too the Ford case [1969] 1 W.L.R. 339.]

union contracts outside the law, this enactment has become fortuitously applicable to collective agreements by reason of the definition of "trade union" laid down in the Acts of 1871, 1876, and 1913, the relevant words of which are:

> The expression "trade union" means any combination, whether temporary or permanent, the principal objects of which are under its constitution the "statutory objects," i.e. the regulation of the relations between workmen and masters, or between workmen and workmen, *or between masters and masters,* or the imposing of restrictive conditions on the conduct of any trade or business, and also the provision of benefits to members [italics supplied].

It is immediately apparent that an employers' association may fall within the legal definition of "trade union" in Britain, and that, therefore, actions for damages or other "direct" enforcement of an agreement made between it and a workers' trade union would not be possible. There are decisions on other parts of section 4 which allow "indirect" enforcement of the contracts there mentioned, by way of remedies of declaration or injunction; but the only decision on subsection (4) in this respect finds the Court of Appeal refusing even such a remedy, with Lord Sterndale, M.R., saying, "I cannot see a much more direct way of enforcing an agreement than by an injunction to prevent a person from breaking it."[2]

Many national or even regional agreements are made between trade unions (in the ordinary sense) and employers' associations which may well be "trade unions" in law.[3] But many other agreements are not. To take but one illustration, agreements are made between a union or group of unions with one company, often a "nonfederated" company like Ford or Imperial Chemical Industries, Ltd., or with a nationalized corporation such as the National Coal Board, Electricity Council, or British Railways Board. These are not agreements between "one trade union and another." But the general view is that they are not enforceable contracts, though there is no clear judicial pronouncement on the issue because no action has ever been launched in a British court to enforce such a collective bargain between the collective parties.[4] The reason usually adopted for the conclusion is as follows. Even if there is clear agreement on precise terms (which would not always be true of British collective agreements) and even if each party contributed

---

[2] *McLuskey* v. *Cole* [1922] 1 Ch. 7; *Cases*, p. 278.

[3] On the uncertainties concerning the status of many such associations, see the excellent review by M. A. Hickling (1964) 27 M.L.R. 625.

[4] The judicial *dicta* bearing on the point are collected in *Cases*, p. 267.

mutual promises to the bargain (thereby satisfying the English demand for "consideration" in contracts), the law goes on to enforce the agreement as a contract only if the parties "intend" that it should give rise to legal obligation. But, as Professor Kahn-Freund puts it:

> The true reason for the complete absence of any attempts legally to enforce the mutual obligations created by collective agreements can, in the writer's opinion, only be found in the intention of the parties themselves. . . . Agreements expressly or implicitly intended to exist in the "social" sphere only are not enforced as contracts by the courts. This appears to be the case of collective agreements. They are . . . intended, as it is sometimes put, to be "binding in honour" only; or (which amounts to very much the same thing) to be enforceable through social sanctions but not through legal sanctions.

This view, if correct, will be seen to be of the highest importance in respect of the institutional and procedural clauses dominating British collective agreements. The arrangements for negotiation between management and union, the agreed facilities for shop stewards, the promises of both sides (which are a regular part of all agreements, as in the United States) not to take hostile industrial action by strike or lockout while the disputes or negotiation procedures are followed—all these are to be enforced in honor, not by legal sanctions. That is undoubtedly the common view on both sides of British industry. As Lord Justice Pearson expressed it when presiding over an Administrative Court of Inquiry into Disputes in the Electricity Supply Industry in 1964:

> The effect of (the collective agreement) was to make the schedule wage rates, with their annual increases, "sacrosanct" for the period of three years. . . . The word "sacrosanct" is convenient but needs to be explained in two respects. First, the three-year agreement was not intended to be legally binding, but the parties by entering into it assumed a moral obligation as is normal in industrial relations.[5]

The discussions before the Royal Commission without exception began from that basis, and the question posed has been whether the law should be *changed* in order to make collective agreements enforceable. Certainly the problems that would then be encountered would be formidable without a complete restructuring of the style and content of British collective bargaining.[6]

This is not to say that an English court might not, before these

---

[5] Report of Court of Inquiry (CMND. 2361; 1964), paras. 139–140.
[6] The difficulties are discussed by Wedderburn in *The Worker and the Law*, pp. 109 ff.; and *R.C.M.E.*, vol. 31, paras. 49–53.

words appear in print, find that a particular agreement did (exceptionally) bear the imprint of contract. For example, subject to the problems created by section 4(4) of the Trade Union Act, 1871, it may be that the agreements in the boot and shoe industry have that character. The national provisions of these agreements are based upon a trust *deed* entered into orginally on March 8, 1898, under which certain sums are deposited by the employer and trade unions to secure the execution of their promises. Although the last penalty awarded by the "national umpire" under these provisions seems to have been in 1913, the trust deed remains the basis of the agreements and a court conceivably could find in that deed under seal a sufficient "intention" to create legal obligation. If it did, however, even in such unusual circumstances, the shock and surprise, especially among trade unionists, would be severe, not least among the unions in the boot and shoe industry itself.[7] Some modern "productivity" agreements, on the other hand, have a sharper and clearer language and might with less difficulty be held to be intended to produce contractual relationships. Even there, however, the presumption seems to be the other way. Even if, as some commentators state, apart from the 1871 Act, the "ordinary law of contract" applies to collective agreements, it still seems that the employer must buy legal enforceability by offering some special economic incentive expressly to buy off the orthodox presumption.

The general structure of British labor legislation supports the orthodox view. Time and again since the early nineteenth century proposals have been made for legislative enforcement of agreements. With rare, and short-lived exception (such as the compulsory arbitration of wartime Orders), no such legislation has been passed. What legislation there is, such as the exceptional Terms and Conditions of Employment Act, 1959 (examined on p. 204) which provides for the "extension" by legal means of an agreement against an employer in the industry who is not observing terms as favorable to his work people, seems to take the orthodox view for granted.

RELATIONSHIP TO INDIVIDUAL CONTRACTS OF EMPLOYMENT

It has been suggested that the union in negotiating collective agreements is acting as the *agent* of its members and that thereby the terms of the agreement find legal expression by binding the union members as principals. The preponderance of such judicial statements as there are militate against this view, except possibly in situations where union

---

[7] On the history of this arrangement, see Sharp, *Industrial Conciliation and Arbitration in Gt. Britain* (1950), pp. 229–236. The guarantee fund under a deed of trust is "unique" to British industrial relations: *ibid.*, p. 215.

officials have negotiated special local arrangements for a few members at plant level and may truly be said to be their agents.[8] Normally, the "agency"analysis is not adopted. The terms of the collective agreement find their legal way into the employment relationship by being incorporated into the individual contract of employment. It cannot be too strongly emphasized, however, that the individual contract of employment need *not* do so. The collective agreement has no automatic effect as it does in some European countries. In two strong decisions of 1945 and 1948, the English courts upheld the supremacy of the individual employment contract with clear express terms, even if those terms are inferior to those of a relevant collective agreement.

The question, therefore, always is: Does the worker's employment contract incorporate the collective terms? It may do so in two ways.

(1) There may be an express incorporation by words in the employment contract, as in *N.C.B.* v. *Galley* (see p. 28) when the obligation to work a "reasonable" number of shifts was in an agreement between the safety deputies' unions and the employers, but the deputies had unequivocally and individually agreed to work on the terms of such agreements as amended from time to time. Such a mechanism has become easier to use since the Contracts of Employment Act, 1963. This act, enables an employer to give written "particulars" referring an employee to another document, which may change from time to time, for his employment terms, without the further obligation to notify of changes, so long as the document is available and accessible to the worker. Inspection of the reported decisions of the Industrial Tribunals confirms the impression that in the last three years increasing use has been made by employers of this method of express incorporation via the written particulars.

(2) If this practice is not followed, and the employment contract says nothing about collective terms, the latter can be incorporated only if they can be regarded by the court as customary or *implied* terms of that contract. Clearly, if the express terms differ from the collective terms, the latter cannot be implied as the terms intended by the parties. In some cases, collective terms have been read into even written employment contracts on matters on which they were silent (as in the case of National Maritime Year Book terms read into a mate's written articles),[9] and where the employer customarily applies such terms to all his workers it will be easy to imply the terms into the employment contracts. It is highly uncertain, however, how far the courts will go in *implying* into employment contracts *new* decisions

---

[8] See Wedderburn, *The Worker and the Law*, pp. 112–114.
[9] *Maclea* v. *Essex Line* (1933), 45 Lloyd's Rep. 254; *Cases*, p. 290.

(e.g., on increases in pay) of collective bargaining institutions (such as Joint Industrial Councils) even where it has been a custom of the employer to observe such awards. In 1967 a County Court judge accepted that an award of a National Joint Council (N.J.C.) Panel for local authority employees of a pay increase of 7 percent was binding on an employing local council (which had regularly observed such awards) "as soon as the award of the N.J.C. was made."[10] On the other hand, in another case, a government employee's handbook referred to his wages as those agreed on by the Miscellaneous Trades Joint Council. The council agreed upon an increase, but the Treasury refused to authorize payment because of the "pay pause" policy. The court decided that, even if a Crown civil servant has an enforceable contract of employment (which is still doubtful), the decision of this "consultative" council did not automatically become part of his contract, despite the long-standing practice of the employing ministry of recognizing its awards.[11]

To this uncertainty is added another legal problem where, as is frequently true, an industry-wide national agreement is supplemented by local agreements. Unless the written particulars solve the problem by clear words, it may be difficult to know which of the two agreements is incorporated. In one claim for wages the High Court construed the contract as incorporating the local agreement.[12] In redundancy decisions concerning building workers, where the question was whether workers' "normal hours" were the 40 hours of the nationally agreed basic week, or longer hours negotiated in "site" agreements, both the tribunals and the High Court have tended to take the view that, where written particulars incorporated the national agreement, the 40-hour week was the obligatory period and the longer hours were voluntary arrangements outside the contractual ambit.[13] There is no rule of law, as in Germany, giving national agreements priority over

---

[10] *Brand* v. *Greater London Council, The Times,* October 28, 1967. We are grateful for the opportunity of studying the record at Southwark County Court.

[11] *Dudfield* v. *Ministry of Works, The Times,* January 24, 1964 (High Court); *Cases,* p. 296.

[12] *Clift* v. *West Riding C. C., The Times,* April 10, 1964; *Cases,* p. 293. (However, in *Loman & Henderson* v. *Merseyside Transport* [1968] 3 I.T.R. 108, the High Court incorporated the national agreement into the worker's employment contract and held that a differently worded local agreement was not legally effective, being only a "gentlemen's agreement"!)

[13] *Turriff Construction* v. *Bryant* (1967) 2 I.T.R. 292 (High Court); *Duff* v. *Taylor Woodrow, Ltd.* (1967) 2 I.T.R. 258; *Caskie* v. *Campbell and Isherwood, Ltd.* (1967) 2 I.T.R. 276. See too the High Court decision in *Pearson and Workman* v. *Wm. Jones, Ltd.* (1967) 2 I.T.R. 471, where the "particulars" referred to the works rules, and those rules referred on to the national Engineering Agreement for terms about overtime which was held to be permissive only and not obligatory.

local. The matter is one of uncertainty and of construction of the employment contract in each case, which could, as we shall see, have important consequences in regard to disputes clauses.

Where, however, collective terms are incorporated into contracts of employment by custom or implication, it seems clear that the courts would resist the contention that this incorporation applied only to the contracts of union members. There is no clear decision on this question; but it is normally the intention of both union and employers to negotiate terms for the trade group concerned irrespective of union membership. As the Ministry of Labour reported to the Royal Commission: "Generally speaking collective agreements are applied by employers to their employees whether unionists or non-unionists."[14] On the other hand, where the agreement itself specifies that the union is negotiating on behalf of its *members* (as in a 1958 agreement between British Film Producers and the Association of Cinematograph Workers), or the agreement states that it "shall apply to — (i) Draughtsmen and draughtswomen members of the (union)" (Agreement between Engineering Employers Federation and Draughtsmen's and Allied Technicians Association of 1947), the inference would be the opposite. Nonunionists would be covered by such an agreement as that only if something were expressly said in their employment contracts or written particulars to that effect, though the employer might, as a matter of course, observe equal terms of employment.

It may be parenthetically noted here that the incorporation of the collective terms into the individual contract does, on occasion, increase rather than limit the employer's disciplinary powers, putting the individual worker, in George Woodcock's words, "at his mercy." When, for example, the union has agreed that those who engage upon unofficial strikes shall lose certain "fringe benefits," such a clause will be incorporated into the employment contract. Such agreements are sought increasingly by management. As a British Railways Board spokesman put it to the Royal Commission: "I am suggesting that the fringe benefit part should come in here. We cannot say, 'We are going to dock your basic pay'; but I think in our case, for instance, we could say with agreement with the unions, 'If you break your contract by unofficial strike action or go slow, or whatever it is, we will withdraw your travel privileges, your sick pay privileges, annual leave privileges or public bank holiday privileges or whatever it is.' In fact there would be a schedule of sanctions." Such a scheme was recently negotiated in

---

[14] Ministry of Labour Written Evidence to the Royal Commission (H.M.S.O., 1965), hereafter cited as Ministry of Labour Evidence, para. 48.

respect of municipal passenger transport workers. Of course, in such situations, it will often have to be part of the settlement terms of the strike that the sanctions will not be applied. To the common "no victimization" clause of British strike settlements would be added a "no fringe-benefit sanctions" clause. What the legal status of such strike-settlement agreements may be poses an interesting question. In one case in 1956, a court held that such a settlement was "not intended to have contractual force" at all, though here much emphasis was placed upon the exact wording used.[15] This was another example of a judicial desire not to give legal force to collectively agreed terms.

A problem of special importance is presented by the fact that even if a collective agreement is expressly incorporated into the worker's individual contract, some of its terms may be *inappropriate* to the individual contract for one of two reasons. First, the matter may be appropriate in substance only to the arrangements between the collective parties, as, for example, a clause providing: "The Shop Stewards elected to the Works Committee shall, subject to re-election, hold office for not more than twelve months" (Engineering Agreement). Second, the actual words of the clause may indicate that the clause is semantically appropriate only at the collective level. The two points tend to converge and create difficulty in actual cases. Thus, one clause of collective "working rules" read: "Overtime required to ensure the due and proper performance of contracts shall not be subject to restriction but may be worked by mutual agreement and direct arrangement between the employer and the operatives concerned." The employees, whose particulars incorporated the working rules agreed by the National Joint Council, without union support refused to work overtime. Lord Denning, M.R., in the Court of Appeal considered that they were individually in breach of contract because the rule meant that each man agreed not to impose officially or unofficially a *collective* embargo on overtime (as had been done) when it was required. Another judge took a different view, maintaining that the words of the clause were appropriate at the collective level only:

> As I see it in my mind's eye, the parties of the joint council round the table said: "Are we in these rules going to fix a ceiling on the hours of overtime worked by any man?" Answer, "No." . . . They then proceeded to say, by way of addition: "It is to be left to agreement between operative and employer." If that be so, it certainly cannot import into the contract of any particular operative an agreement not to limit or refuse to work overtime save for a reason special to himself.[16]

---

[15] *Ardley and Morey* v. *London Electricity Board*, *The Times*, June 16, 1956; *Cases*, p. 268.

This issue of the doubtful propriety of certain collective terms for incorporation into employment contracts assumes even greater importance if we turn from clauses dealing with substantial terms of the employment to the "procedure" clauses described in Part II. Most British collective agreements include a series of stages through which disputes and grievances are to be taken and provide that: "Until the procedure provided above has been carried through there shall be no stoppage of work either of a partial or a general character" (Engineering Agreement); or:

> The parties hereto being agreed that in the event of any dispute or difference arising between their respective members or any of them, every means for effecting an amicable settlement should be exhausted before resorting to direct action, hereby undertake not to instruct their members to strike or lockout or othewise to take such action as would involve a cessation of work without complying with all the agreements then in existence between the parties and giving the customary notice to terminate the employment.[17]

Do such clauses impose obligations upon the individual workers? There is no clear judicial decision on the matter. In the few cases where it has arisen, it was *conceded* without argument by the defendants that the procedure clauses in question were incorporated in full into the employment contracts; as in one where the clause said, "The Employers . . . and the employees . . . undertake that no lockout or strike shall take place." Such an exceptional absolute obligation never to strike at least is clear in its meaning; and if the test be that of semantic appropriateness, then a clause that speaks of the "employees" undertaking obligations will plainly be more readily incorporated than one that merely records the promise of the collective parties (e.g., the trade union on the workers side). But a purely semantic test of this kind would produce bizarre results. For example, the standard clause quoted in the Engineering Agreement has been inserted in many agreements made by the Engineering Employers' Federation. Contrast the agreement made with the Draughtmen's Association ("This Agreement shall apply to draughtsmen and draughtswomen members of the [union]") with that made with the Clerical and Administrative Workers Union ("The . . . Employers intimated to the Union . . . that they would be prepared to recommend the recognition of the . . . Union

---

16 Russell, L.J., in *Camden Exhibition & Display, Ltd.,* v. *Lynott* [1966] 1 Q.B. 555, disagreeing with Lord Denning, M.R.; *Cases,* p. 306.

17 Clause 2 of Emergency Disputes Agreement, 1927, between Building Trades Employers and Building Trades Operatives, under National Joint Council Rule 9.

as representing clerical workpeople employed in engineering and allied establishments, subject to the following conditions . . .") . On a purely semantic test the "no-strikes-until-procedure-is-exhausted" clause would, in the first case, bind individual workers; in the second, the clause would seem appropriate only as an agreement at the collective level.

It is thought that a court would not be guided only by such semantic factors but would ask whether a "no-strike" or "procedure" clause is in *substance* appropriate for incorporation. The worker is always in breach of his contract of employment if he strikes without giving notice to terminate employment. What can the collective term add to that? If Lord Denning's approach to the overtime clause were applied by analogy, the answer might be that the normal procedure clause obliged each worker not to *organize,* officially or unofficially, a collective cessation of work, even by means of notice of termination. while the procedure was being exhausted.[18] This extreme interpretation is the only way to give meaning to the incorporation and thereby make procedure clauses "normative" on each worker in the average industrial situation. Objection has been raised to this view. Professor Kahn-Freund has said that "It goes almost without saying that neither an individual employer nor an individual employee could be bound by the agreement as a contract . . . in a recent case it was admitted that the "no-strike" obligation had become a term of the individual contracts of employment but this must be quite exceptional."[19] This, too, is the view of the Trades Union Congress (T.U.C.) spokesman expressed in its oral evidence to the Royal Commission, where the Assistant General Secretary said:

> The procedure agreement is not part of the contract of employment, I think; the procedure agreement is really an agreement between the union or unions and the employer as to the way in which they will resolve difficulties which arise. . . . Really it sets out the way in which disputes will be settled. This is not part of the contract, I think, between the employer and the employee."[20]

---

[18] [Plainly, such an interpretation would oust any implied term to the effect that strikes engaged upon after due notice suspend the modern employment contract, which Lord Denning, M.R., suggested in *Morgan* v. *Fry* [1968] 3 W.L.R. 506 (C.A.) (above, p. 18). The express terms of an English contract always oust any implied terms; even Lord Denning had to agree that this would be the effect of a "no-strike" clause incorporated into the employment contracts, as in *Rookes* v. *Barnard* [1964] A.C. 1129 (H.L.).]

[19] *Labour Relations and the Law* (1965), p. 27.

[20] R.C.M.E., vol. 61, p. 2688, para. 9662.

Some indirect support for this view can be found in two legal sources. First, under Industrial Disputes Order, 1951 (repealed 1958; below, p. 210), issues concerning recognized terms and conditions of employment could be reported to the minister for reference to the Industrial Disputes Tribunal. In 1955 the Court of Appeal decided that a procedure clause was "not properly speaking one of the terms and conditions of employment at all. It is only machinery for settling a difference."[21] Second, the Industrial Court has taken a similar view under its exceptional jurisdiction to "extend" collective terms that are "recognized terms or conditions of employment" within section 8 of the Terms and Conditions of Employment Act, 1959. In Case 3059, the court was presented with a clause in the Agreement between the U.K. Joint Wages Board for Employers for the Vehicle Building Industry and the relevant unions setting out a procedure for settling disputes and ending:

> There shall be no stoppage of work or lockout of a partial or a general character but work shall proceed under the conditions prevailing prior to the question being raised until either side, at the National Conference [the last step in procedure], declares disagreement.

The court considered that these clauses were "not terms or conditions of employment" within the act.[22]

This fundamental point is, however, not clear. Two questions may be raised if the opposite view is taken and procedure or no-strike clauses *are* regarded as appropriate for incorporation. First, is the nonunionist bound equally with the unionist worker alongside him? We have seen that the normal understanding is that collective agreements apply to the former if they apply to the latter unless their language forbids that interpretation; and anyway a nonunion worker's particulars may state that the collective terms are incorporated. But the nonunion worker is usually not in any position to initiate use of the procedures, which can be operated only by union representatives. If the limitation on strikes were normative, he might complain that he had all the burdens without any benefit from this part of the collective agreement (though that might be said to be the penalty of not belonging to the union). Lastly, if the procedure clause is used and procedure is exhausted, the limitation on strike action no longer applies. In industrial parlance a strike is then said to be "constitutional"; but it is not clear whether this is

---

[21] *R. v. I. D. T. ex parte Portland U.D.C.* [1955] 3 All E.R. 18; *Cases,* p. 303.
[22] Following its earlier Award 3069, National Society of Metal Mechanics against Newtown Polishing, Ltd. (No. 2); *Cases,* pp. 359–366.

thought to affect the legal position of the striking employee. We have seen that the bulk of modern legal authority favors the view that most strikes involve a breach of the contract of employment where no notice to terminate employment has been given. If, then, the industrial parties' parlance were to be translated into legal meaning, it could only be done by means of a further term, implied into the contract of employment, whereby the employer *agrees* to allow a strike after procedure is exhausted. It seems very uncertain that this is what most employers believe that they are agreeing to when they sign a procedure clause.

These are by no means the end of the complex problems that British legislation and case law leaves obscure in regard to the relationship between individual employment contracts and collective agreements, especially the procedure clauses. Foreign observers often express surprise that such fundamental issues as the legal import of procedure clauses, some of which have been in agreements since the turn of the century, have still not been decided. The difficulties discussed in this section have, perhaps, served to illustrate the manner in which the industrial parties have rarely been interested in probing that legal meaning. That is why there are so few cases litigated on basic and moot points. The operation of collective bargaining, and especially of procedure, tends to be carried on without regard for either legalism or, even, its legal meaning.

Part Two
COLLECTIVE BARGAINING AND PROCEDURE

4.

THE MACHINERY OF
COLLECTIVE BARGAINING‹

NATIONAL INSTITUTIONS AND PROCEDURES

B etween 1914 and 1918 British trade union membership doubled. It was in this era that it came about, in Professor Phelps Brown's words, "that the typical British bargaining unit which in 1914 was still made up of certain occupations in one district of one industry, had become by the end of the war the whole of the wage earners in the whole of an industry."[1] Many of the national negotiating machineries owe their inspiration to the recommendations of the famous Whitley Committee's five reports after its appointment in 1916, which were based upon "the advisability of a continuance, as far as possible, of the present system whereby industries make their own arrangements and settle their differences themselves." To this end it recommended the improvement of both employers' and employees' organizations; the establishment of Works Committees in individual enterprises; and, most important, the establishment of Joint Industrial Councils in every well-organized industry. "The J.I.C. was to be an organization representative of employers and workpeople, to have as its object the regular consideration of matters affecting the progress and well-being of the trade from the point of view of all those engaged in it, so far as this is consistent with the general interests of the community." From the beginning such bodies dealt with all types of disputes and grievances without dis-

---

[1] *The Growth of British Industrial Relations*, p. 362.

tinguishing "rights" from "interests." Between 1918 and 1921, 73 Joint Industrial Councils were established. In 1965 there were over 200.[2]

With two main exceptions, the industrywide collective bargaining structures have been created without serious legal intervention. Apart from the Terms and Conditions of Employment Act, 1959 (described below, p. 204), there are only two exceptions. First there are industries where the Minister of Labour, because of the inadequacy of voluntary bargaining arrangements, has established wages councils or boards through which compulsory minimum wages and holidays may be set by legal order (now the Agricultural Wages Act, 1948, and the Wages Councils Act, 1959). Some four million workers are covered by such exceptional legal arrangements. These councils are set up on a tripartite basis (i.e., with representatives of employers and employees and an independent chairman). Each one thus resembles a bargaining body containing a conciliation element; but where voluntary arrangements for bargaining improve, the minister may, and should, abolish such a wages council, thereby removing the legally enforceable minimum and allowing the industry to revert to voluntarism. Ten such councils have been so eliminated since 1945. Second, the nationalized commercial corporations (for example the National Coal Board, Electricity and Gas Boards, or Railways Board) are under statutory duties to enter into or "seek consultation with any organization appearing to the Board to be appropriate" to settle terms and conditions of employment (Transport Act, 1962, sec. 72) and like matters. The industries in question have all been so well organized for many years that the vague legal formulas (scarcely open to enforcement in court since they always leave the choice of appropriate unions to the employer) have not, in the opinion of the corporations concerned, added anything significant to the practice.[3]

With that one exception, there is no legal obligation upon an employer in Britain to recognize or bargain with a trade union. Indeed, there are still pockets of nonrecognition, especially in regard to white-collar workers. A Trades Union Congress survey in 1967 revealed that trade union organization was most difficult in small firms; firms with a high proportion of female labor; firms where labor turnover is high;

---

[2] Much of the information here is based upon the Written Evidence to the Royal Commission, Ministry of Labour (H.M.S.O., 1965), and the *Industrial Relations Handbook*, Ministry of Labour (H.M.S.O., 1964); and the most valuable *Disputes Procedures in British Industry*, Research Paper No. 2 (Part 1) for the Royal Commission on Trade Unions and Employers' Associations, by A. I. Marsh.

[3] See e.g., R.C.M.E., vol. 4 (National Coal Board Evidence); vol. 21 (Electricity Council); vol. 14 (British Railways Board); vol. 11 (Gas Council).

firms offering nonmanual employment; and firms under foreign owner-ship and control.[4] Despite the gaps, however, in 1965 the Ministry of Labour listed some 500 separate pieces of negotiating machinery at the national level (including the wages councils) for manual workers alone, and estimated that about 14 million workers were covered by such machinery out of a total of some 16 million in employment. Of the 7 million nonmanual workers, less than 4 million were thought to be so covered; and most of those were found in the public sector of employment.

The figure of about 18 million workers covered by national machin-ery of collective bargaining confirms the view that nonunion members in practice receive its benefits, for trade union membership in Britain does not exceed 10 million. Theoretically, this number was distributed among a total of nearly 600 workers' trade unions; but of those, 44 percent have under 500 members. In 1965, the number of unions affili-ated with the Trades Union Congress (the central body set up in 1868) was 175 with a membership of 8,867,522; but even among these, the largest eight unions accounted for 6¾ million members, thereby dominating the movement. To name those unions illustrates the di-versity of British collective bargaining, for they include unions whose origins lie in the early craft unions; unions based on an occupational structure; and some "general unions." They are the Transport and General Workers Union and the Amalgamated Engineering Union (each with over one million members); the National Union of General and Municipal Workers; National Union of Mineworkers; Union of Shop, Distributive and Allied Workers; National and Local Govern-ment Officers Association; National Union of Railwaymen; and the Electrical Trades Union. A current study has suggested that, despite a gradual process of amalgamation or absorption of smaller unions into these bigger ones, the frontiers between unions are not emerging on clear-cut industrial lines. Rather, each large union is tending to diver-sify.[5] Yet another study has shown that the smaller white-collar unions have done no more than keep pace with the rapidly increasing propor-tion of white-collar employees in the work force. Despite a fast ex-pansion of the white-collar unions, this "density" (i.e., percentage of potential membership) which was 28.8 in 1948 rose to only 29.0 in 1965.[6]

---

[4] *General Council Report*, Trades Union Congress, 1967, para. 33.

[5] See John Hughes, *Trade Union Structure and Government*, Research Paper No. 5 for Royal Commission on Trade Unions and Employers' Associations.

[6] George Sayers Bain, *Trade Union Growth and Recognition*, Research Paper No. 6 for the Royal Commission on Trade Unions and Employers' Associations. Both this and the paper cited in note 5 are exceedingly valuable additions to knowledge about British trade unions.

In the light of these facts it is scarcely surprising that in collective bargaining, "as negotiations are conducted on an industrial basis the worker's side at such negotiations commonly comprises a number of unions."[7] Sometimes the unions have formed federations such as the Federation of Building Trade Operatives or the Confederation of Shipbuilding and Engineering Unions, with 34 constituent organizations. Such federations of unions become bargaining parties, though it is rare for any individual union to relinquish much of its sovereignty to the federation. By contrast, the T.U.C., unlike its equivalent in other countries such as Sweden, is not in Britain a bargaining party. Its functions are largely consultative. Originally, it acted mainly as a coordinating body for the member unions and it still fulfills that function, as when it operates the Disputes Committee machinery to settle jurisdictional disputes between member unions under the principles of an agreement made at Bridlington in 1939 (the Bridlington Agreement). But today it increasingly performs the role of consulting with and advising government on behalf of the movement through membership of such bodies as the National Economic Development Council or representations to the new National Board for Prices and Incomes.

As for the employers' side, in 1965 the Ministry of Labour knew of 1,411 employers' organizations, many of them local bodies subordinate to industrywide federations. Some 750 were estimated to be autonomous. A few, like the Engineering Employers Federation or Shipbuilding Employers Federation, are nationwide in extent.[8] These are organized on an industrial basis, and the overlapping found on the trade union side is not present in their bargaining structures. We have already seen how legally relevant the question whether such a federation is a trade union in law can be for the purposes of section 4(4) of the Trade Union Act, 1871. On the other hand many large employers either do not belong to the relevant federation (like Ford Motor Co. or Esso Petroleum), or bargain separately with unions even though a member of an association (like Imperial Chemical Industries). In these cases the 1871 Act is usually irrelevant. We have written "usually" because recently interesting practical issues have arisen in union bargaining with "groups" or "consortia" of individual companies[9] and

---

[7] Ministry of Labour Evidence, p. 13, para. 15.

[8] For details on these bodies, see R.C.M.E. vol. 48 (Shipbuilding Employers Federation); and the Engineering Employers Federation Evidence published separately (St. Clements Press, 1965), oral evidence by Engineering Employers Federation, in R.C.M.E., vol. 20.

[9] See G. H. Doughty, "Negotiating with Consortia," *Trade Union Affairs* (Spring, 1961).

it might be for consideration whether such a consortium was not a "temporary combination" within the definition of "trade union" if it had any kind of "constitution" containing the principal objects that would bring it within the current legal definition of a trade union (see above, p. 43). At the national level, the British Employers' Confederation, founded at the beginning of the modern era in 1919, merged in 1965 with two other bodies to form the Confederation of British Industry (C.B.I.). Like those of the T.U.C., the powers of the C.B.I. are largely coordinating and advisory. It does not take part itself in any collective bargaining.

When therefore one looks at the national structures of bargaining, one finds a great diversity, an appreciation of which is needed to understand the operation of disputes procedures. Thus the Ministry of Labour gave to the Royal Commission a picture of methods for negotiating or settling the wages of industrial groups consisting of 100,000 workers or more. This disclosed that of the major industrial groups, eleven made use of a Joint Industrial Council or similar body;[10] three used a "Whitley Council" or similar body;[11] whereas five engaged in "direct" negotiations;[12] and six were covered by statutory wages councils.[13] The C.B.I. told the Royal Commission that in the private sector, six major industries used Joint Industrial Councils or the like,[14] while in two major industries wages were settled by direct negotiations, usually between employers' associations and groups of trade unions.[15] When it is appreciated that each of these industry-wide machineries has its own "disputes procedures," and that large individual firms (such as the Imperial Chemical Industries) will have their own, some measure of the variety can be taken. The C.B.I. also presented an

---

[10] Ministry of Labour Evidence, Appendix ix, pp. 54 *et seq.;* group (number of unions): building (federation: 11), electricity supply (5), food manufacture (3), coal mining (1), civil engineering (6), co-operative service retail trade (15), British railways (5), local government (7), national health service (manual) (5), road passenger transport (6), motor vehicle retail and repair (5).

[11] National government (20), education (8), nurses and midwives (12).

[12] Engineering, manual (confederation: 26 affiliates plus 4 other unions); engineering, nonmanual (3); shipbuilding (confederation); cotton (8); woolen (federation: 13); general printing (federation: 8).

[13] Agriculture (2), clothing (1), retail drapery (2), road haulage (4), retail food (4), catering—three councils (17).

[14] C.B.I. Evidence, Appendix 2; industry (approximate number of workers): electrical cables (25,000), heavy chemicals (65,000, excluding I.C.I.), pottery (60,000), rubber manufacture (80,000), building (900,000), civil engineering (250,000).

[15] Iron and steel (250,000), engineering (2,000,000), shipbuilding (80,000), cotton (80,000), woolen (125,000), textile finishing (50,000), leather (20,000), paper and board (70,000), general printing (280,000).

analysis of types of procedures, of which a summary is difficult to make. But we may note that the following large industries were listed as having national procedural arrangements providing for discussion at three levels, company, local or regional, and national: building, engineering, ropemaking, shipbuilding, and cotton. The following were listed as providing a two-tier structure, viz., discussion at company or similar level, followed by a national level: civil engineering, chemicals, iron and steel, leather, oil distribution, pottery, printing, and rubber manufacture.[16]

The distinction between "direct negotiations" and "joint councils" relates also to a division traditionally made of British procedures into two categories. Some agreements refuse to fit neatly into the categories, but the dichotomy is useful. On the one hand are the machineries that allow at various stages (works, district, national) for the joint settlement of disputes by bodies on which both employers and union representatives sit. Normally there will be no independent chairman, the chair alternating between employer and union member. This was the form recommended by the Whitley Committee in the guise of Joint Industrial Councils and it is often thought by foreign observers to be uniformly typical of the British scene. The other category is that used in the engineering industry. It springs from a much stronger notion of management prerogative than the joint council idea; the conceptual apparatus with which it works is, in theory, the idea that grievances and disputes are to be brought to *employers'* panels. The practice in engineering itself is, as we shall see, rather different. But because the employers reaching the decisions at the various levels of such a procedure are acting partly as managers and partly as conciliators, Marsh has dubbed this type of ad hoc procedure "employer conciliation." Of the two types he writes:

> The joint standing committee notion has undoubtedly taken deeper root in the British industrial relations system, but some industries have, in comparatively recent years, adopted the engineering system. Most procedural machinery developed in the past half century, however, has regarded the Joint Industrial Council device as more natural, and has been encouraged in this by the commitment of the Ministry of Labour to Whitley type machinery. There are illogicalities in either form; but the joint standing committee approach has usually been thought to lead to closer relationships between employers and trade unions and, although older in origin, to be the more modern approach to procedure.[17]

---

[16] C.B.I. Evidence, Appendix 3, Annexure A. The C.B.I. oral evidence is in R.C.M.E., vols. 6, 9, and 22.

[17] Marsh, *Disputes Procedures in British Industry*, p. 13, para. 55.

Union attitudes to the two types of procedure vary according to the position in which they find themselves; but in a number of sectors, employer conciliation has recently come under hostile criticism. The Electrical Trades Union has, for example, for some time criticized the procedures used in engineering. And in the papermaking and board-making industry where a similar procedure is followed, a delegate meeting of the main union of manual workers, National Union of Printing, Bookbinding and Paper Workers, recently instructed its executive to withdraw from the procedure. Seeing such tendencies, some observers conclude that they represent a desire to set up a more "judicial" style of determining disputes and grievances in such industries. Such a conclusion is of doubtful validity. The unions are, in effect, usually seeking methods that will give them a better opportunity to negotiate (especially at levels above Works Conference) on matters management now tends to regard as well within its own prerogatives.

If one turns to the "public sector" (i.e., the nationalized corporations plus local government and national civil servants), the picture is very similar though rather more systematized. That is to say, the public industries concerned, in each case having one employer rather than a group of firms, each have their own negotiating procedures. They usually involve joint bodies, but not always. Two of these joint bodies —in coal mining and the railways—are examined further on pages 98 and 102. Government servants largely fall outside the scope of this study; but it may be noted that "civil servants" of the Crown, who enjoy perhaps the weakest position in law (since it is not even clear that they have enforceable contracts of service), if "established" enjoy in practice much greater protection and security of tenure than ordinary industrial employees. Their machinery will invariably involve joint machinery of a "Whitley Council" type at national and departmental level. In such a system, "each side (union's and employers') speaks as a whole"; as the Treasury explained it to the Royal Commission, "If the two sides disagree there can be no question of one side overriding or out-voting the other within the Whitley machine."[18] One department permeated with the "spirit of Whitleyism" is the General Post Office. In 1969, the Post Office will cease to be a department of state and become a commercial public corporation, like the National Coal Board. Some features of its procedures have therefore been investigated in outline for this study.

The major difference, however, between the private and public industrial sectors lies in the fact that in the latter the procedures nearly

---

[18] H.M. Treasury Evidence, R.C.M.E., vol. 10, p. 347, para. 13.

always have as a last stage some form of arbitration to which the parties have either bound themselves in advance or which they are under some moral obligation to consider using. Arrangements for arbitration may, broadly, take one of three forms in Britain: reference to an umpire or arbitrator chosen ad hoc; reference to machinery provided by statue, such as the Industrial Court, or persons appointed by the Minister of Labour (single arbitrator or board of arbitration); or reference to a standing body created by the industry for its own purposes (such as the Railway Staff National Tribunal, Civil Service Arbitration Tribunal, or National Reference Tribunal and equivalent local umpires in the coal mining industry). Sometimes the commitment will be clear, as in the case of the electricity procedure:

> In case the National Council is unable to determine any matter falling within the scope of their functions they shall at the request of either the Electricity Boards' members or the Unions' members refer the difference to the Industrial Court or to any other agreed Tribunal for arbitration and any award made in relation to the difference shall be binding upon the Electricity Boards and the Area Boards and the Unions and the members of the Unions.[19]

In the light of such words it is interesting to remember that the award would not be contractually binding between the parties on the orthodox view of the present law. An analysis of the procedures in use in the public sector, as described in the Ministry of Labour's *Industrial Relations Handbook* (1964) by broad industrial classifications, reveals that of a total of 14 headings, at least 10 may be said to have obligatory or near-obligatory arbitration as the last stage of procedure (including coal mining, gas, electricity, atomic energy, civil service, railways, and waterways). It may also be mentioned here that when arbitration is met with, it assumes in the majority of cases in British practice an award *without* reasons. The Treasury representative remarked to the Royal Commission concerning civil service arbitration:

> The general view in the past has been that it is much better that reasons should not be given. Very occasionally they have been given by the Civil Service Arbitration Tribunal, but this is the odd occasion in four or five years. Normally the reason has been brief, quite short; but the feeling has been in the past, I think, that it is much better that "God" should not give the reasons for His Commandments because whilst God without quotes is infallible, arbitration tribunals are not.[20]

---

19 Electricity Council Evidence, R.C.M.E., vol. 21, p. 762, para. 11.
20 R.C.M.E., vol. 10, para. 1703. [From 1968 the Civil Service Arbitration Tribunal intends to increase the number of occasions on which reasons are given.]

As discussed on page 171, the practice of the Industrial Court gives encouragement to the secular aspect of this belief.

In private industry, agreements to use arbitration of this kind as a final stage in procedure are much more rare, though use at a lower level through reference of local issues to ad hoc arbitrators appears to be increasing. Sometimes, however, the national agreement does so provide. In the famous Boot and Shoe Agreement, which originates in the settlement of a major lockout in 1895, the local and national procedures both make provision for the use of an umpire as the final arbiter. Some new agreements include such clauses. For instance, in the important agreement between the Shipbuilding Employers' Federation and the Amalgamated Society of Boilermakers, Shipwrights, Blacksmiths, and Structural Workers reached in August 1966,[21] the procedure aims at ending "demarcation disputes" over jobs between workers by: (1) reporting the issues to the foreman and management who will arrange a meeting with shop stewards at the yard; (2) if the shop stewards fail to find a solution within 48 hours, reporting the issue to the District Delegates of the workers. The agreement continues:

> (4) If no settlement acceptable to the management has been reached within 24 hours of the issue being reported to the District Delegates . . . the matter will be referred forthwith to arbitration.
> (5) To enable matters to be dealt with under clause (4) the District Delegates . . . whom failing the management, shall advise the appropriate Industrial Relations Officer of the Ministry of Labour . . . of the question at issue and request the appointment of an arbiter to determine the issue forthwith . . . .
> (7) The decision of the arbiter which shall be given within 24 hours of the conclusion of the hearing will be final and binding on all parties, including the management.

Perhaps it says something for the novelty of any such arrangements in private industry in Britain that the same agreement does *not* allow questions of interpretation to go to arbitration; for in clause 12, it provides: "In the event of any difficulty arising over the interpretation of this agreement . . . the matter shall be dealt with by the President and Director . . . of the Federation and the President of the Society . . . ." Indeed, all the published sources confirm the Ministry of Labour's comment that, "in a few agreements there is an unqualified commitment to arbitration but more usually the agreement provides for arbitration only by agreement between the two parties." A similar analysis

---

[21] Appendix D of Shipbuilding Employers Evidence, R.C.M.E., vol. 48, p. 2065.

of the procedures described in the *Industrial Relations Handbook* for private industry reveals only six procedures out of twenty-two in which arbitration could be said to be obligatory. In certain others it was an expected last stage or an optional stage. In nine no kind of arbitration appeared to exist, though the chairman of a National Joint Council might, of course, on some issues exercise a similar function by means of a casting vote. In the C.B.I. Evidence, the following picture emerged from an analysis of procedures that could be used to settle local disputes: in four industrial groups provision was made for arbitration or an independent award as the final stage of procedure (in one, building, it is not used); in a further four there could be arbitration if both sides agreed; and in ten no provision was made for arbitration.

The Transport and General Workers Union kindly provided us with an estimate of the position under some 144 national agreements to which that union is a party. They found that some 60 of these agreements included arbitration clauses of one kind or another, of which 35 were obligatory. Evidence of this kind seems to indicate that a reasonable estimate would be that, counting by industrial categories or by different procedures, not more than one half, and probably considerably less, of the procedure agreements include any arbitration provision. Moreover, those that do not include such provisions will involve an even higher proportion of employees, covering as they do the larger industrial groups such as engineering. Even where provision for arbitration exists, it is apparently used more often for disputes of "interest" than those over "rights." Indeed it is often very infrequently used and may be no more than an encouragement to the parties to reach agreement between themselves before arbitration is forced upon them. The Imperial Chemical Industries Agreement with 22 unions ends, for example, with a procedure at "Headquarters Conference," and if that fails to produce agreement, no strike or lockout is to be engaged upon "until the question as to whether arbitration on the particular issue is mutually acceptable has been discussed between them." The company was good enough to tell us that between 1964 and June 1967, a dispute was taken to arbitration only once (below, p. 96).

THE ACTUAL USE OF PROCEDURES

The procedure clauses of collective agreements are used by the parties to determine *all* kinds of disputes. It is true that on occasion something in the nature of a "rights" dispute will be treated in a manner slightly different from that of an ordinary economic dispute,

but even then this will usually arise from a flexible use of one procedure (apart from the special case of discipline and dismissal discussed on p. 129). The Trades Union Congress, in its Evidence to the
Royal Commission, stated on this distinction between disputes over
existing agreements and disputes over the application of these provisions:

> In practice this may not be reflected so much in the existence of
> separate procedures as in the clear recognition by representatives of
> both sides as to the different approach in the two cases . . . .
> It may be argued that rights procedure inherently requires a "judicial"
> rather than a conciliatory function as the question is not so much how
> to reach a mutually satisfactory bargain as whether a man has received
> what he is entitled to . . . .
> However, a conciliatory function is in some circumstances not only
> more appropriate but often the only realistic way of approaching a situa-
> tion where the rights involved are not laid down with clarity and the
> problem is therefore not so much to discover what the facts are—the
> decision then being automatic—as to establish in the light of the facts
> what should be done to the satisfaction of both parties so that the situa-
> tion can be resolved.
> It is generally true to say that whereas a conciliatory approach is
> generally recognised to be appropriate within negotiation procedure, in
> the case of conflicts over interpretation of rights, the approach is inher-
> ently more judicial though it is quite often found expedient not to
> interpret a substantive agreement too rigidly in the interests of concilia-
> tion. Certainly it would be an exaggeration to equate the conciliatory
> approach too closely with negotiations or the judicial approach too
> closely with interpretation, and it should be recognised that the choice
> always exists. The fact that an agreement, or rule, is a formal instrument,
> the text of which is indeed carefully negotiated, does not mean that it is
> the intention of the parties in making this agreement to absolve their
> constituents from using their common sense in making it a working
> document rather than, in observing its letter, eliminating all flexibility.[22]

One would quarrel with this assessment only in that it probably
overstates the "judicial" approach taken even to many "rights" issues.
A. Marsh in his authoritative survey of disputes procedures has described five features that characterize the actual operation of present
day procedures:[23]

(1) *The preference for voluntary rules.* "There can be no industrial
relations system in which preference for voluntary procedural rules is

---

[22] "Trade Unionism," extracts from paras. 317–319.
[23] Marsh, *Disputes Procedures in British Industry*, pp. 14–19, from which the
quotations in this section are taken unless otherwise specified.

stronger than in the British, nor one in which voluntary rules are regarded so flexibly by the parties concerned." Here we can add not merely the avoidance of legal enforcement, which is fundamental, but also a preference to avoid third-party arbitration. In their evidence, the Motor Employers express "reservations" about arbitration as a feature of disputes procedure on ordinary claims; and while they thought there might be more scope for it on interpretation of agreements or discipline cases, they also warned that "we might be led towards the American practice of extremely detailed conditions of service Agreements which prima facie appears to be highly restrictive of Management."[24] This is an excellent illustration of the second feature:

(2) *Preference for procedural over substantive rules.* The substantive rules in the national agreements lay down a framework, mainly of *minimum* wages and conditions in the national agreements. The "interpretation" of an agreement as such (though exceptions could easily be found) is not characteristically the issue in a British dispute. If such points arise, "it is commonly thought proper," Marsh says, "for these to be referred not through normal procedure but by other means back to the parties who made the original agreement." This fits in with "the conviction that in making a procedural settlement of a grievance the parties are merely settling the matter at issue preferably at the level at which it arose."

(3) *Preference for general procedures.* Procedures are multipurpose. Such distinctions as that between a "judicial" approach to a dismissal and the approach to an economic dispute "are rarely made either in the main procedure agreements between the parties or in subsidiary agreements at lower levels. The tendency is to regard procedures as all-purpose agreements to be used flexibly as particular situations arise and as common sense seems to dictate." Here we touch on the use of that same procedure in "rights" and "interest" questions to produce a "durable compromise," of which Allan Flanders has spoken (above, p. 3). The point touches too upon the probable inadequacy of some procedures to bear the burden of all types of issues, a point not unrelated to the use of the small-scale stoppage in some sectors of industry as a well-recognized modern method of processing an employment dispute.

Marsh's fourth and fifth headings are (4) *The flexibility of work place procedures,* and (5) *The decline of formal (joint) consultation.* Both of these points relate to the place of the shop steward in negotia-

---

[24] R.C.M.E., vol. 23, p. 838, para. 34.

tion and procedure in Britain, and two surveys have been made on this subject.[25] W. McCarthy and S. Parker estimate the total number of stewards at 175,000 (an increase of 14 percent over the last ten years), and their survey shows that shop stewards are found in most industries and firms where unions are recognized and are not confined (as is sometimes alleged) to engineering and shipbuilding. They are usually elected and periodically reelected by workers at the place of work (often unopposed), and are in different ways accredited by their unions (though few union rule books, McCarthy shows, make detailed provision in that regard). The growth of the power of shop stewards, and in large enterprises the senior shop steward or "convenor," and of committees of shop stewards (which could themselves even be "trade unions" in law; see above, p. 43) has been the counterpart of the decline of "joint consultation," which it had been for many years the policy of the Ministry of Labour to foster alongside bargaining procedures. McCarthy writes:

> First plant consultative committees in the strict sense of bodies intended simply to advise management on how to raise efficiency and discuss other matters of assumed "common interests" without reaching binding agreements cannot survive the development of effective shop floor organisation. Either they must change their character and become essentially negotiating committees carrying out functions which are indistinguishable from the formal processes of shop floor bargaining, or they are boycotted by shop stewards and, as the influence of the latter grows, fall into disuse. Secondly shop stewards themselves do not subscribe to the assumptions which lay behind the provision of separate institutional arrangements for the purpose of dealing with so called "conflicting" and "common interest" questions; and any committee on which they serve which cannot reach decisions, albeit informal ones, they regard as essentially an inferior or inadequate substitute for proper negotiating machinery.

McCarthy's explanation ties in with the place of shop stewards in local use of procedure. It is *their* use of procedure which in many ways demonstrates its "flexibility." The ways in which they are brought into contact with union members and "procedure" are summarized in Table 3, which is based on a survey of the relative importance of a

---

[25] McCarthy, *Shop Stewards,* and the results of a study undertaken by the Government Social Survey and appearing as *Shop Stewards and Workshop Relations,* by W. McCarthy and S. Parker, Research Paper No. 10 for the Royal Commission on Trade Unions and Employers' Associations, hereafter cited as McCarthy and Parker.

shop steward's activities made by Clegg, Killick, and Adams. With this wide range of activities it is not surprising that the stewards' powers and functions vary according to the attitude and strength of management. Thus in engineering, although the agreement makes no provision for recompensing stewards for lost working time, none for allowing stewards to meet in working hours, and none for recognition of a hierarchy of shop stewards, Marsh has found that in practice some managements do pay stewards out-of-pocket expenses, allow them to meet in working time, and accept the fact that there are convenors or chief stewards.[26]

TABLE 3
Shop Stewards: Main Duties

Duties	Percentage of time spent	
	All stewards	Senior stewards
Dicussions with members and shop stewards	32	33
Negotiation with management above foremen level	21	36
Taking up grievances with foreman............	16	7
Serving on joint consultative committees........	11	10
Attending other meetings	8	5
Fixing rates	6	5
Correspondence	6	4
	100	100

SOURCE: Clegg, Killick, and Adams, *Trade Union Officers* (1961), p. 157

The Government Social Survey has added general statistical backing for these trends. While only 1 percent of informants devoted all or most of their working time to union work, the average steward spent six hours (rising to ten in the case of senior stewards) in this way. It may be stated to be generally true that stewards may leave their jobs to contact members (87 percent were in this position), though usually only after asking permission; that meetings can be held at the place of work (75 percent, and by 35 percent during working hours if permission is obtained); that meetings of stewards in the workplace, whether of the same union or not, are frequently held (75 percent and 80 percent, respectively, of informants took part in such meetings); that meetings of stewards from different workplaces, whether in the same union or not, are also held, but less freqently and are likely to be organized by full-time officers as by the stewards themselves; that most workplaces have a "senior steward" system and joint committees

---

[26] *Industrial Relations in Engineering* (1965), pp. 81–82.

of stewards from different unions to discuss problems with management. It is also true that the range of topics over which stewards bargain is extremely wide: of 28 issues put forward in the Social Survey, at least 20 percent of the informants in each instance bargained as a matter of standard practice on 24 of them, but the *number* of issues bargained on as a matter of standard practice by the average steward was only 7, and 16 percent of them had no bargaining function at all. Further, 44 percent of stewards and 76 percent of full-time officers said there were issues they wanted to settle with management but which management regarded as not open to joint regulation, notably financial policy and discipline. Thirty-eight percent of the stewards said they had a written domestic procedure.[27] In one chemical firm investigated by McCarthy and Coker, the national framework for the industry had been supplemented with a precise "Factory Negotiating Procedure," laying down a ratio of stewards to members, and so forth.[28] Firms belonging to no employers association often go much further in this direction.

Turner has described in detail how senior shop stewards at one car firm (Austin's) act "as part-time negotiators responsible for handling the grievances of 26,000 men."[29] The works handbook now makes provision for meetings of and payments to members of a Works Committee; and the chief shop steward now spends "almost all his time" in negotiation, the firm paying him average factory earnings, or sometimes more. He has a telephone by his machine. "In effect the Works Committee—and particularly the convenor, the apex of several stages of internal grievance procedure before the local union and employers' association officials are called in—are skilled and near-professional negotiators." Turner points out that "in the motor industry at least (though a similar development seems evident in several other sectors) there are now in effect two separate forms of workers' organisations which, while they are not necessarily in conflict—indeed, interact in many ways which involve co-operation rather than friction—must nevertheless be sharply distinguished." Shop steward organization serves as a supplement to the written procedure, as well as a method for making it work. Both Turner and McCarthy in their studies show that shop stewards frequently do more to prevent stoppages of work than to encourage them. Having become the "main agency" for bar-

---

[27] McCarthy and Parker, paras. 61–84 and Tables 3, 8, 8A.

[28] McCarthy, *Shop Stewards*, pp. 8–9.

[29] H. Turner, *Motor Industry*, pp. 209–210, p. 192, p. 222. Of course, the type of shop steward described here is still exceptional.

gaining at shop floor level, "the senior stewards like the full-time union officials before them," comments Turner, "are forced to assume something of the role of buffer between the employer and the operatives." This view is confirmed by the Government Social Survey which reports that the great majority of managers preferred to deal with stewards rather than full-time officials and assessed their stewards as "reasonable." McCarthy and Parker comment that the average steward cannot be seen as "an embattled opponent of management" and is regarded by all participants as "an accepted, reasonable and even moderating influence; more of a lubricant than an irritant." This does not, of course, imply an absence of disputes with management or of strikes (even unconstitutional ones); rather these are not necessarily seen as "incompatible with mutual toleration and acceptance, and a judgment on the over-all state of industrial relations which is regarded as generally satisfactory."[30]

If this observation is true of the structure of shop stewards' functions, it is even more true of substantive and procedural arrangements negotiated by them. In the main the special agreements remain informal, as McCarthy explains.[31] Employers prefer to have it this way because the arrangements if unwritten will "set as little precedent as possible"; while stewards prefer to have the freedom to argue about the meaning of old settlements, sometimes realize that their privileges can be granted only if they are not quotable precedents, and know that they can reach further into matters regarded as management's "prerogatives" if they proceed on an informal basis. Thus a situation arises which Marsh describes as follows:

> There are probably in the British economy as a whole more establishments in which domestic procedures work by custom and practice than by agreements which have a written format . . . it can seldom be said that the rights and duties of the parties are clearly defined. While this may have virtues in laying emphasis on the need for workers and managements to adopt a flexible approach to the settlement of workplace problems, it has a number of concomitant disadvantages. In the first place it tends to provide an imprecise framework for trade union workshop organisation . . . . Second, it is seldom clear precisely what procedures are to be followed in particular circumstances except by

---

30 McCarthy and Park, paras. 123, 194–195, and Table 12. Of course, the text must not be taken to imply that the authors cited regard the state of industrial relations in all sectors of the motor industry as satisfactory.

31 McCarthy, *Shop Steward*, p. 28, citing Phelps Brown, *Industrial Relations: Contemporary Problems and Perspectives*, p. xii.

custom and practice. Even where workplace procedures are written they are seldom implemented in the precise form laid down.[32]

This emphasis upon *custom* and *practice,* and the *im*precision that goes with flexibility is confirmed by McCarthy. In particular he and other research workers have noted the way in which the normal first stage of procedure (the demand that the worker raise the matter with the foreman) is so often ignored. McCarthy and Coker, for example, found that workers usually approached their steward, and in some firms the steward would go straight to second-level management, or even directly to the personnel or works manager. Similarly investigations of the coal industry have shown that union branch secretaries often did not take grievances to the under manager as the machinery provided, but went straight to the manager. These findings have been supplemented by the Government Social Survey which reports that 70 percent of stewards said that they had ways of approaching management outside formal procedure, 50 percent of those who had a foreman said they could by-pass him in this way, 25 percent claimed they were able to approach top management directly, and that more workers approached their steward first over any problem than approached the foreman.[33]

This degree of flexibility and imprecision in the actual practice is important to what has gone before and to what comes later in this part. For example, if it becomes necessary to ask whether workers have acted in breach of procedure in a situation where the procedure clause has been incorporated into their employment contracts, to what extent should account be taken of these local customs and practices without which in truth the procedure probably would never work at all? It is sometimes suggested that such imprecision is caused by the fact that no effective legal sanction is provided in Britain for collective agreements. Certainly it is believed, as the Motor Employers suggested, that further sanction, or even an increase in arbitration, would necessitate more detailed formal agreements. But McCarthy has replied that verbal understandings appear in systems where detailed

---

[32] Marsh, *Disputes Procedures,* pp. 18–19. In this context it is interesting to note that the Government Social Survey reports that 58 percent of stewards thought that procedure within the firm had been exhausted before their last strike took place, whereas only 19 percent of personnel officers were of this view (Table 17, p. 89).

[33] McCarthy, *op. cit.,* pp. 30–32; quoting Scott, Mumford, McGivering, and Kirkby, *Coal and Conflict: A Study in Industrial Relations at Collieries* (1963), p. 161; McCarthy and Parker, *op. cit.,* paras. 85–86.

bargains are legally enforceable, in the United States for example where "unwritten supplementaries" are partly the result of shop stewards using unofficial shop floor sanctions to improve the position of their members. Such informal arrangements are, he suggests, the result of the conflicting but complementary interests of management and stewards.[34]

---

[34] McCarthy, *op. cit.*, pp. 26–27, where he cites in particular J. W. Kuhn, *Bargaining in Grievance Settlement* (1961). On details of shop steward organization into which it has not been possible to go here, see too Marsh and Coker, "Shop Stewards Organisation in the Engineering Industry" (1963) I *British Journal of Industrial Relations* 170; Lerner and Bescoby "Shop Steward Combine Committees in the British Engineering Industry" (1966) vol. 4 *British Journal of Industrial Relations* 154.

5.

EXAMPLES OF PROCEDURE
IN CERTAIN INDUSTRIES

BUILDING

A s has been mentioned already, there exists a National Joint Council (N.J.C.) for the Building Industry, to which the Employers' Federation and twelve unions are parties. Two different procedures exist, however, within its scope.[1] The first is provided for by Rule 9 of the council constitution. This rule applies to "all differences or disputes referred to (the Council) under its Constitution and rules, whether concerned with the interpretation of its own decisions or otherwise." The stages in practice are:

Stage 1: The shop steward takes up the matter with management on the site. This stage is not mentioned in National Working Rule (N.W.R.) 9 but has existed since 1964 under the provisions of N.W.R. 7, which for the first time recognized shop stewards on the sites.

Stage 2: The dispute is considered by a Local Joint Committee. The

---

[1] For an analysis of examples of procedure in certain industries, see generally A. Marsh and W. McCarthy, *Disputes Procedures in Britain*, Research Paper No. 2 (Part 2) for the Royal Commission on Trade Unions and Employers' Associations (1968), hereafter cited as *Marsh and McCarthy*.

In general, information for this chapter came from the National Constitution and Working Rules of the National Joint Council, and from the minutes of its meetings and of the hearings of Disputes Commissions. We are most grateful in particular to F. W. Beazley, clerk to the council, for his assistance. See too the Evidence of the Federation of Building Employers, R.C.M.E., vol. 16, and the Federation of Building Trades Operatives, R.C.M.E., vol. 19.

constitution does not formally recognize these committees as having a conciliation function, but in practice they often act as one stage in the procedure.

Stage 3 (or 2, where there is no local committee): The dispute is considered by a Regional Conciliation Panel. There are ten regions. The panel must hear the dispute within 21 days, and its decision is "final and binding" subject to an appeal to the National Conciliation Panel within 21 days. Decisions are not to be used as "precedents." If there is failure to agree, the panel or either of the parties may proceed to the National Conciliation Panel.

Stage 4: National Conciliation Panel of N.J.C. This panel sits on fixed dates each year and hears disputes at the next following hearing. Decisions are "final and binding." If the panel cannot agree, the full National Joint Council considers whether it can suggest a solution, and if so, it refers the matter back to the conciliation panel. If it cannot, it refers the matter on under Rule 13 (the "deadlock procedure").

Stage 5: Under Rule 13 the council appoints a special committee to examine the position and find terms of settlement. This committee must report within one month.

Stage 6: Where the special committee fails to find terms of settlement, it is "the duty of the council to refer the matter to arbitration." The method of arbitration is determined by a majority vote on the council.

It goes without saying that the rules also prohibit any stoppage of work "on any pretext whatever" until completion of this procedure. Also, we have noted already that the Confederation of British Industry described an arbitration as having "never happened" under this procedure; it certainly has not been used for the last 40 years (though, as we shall see, the same is not true under the other procedure). In some respects the work of the council is surrounded by unusual rules. For example, the council (and its committees) is allowed only to hear witnesses giving evidence "within their personal knowledge and hearsay evidence shall not be admitted," and witnesses are limited to five minutes for their evidence unless allowed more by resolution (Regulations 3 and 2 Governing the Procedure, dating from 1904). Other regulations make similar demands for unusual strictness in procedure; but in practice there seems no doubt that the chairman has some discretion in the way these regulations are enforced. The National Joint Council Panel meets every six weeks throughout the year, and consists of seven members from each side plus the officers, each case usually being heard by three a side plus the officers (chairman, vice-chairman, secretaries, and the clerk). Regional panels are convened as required, and it is the council's belief that the time limits of the procedure are regularly adhered to, although no clear figures on this aspect of the procedure were available. This last gap may not be unrelated to the fact that many cases are disposed of in local panels, whose existence is not officially recognized at all in Rule 9. The C.B.I. in its Evidence to the Royal Commission comments that "no record is kept of the cases settled informally by over two hundred joint committees in the industry." One interesting feature is that, with the consent of the firm involved, the N.J.C. Panel is willing to allow its machinery to be used for employees of a nonfederated employer. No similar record exists of any use of the machinery by nonunion workers.

Side by side with this machinery is the "Green Book Procedure" set up by the National Emergency Disputes Agreement of 1927. This applies to "any dispute or difference" between the parties or any member of them which *threatens to cause a stoppage of work*. Such disputes are to be reported to appropriate local officials of both sides "in triplicate." The officials must then meet "without delay" and cooperate to prevent the stoppage either (1) pending reference to the ordinary Regional Panel, or (2) pending reference to an Emergency Disputes Commission. The same obligations apply to regional and national officials. In cases where stoppage seems unavoidable, the officials must "confer with a view of bringing about an *immediate* reference of the dispute to an appropriate Regional or National Joint Emergency Disputes Commission. The existence of official machinery to deal with disputes threatening or actually causing a stoppage of work sheds considerable light upon how the parties must view the "peace obligation" in the N.J.C. procedure, especially as in practice the parties are prepared to hold Disputes Commissions even though the workers are still on strike. Clearly, the parties do not attach great formal significance to the distinction between constitutional and unconstitutional acts.[2] This attitude obviously contributes to the lack of litigation in the courts on such questions. Even more important it illustrates how inappropriate it might be to "incorporate" such a peace obligation into each individual worker's employment contract, as was suggested earlier.

The stages of the emergency Green Book Procedure are:
Stage 1: Regional or National Emergency Disputes Commission consisting of three employers' and three employees' representatives from the region and two officials as permanent members (regional or national as the case may be). The commission must hold an inquiry

---

[2] Marsh and McCarthy, *op. cit.*, pp. 54–55, paras. 23–24.

without delay at the place of dispute, take evidence as to the cause, decide whether the dispute is referable to the ordinary Rule 9 procedure, make a report to the National Executive Committees of the employers and the unions, and give directions as it sees fit to prevent or end a stoppage.

Stage 2: A regional decision may go up to a National Emergency Disputes Commission for further consideration.

Stage 3: The national executives of the Employers' Federation and of the unions may approve the recommendations of the commission. If they do not they must jointly consider what further steps can be taken.

Stage 4: In principle, if there is still a failure to agree, the "deadlock" provisions of Rule 13 apply (i.e., consideration by a special committee and by the N.J.C. itself if necessary).

Stage 5: Under the same rule, the arbitration provision applies.

It must be said at once that the emergency disputes procedure certainly has not prevented all stoppages in the building industry. No separate figures can be obtained for building, but in the construction industry as a whole, of which building forms a sizable part, in 1964 and 1965 the number of stoppages was 222 and 261; number of workers stopping, 25,800 and 27,800; and number of working days lost through stoppages, 125,000 and 135,000, respectively. This total included some of the stoppages at two South London building sites which eventually caused the appointment of a Court of Inquiry that reported in September 1967 (below, p. 228). There long drawn-out unofficial stoppages had continued despite 16 Regional and 8 National Disputes Commissions, one Regional Joint Conciliation Panel, and one deadlock procedure special committee between August 17, 1965, and December 21, 1966. The Court of Inquiry condemned some shop stewards and some employers for not really wanting to end the strikes.[3] Except for some efforts to obtain injunctions against allegedly violent pickets, no legal action was taken. Also it may be noted that an arbitration did take place under the emergency procedure, with three outside persons acting as arbitrators and making their report on February 10, 1965. But this was in effect an arbitration to settle a long-standing dispute between two of the unions in the industry (the Building Trades Workers and the Operative Plasterers) as to which of their members should do certain work; and the national executives had followed a recommendation of the National Emergency Disputes Commission in asking the N.J.C. to appoint a Special Arbitration Tribunal.

---

[3] Report of a Court of Inquiry into trade disputes at the Barbican and Horseferry Road construction sites (CMND. 3396; H.M.S.O., 1967).

The N.J.C. asked the Trades Union Congress, the Royal Institute of British Architects, and the Institute of Builders to appoint three arbitrators, who heard the case—and decided that members of either union were competent to do the work.

It may be thought that the two procedures clearly overlap to such an extent that they are in effect interchangeable. The National Federation of Building Trade Operatives in its Evidence to the Royal Commission distinguished sharply between the two forms of procedure:

> We have two forms of procedure. We have the conciliation machinery, which concerns itself with conciliation—that is, deals with differences in the interpretation of the rules themselves and that is its function . . . the emergency disputes machinery deals with matters that are not concerned with the interpretation of rules, deals with the more emotional aspects—a sudden flare up of temper, dismissal of a man unjustly, and so on. That is what the emergency disputes machinery does. Otherwise the only way to deal with a matter of that kind would be a strike.[4]

The Confederation of British Industry accepted this dichotomy in analyzing the 112 disputes going through the procedures in 1964 as 59 emergency disputes (42 settled by regional and 17 by national commissions) and 53 "questions of interpretation of the Rules and decisions of the N.J.C. . . . accordingly dealt with under the conciliation machinery" (39 settled at regional and 11 at national conciliation panels; 3 unresolved).[5]

It certainly seems to be true that the emergency procedure is used as intended viz where strikes happen or are threatened. Of 17 such instances in 1965, 15 involved actual or directly threatened stoppage. But our analysis of recent minutes of National Conciliation Panels and of the decisions of National Emergency Disputes Commissions failed to sustain the substantial differences of the *character* of disputes going through the two procedures. Both could involve the interpretations of the National Working Rules, though only the former were usually couched in the form of an interpretation of these rules. This is confirmed by Marsh and McCarthy who say that in 1965 about half the cases handled by the emergency procedure concerned primarily the meaning and application of the National Working Rules.[6] Of the 48 N.J.C. cases, 8 were certainly not merely interpretations of N.W.R. provisions. One, for example, made an award for the claimant workers in 1965 stating:

---

4 R.C.M.E., vol. 19, p. 669, para. 2792.
5 C.B.I. Evidence, Appendix 3, Annexure A.
6 *Op. cit.*, p. 55, para. 25.

While in these circumstances no claim arose either under the Holidays with Pay Scheme or the Working Rules Agreement, it is the rule of the Panel that when an employee has had a long period of employment with a firm—in each of these cases over eight years—it would be in accordance with good industrial practice for him to be placed on leaving the employment in a position no less favourable than he would have enjoyed had he been covered by the Holidays Scheme throughout the employment.

TABLE 4

Subject Matter of National Emergency Disputes Commission, 1960-1966

Subject	Number of cases
Dismissal and reemployment including alleged victimization	46
Demarcation disputes	9
Union recognition and membership	7
Wage rates	
Particular jobs	2
Incentive bonus schemes	4
Hours (interpretation of N.W.R. 2)	12
Recruitment or transfer of workers	8
Labor—only subcontracts	8
Miscellaneous or not analyzed	12
Total	108

Source: Disputes Commissions records, 1960-1966.

TABLE 5

Subject Matter of N.J.I.C. Panel Cases, 1962 - 1966[7]

Subject	Number of cases
Wage rates (N.W.R. 1)	7
Working hours (N.W.R. 2)	4
Time lost (N.W.R. 2A)	5
Dismissals and other termination of employment (N.W.F. 2B)	19
Extra payments (discomfort pay), tool allowances etc. (N.W.R. 3)	5
Overtime (N.W.R. 4)	4
Daily travel pay (N.W.R. 6)	1
Miscellaneous	3*
Total	48†

*Two cases concerned interpretation and application of site bonus agreements.
†Where the regional panel had agreed on a decision (13 cases), it was overruled in only 2 cases.

Source: Minutes of N.J.C. meetings, 1962 - 1966.

[7] The National Joint Council kindly made available to us records of 48 cases in the period 1962 to 1966. The figures in Marsh and McCarthy (Table 18, p. 59) are confined to 24 cases in the period 1962 to 1965.

Such a decision would only be possible in a system where the parties knew they were not setting a precedent and did not stop to ask themselves whether they were making new rules or extending old ones.

A similarly realistic insistence upon an "industrial jurisprudence" rather than the letter of the agreements is found in the flexible remedies used. For example, in the special committees dealing with apprenticeship disputes, we found in Case 32, 1966, a situation in which the committee accepted that an apprentice had such a record of unpunctuality and sporadic attendance at classes that his master might have been entitled to cancel the apprenticeship deed before the necessary five years had been served. But this would so "seriously prejudice" his future employment that the committee, in view of his having served four years (to which period an apprenticeship in the industry was currently being reduced), directed that the apprentice be "deemed to have completed" his apprenticeship.

The Emergency Disputes Commissions' records show great variations in the time taken to hear cases when they went from regional to national commissions, though parties could reasonably expect to have a national hearing after a delay of less than 3 weeks. Some 68 of the 108 cases went through both stages; and of these, 8 were delayed less than a week between stages; 22 took 8 to 14 days; 12 took 15 to 21 days; 9 took 22 to 31 days; and 17 took more (one of them 82 days!). The N.J.C. procedure is equally speedy: in 1965, cases took an average of 16 days to reach regional level and a further 18 to reach national level, if the case was taken that far. Both procedures show satisfactory disposal rates of about 70 percent at regional level, while failures to agree at national level are rare. There is little evidence of increased use of the procedures in recent years.[8] More important, an investigation of the subject matter of the emergency cases disclosed that 40 percent of them were concerned with discharge (the same percentage as in the N.J.C. cases). In neither machinery are the decisions concerned with legalistic differences between "rights" and "interest," although where an interpretation of the National Working Rules was primarily in issue, a panel or commission would naturally require some good industrial reason to go beyond them.

Thus the building procedures operate speedily and with a low proportion of failures to agree. The most serious criticism of them, however, is that they cannot be used to handle certain important classes of dispute arising in the industry. This failing can be explained historically by the fact that the two sides in the industry have been com-

---

[8] Marsh and McCarthy, *op. cit.*, pp. 57–58, paras. 34–37.

mitted to an attempt at close, centralized regulation of the terms and conditions of employment. On the one hand, the National Working Rules lay down maximum rates, and on the other, the extra payments that may be made to various classes of worker for various extra duties or discomforts, or for work in particular areas of the country, are precisely stipulated, and there is a regulator providing for automatic increases in the wage rates when the cost of living increases. The procedure agreements are intended to reinforce this system. The National Joint Council Procedure allows for the flexible settling of disputes but only within the overriding principle set out in clause 2 of the Memorandum of Agreement that the parties will not "permit, endorse, sanction or otherwise condone any claim or agreement to vary any of the Rules, Regulations or Working Rules hereunder and having as its object the determination of any of these matters on any other than a National basis." As for the emergency procedure, it "is mainly intended to facilitate joint action to prevent the undermining of national regulations by the use of work-group sanctions at site level."[9]

The first modification of this system came shortly after World War II when the employees' side of the N.J.C. was induced by pressure from the employers, the Ministry of Labour, and the National Arbitration Tribunal to accept the present N.W.R. 1, which allows for the negotiation at site level of incentive plans provided the national rates are taken as the basis for calculating earnings. The majority of workers in the industry (unless they are self-employed or employed by labor-only subcontractors) are still employed on the time rates, yet their earnings on an average over the whole country are, if overtime is included, 30 percent above what the national rates allow, or 10 percent, if overtime is not included.[10] The addition consists of plus rates and standing bonuses paid by employers in contravention of the rules. Since many workers have no difficulty in obtaining the national rates, the disputes that arise concern the extent of the additional payments; but such disputes, unlike in the engineering industry, cannot be entertained within the official procedures. Furthermore, partly because the national rates are supposed to be applied and partly because of the nature of the industry, there is usually no official procedure at site level for the negotiation of the additional payments and the handling of disputes. Shop stewards may now be recognized, but procedure itself does not reach down far enough into the site.

Second, there are problems raised for the procedures by the practice of labor-only subcontracting and the use of workers on a self-employed

---

[9] *Ibid.*, p. 56, para. 28.
[10] *Ibid.*, p. 67, paras. 63 and 65.

basis. Historically, both these practices have been resisted as being synonymous with employment on piece rates and thus with the undermining of national regulation. Other reasons still compel their control.[11] Consequently, neither practice has received official recognition except to the extent that N.W.R. 8, introduced in 1964, provides that the subcontractor must observe the National Working Rules and the main contractor is to ensure that he does so. But the rule does not formally provide for the employees of subcontractors to use the official disputes procedures, and there is a decision from the National Joint Council Procedure that self-employed workers cannot use it. Estimates of the number of people thus employed range from 50,000 to 350,000, and it is agreed that the number is growing.[12]

ENGINEERING

As has already been indicated, engineering procedure is very difficult, relying as it does upon "employer conciliation panels." Recently a great deal of information has been collected about its working, and what is attempted here is merely a sktech of the main findings.[13]

The modern Agreement for Manual Workers, often called the York Agreement, made in 1922 and subsequently amended in 1955, may be summarized as follows:

Stage 1: The individual employee raises the question with his immediate supervisor.

Stage 2: If shop stewards have been appointed, the employee and his steward discuss the question with the shop steward or head shop foreman.

Stage 3: If a Works Committee has been appointed and the parties wish to use it for this particular question, it is discussed by the committee. The committee consists of not more than seven representatives from either side. (The employees' representatives are shop stewards nominated and elected by all the workshop members of the trade unions party to the agreement. Each steward must retire or be re-

---

[11] R.C.M.E., vol. 19; Clark, 30 Mod. L.R. 6 (1967); Samuel and Lewis, *Personnel* (April 1968), p. 20.

[12] If union officials knowingly or recklessly induce a breach of contract to supply workers on a labor-only basis, they commit a tort: *Emerald Construction Ltd.* v. *Lowthian* [1966] 1 W.L.R. 691 (discussed above, p. 14).

[13] See A. Marsh, *Industrial Relations in Engineering* (1965), hereafter cited as Marsh, *Industrial Relations;* A. Marsh and R. S. Jones, "Engineering Procedure and Central Conference at York in 1959" (1964) II *British Journal of Industrial Relations* 228, hereafter cited as Marsh and Jones; Turner, *Motor Industry;* Marsh and McCarthy, *op. cit.,* chap. 2.

elected after at most one year. If a question arises concerning a department having no shop steward on the committee, such a steward may be co-opted. Local trade union and Engineering Employers' Federation officials may be present.)

Stage 4: The matter now proceeds to a *Works Conference*: "deputations of workmen . . . shall be received by the Employers by appointment without unreasonable delay for the mutual discussion of any question in the settlement of which both parties are directly concerned." If the local trade union official exercises his right to be present, as is usual, the local employers' association official *must* also attend. The agreement does not further regulate procedure at the Works Conference, but each trade union and each local employers' association will frequently have its own rules. For example, the Amalgamated Engineering Union limits, by executive council instruction, attendance at a Works Conference to "selected members actually employed" in the establishment "who may be accompanied by the Divisional Organiser or his deputy."[14]

Stage 5: Failure to settle at Works Conference allows for reference to a *Local Conference*. This must be held within seven days of an application for the meeting. A panel of employers drawn from federated firms in the district but not directly involved in the dispute hear the case. Once again, the detailed composition and procedure are not laid down. Employers' associations vary in their precise practice; and unions regulate their own side (the Amalgamated Engineering Union, for instance, restricting the number of delegates attending to three). Local Conferences can constitutionally be called at the request of local officials on either side without the use of the lower stages, but this practice is rare.

Stage 6: If there is no settlement at Local Conference, either side can refer to *Central Conference* at York. (A special Welsh section has a separate Central Conference, for some time in Cardiff, now in Bristol.) Fourteen days' notice is required, time running from the date of application; and the meetings are held on the second Friday of each month. Thus, even when operated as speedily as possible, procedure may delay a hearing for more than a fortnight; and if an application for a hearing is held up for tactical reasons by the parties to within a fortnight of the next meeting, the hearing will not take place within a month. The employers constitute their national representatives into a number of "courts," each usually numbering four or more members and a chairman, and dealing with five or six cases. The cases are

---

[14] Marsh, *Industrial Relations*, p. 84.

screened in formal discussions on the Thursday evening between the two sides; and relevant local trade union officials are in attendance on their national officials, though they never go into the "court" but are only consulted in adjournments.

There are eight possible outcomes to a Central Conference: (1) issue settled; (2) "parties unable to arrive at a mutual recommendation" (often called by commentators "failure-to-agree," though that is not the same thing); (3) "issue referred back for further *discussion*"; (4) "issue referred back for works (or local) *settlement*"; (5) "issue retained in the hands of the central authorities"; (6) "adjourned"; (7) "withdrawn"; or (8) "not proceeded with."

There are similar agreements in force with six "staff" unions. Central Conferences for these unions are held in London. Special problems attend the recognition of "staff" workers, of course, concerning which engineering employers have been traditionally reluctant; but these cannot be pursued here.

The number of hearings at the different levels is large and growing. It may be remarked that this is particularly important when one remembers that until procedure is exhausted (i.e., ends with either solution (1) or (2), a stoppage of work is not constitutional, and the situation resulting from the act of management complained of is maintained, under management prerogative, during procedure except where questions arise which result in one class of workpeople being replaced by another. The proportion, however, of Central Conference hearings which end in (2), "failure to arrive at a recommendation," is relatively constant. The figures in Table 6 illustrate these points.

TABLE 6

Number of Conferences Held

12 months ending	Manual workers				Staff				Total
	Works	Local	Central	Total	Works	Local	Central	Total	
June 30, 1955	1564	282	113	1959	154	20	12	186	2145
Dec. 31, 1959	2033	359	147	2539	254	70	41	365	2904
Dec. 31, 1959	2990	656	296	3942	663	192	83	938	4880
Dec. 31, 1964	3271	789	335	4395	793	268	116	1177	5572

SOURCE: Engineering Employers' Evidence to the Royal Commission, Appendix P.

By far the greater number of issues are initiated by trade unions. At local and works level, the confederation may coordinate trade union activity; but it operates only with the authority of the particular trade union involved in the case, and the presence, for example, of a confederation official does not exclude the necessity of attendance by the individual union's own officer. At Central Conference level, Marsh and Jones found that in 1959 some 91 percent of the issues referred to York were brought by the trade unions (only 2 of them by the confederation itself). Employers in engineering have been reluctant to make use of procedure. No information seems to have been collected concerning the processing of grievances raised by nonunionists. If any such grievances were put through procedure, they would, of course, need to be taken up by a trade union.

Marsh has revealed that the manual workers figure for 1966 conferences is 5,406 (3,854, 1,033, and 519), and that the *rate* of all conferences has increased from 1.54 per 1000 manual workers employed in 1955 to 4.02 in 1966. Further, Central Conference hearings have increased from 7.2 percent of Works Conference figures in 1955 to 13.5 in 1966.[15] It may be noted that the number of *hearings* always exceeds the number of *issues* since one issue is often reheard. For example, the 147 Central Conferences for manual workers in 1959 represent 125 issues.[16]

Of the 113 Central Conferences in 1955, 9 were (1), settled; 45 ended in (2), a failure to arrive at recommendations; 29 were referred back, (3) and (4); and 25 were "retained," (5). The equivalent figures for other years are given in Table 7.

TABLE 7

Year	(1)	(2)	(3) and (4)	(5)	Total hearings
1959	14	59	23	42	147
1963	42	130	47	70	296
1964	34	157	64	74	333
1965	60	181	93	93	436
1966	55	239	85	127	519

SOURCE: A. Marsh and W. McCarthy, *Disputes Procedures in Britain,* Research Paper No. 2 (Part 2) for the Royal Commission on Trade Unions and Employers' Associations (1968), p. 21.

Marsh records that the disposal rate has not changed very markedly over the years. The percentages of issues settled at Works and Local Conferences, or dealt with at Central Conferences in any fashion other than (2), failure to make recommendations, were in 1953, respec-

---

[15] Marsh and McCarthy, *op. cit.,* pp. 27, 28. See too Marsh and Jones, *op. cit.,* Tables 1 to 4, for further details.

[16] Marsh and Jones, *op. cit.,* Table 2, where it is shown that 77 of these originated from firms with over 1,000 workers, representing 8.7 percent of the firms in the industry and employing 58.9 percent of the workers.

tively, 81.9, 59.9, and 54.9. In 1966 they were 73.1, 49.8, and 53.9; and this was the least successful of recent years. There is generally a slight falling off in Works and Local Conference settlement rates, while that at Central Conference remains more or less stable.[17] Turner's analysis of precedure in the car industry produced similar results, though with a caveat that "disposal" at Works Conference can mean many different things and that the rates of agreement in the motor car section of the industry are significantly lower.

It must be remembered in discussing the increasing use of procedure that a system of informal conferences has grown up to supplement formal meetings within procedure. Such informal conferences are in fact direct consultations between management and the full-time union officials, usually at district level, at which the local employers' association may not be present and of which it may not even be aware. The Engineering Employers' Federation noted some 2,000 informal conferences in the industry in 1966.[18] Turner also points out that many local disputes are, of course, settled without reference to procedure, formal or informal, and that an inquiry at the Morris (Cowley) Works revealed that less than 5 percent of disputes brought to the works superintendent were taken to Works Conference.[19] Marsh also reports that "in one engineering group employing some 60,000 manual workers about 1,500 items were raised at superintendent level during one recent year, of which 4 per cent were taken up at Works Conference."[20] What is clear is that here, *below* procedure as it were, the shop steward is all important.

On the type of decision taken by Central Conference, Marsh comments concerning "reference back" that it is more than a mere procedural device. "It is a tacit admission by Central Conference that it is not in the position of an arbitrator whose findings are the last word and must be applied. The position of Central Conference is rather that of a conciliator whose recommendations must be tried in good faith by the parties directly concerned."[21] In similar vein he describes the methods of Central Conference:

---

[17] Marsh and McCarthy, *op. cit.*, Table 1, p. 20. This means overall disposal of 95 percent of cases raised above domestic level.

[18] *Ibid.*, p. 28, para. 60.

[19] Turner, *Motor Industry*, pp. 250–252. The Motor Industry Joint Study Group found in 1965 that of 190 cases in one firm which went to the Works Superintendent Level only 9 went to a Works Conference: Motor Employers' Evidence, R.C.M.E., vol. 23, p. 851.

[20] *Industrial Relations*, p. 129.

[21] Note also that cases "retained in the hands of Central Conference" (127 in 1966) are often ultimately settled at establishment level, and cases "settled" (55 in 1966) often merely reflect settlements achieved domestically.

Neither side has any intention of creating "case law" in handling issues at Central Conference. The tradition is that each case is regarded only in terms of its own content and circumstances, and that Central Conference findings on particular issues do not suggest that similar issues will always be dealt with in the same fashion. To accept the notion that a system of precedents should be applied appears to the central authorities to suggest that Central Conference would become a body for making national agreements. This, assuredly it is not. Its functions lie, not in making agreements, but in providing the final stage in a process of stage by stage conciliation in grievance settlement.[22]

This significant passage points both to the determination in engineering "employer conciliation" as in the building Joint Industrial Councils, in an industry where national substantive agreements have been most imprecise, as well as in one where the opposite has been true, to avoid "precedents," and, more important, to the strength of the belief in British industrial practice that in making decisions on grievances the parties will usually—especially in arbitration—be "making agreements." Nothing could be further removed from the legalistic distinction between disputes over rights and over interests.

In regard to the type of issue raised, we find, as is normal, that there is scarcely any limitation to the issues put through the one procedure. Marsh and Jones analyzed the issues of 1959, describing in detail, among other items, their subject matter. They reported:

Almost 65 per cent of the issues raised at York in 1959 were primarily concerned with wages and earnings. In view of the fact that it is sometimes asserted that Central Conference attempts to make decisions about detailed workshop arrangements which are too remote from its experience, the eighty-one issues involved were further broken down. Only nine issues (11.1 per cent) were concerned with piece-work prices. A similar proportion primarily related to the application of the industry's piece-work agreements. Sixty-five (76.5 per cent) were concerned with relatively straightforward domestic claims for higher rates or earnings.

About 13 per cent of Central Conference issues in 1959 concerned termination of employment or discipline. Most of these involved individual dismissals, but one suspension and four redundancy cases were included in the group. Among issues on conditions of work (8.8 per cent of the total) were clocking arrangements, overtime arrangements and holidays. Issues involving allocation of work comprised only four cases and trade union facilities in the workplace and non-membership of unions seven cases.

Table 8 summarizes the subject matter, time taken, and unconstitution-

---

[22] Marsh, *Industrial Relations,* pp. 88–90.

al stoppages of work on issues referred to Central Conference at York in 1959.

TABLE 8

Subject Matter, Time Taken, and Unconstitutional Stoppages of Work on Issues Referred to Central Conference at York, 1959

Time interval,* weeks	Number of issues	Subject Matter of Issues						Number of issues involving stoppages
		Wages and earnings	Conditions of work	Termination of employment	Trade union conditions	Allocation of work	Miscellaneous	
Under 5	7	2	1	3	—	—	1	(3)
5 through 9	43	27	3	6	3	4	—	(7)
10 through 14	39	27	4	5	2	1	—	(5)
15 through 19	16	10	1	1	1	1	2	(1)
20 through 24	10	9	1	—	—	—	—	(2)
25 through 29	2	1	1	—	—	—	—	—
30 through 39	4	3	—	—	—	—	1	—
40 through 49	4	2	—	1	1	—	—	(1)
Total	125	81(8)	11(1)	16(7)	7(2)	6(1)	4(0)	(19)
Average time interval	12.9	13.7	12.6	8.2	14.0	9.5	18.5	(11.3)
Median time interval	11.0	12.0	12.0	8.0	10.0	8.0	17.0	(7.0)

*Between first formal Works Conference and Central Conference.

SOURCE: Marsh and Jones, Tables 9 and 10, II *British Journal of Industrial Relations*, pp. 243, 244.

In another investigation Marsh found in one large engineering firm that, of the 1,500 issues raised in procedure at superintendent level during 1961-1962, one half related to payment problems and four out of ten of these involved the straightforward question of piecework prices. Of the others, some 16 percent concerned working hours and conditions, and 12 percent, staffing and transfers.[23] McCarthy, citing this, comments that it appears generally to be true that "where some form of piecework or bonus was in existence the main job of the workplace representatives tended to become the processing of grievances

[23] Marsh, *Managers and Shop Stewards* (1963), p. 12.

and claims arising out of the system of wage payment."[24] An investigation in a motor car factory in 1965 showed that of 126 grievances processed between June 1964 and October 1965, 32 concerned piecework prices; 19, union matters; 18, staffing and transfer; 18, working hours and conditions; 11, mobility of labor; and only 3, discipline.[25] It need not now be added that procedure does not distinguish between "grievances" and "claims" in the American sense.

As for stoppages, the figures for later years show an increase:

TABLE 9

"Unconstitutional"* Stoppages of Work by Manual Workers
in 1000 Federated Firms

Year	Number of stoppages	Percentage of firms involved	Percentage of manual workers involved	Average working hours lost per manual worker employed (all firms)
1960–61	241(7)	7.9	9.6	3.46
1961–62	101(12)	9.5	10.4	2.61
1962–63	162(9)	8.3	5.6	0.89
1963–64	207(21)	9.7	14.0	1.27
1964–65	267(29)	11.2	13.0	1.77
1965–66	232(28)	8.7	9.2	1.06

*Numbers of constitutional stoppages are given in parentheses.

Source: A. Marsh and W. McCarthy *Disputes Procedures in Britain,* Research Paper No. 2 (Part 2) for the Royal Commission on Trade Unions and Employers' Associations (1968), p. 24.

On the basis of his research on the question of delay, Marsh has pointed out that Local Conferences very rarely take place within the required 7 working days. In 1959, about one half took up to 4½ weeks. In practice, "average time taken for an issue to be processed from formal Works Conferences to Central Conference seems," he wrote, "to be about 13 weeks. In 1959, 25 per cent of issues took six weeks or less; 50 per cent 11 weeks or less and 75 per cent 17 weeks or less. Cases involving dismissals and redundancies and issues involving allocation of work are commonly dealt with with greater dispatch than normal and in 1959 took on the average between 8 and 10 weeks."[26]

But this figure of 13 weeks may be too low, and the delays in engineering procedure are probably slightly greater than the Marsh and

---

24 McCarthy, *Shop Stewards,* p. 15.
25 "State of Labour Relations at Rover Co. Solihull" (November 1965), unpublished first report of Motor Industry Joint Labour Council. See below, p. 121.
26 *Industrial Relations,* p. 130.

Jones survey of 1959 suggested. For example, Turner's analysis of car firms put the delays between Local and Central Conferences at eleven weeks, giving an average total delay of 17 weeks.[27] And the general report by A. J. Scamp, Chairman of the Motor Industry Joint Labour Council (described below, p. 121), showed that of 60 cases examined in 1965, which were taken to Central Conference from six motor car manufacturing firms, two thirds were taken from Works Conference to Central Conference in periods not exceeding four months while the rest took longer.[28] Furthermore, evidence given by the Austin Joint Shop Stewards to the Royal Commission suggests that in that firm (despite the recognition given there to Works Committees and to shop stewards) the average time from Works to Local Conference is 7½ weeks, and from Works to Central Conference, 23 weeks.[29] There seems little doubt that the delay in car firms is greater than elsewhere in engineering; but there is also the possibility that the figure of 13 weeks should be adjusted upward for engineering as a whole.

A NONFEDERATED CAR FIRM

Since the motor car sector appears to be that part of the engineering industry in which the procedure works least smoothly, it is worth glancing briefly at the different procedure used in a nonfederated motor manufacturing company in Britain with some 45,000 manual workers.[30] The firm "encourages" union membership, and about 97 percent of the manual work force are union members, but does not make it compulsory. The Procedure Agreement reached with 22 unions in 1955 makes specific provision for "reasonable facilities" to be provided for shop stewards' activities at the workplace; and states that "actions taken by stewards in good faith in pursuance of duties recognized in the agreement shall not in any way affect their employment with the Company," though in other respects stewards must comply with normal working conditions, and they need the written permission of their supervisor to leave the department for union duties. (Apart from the agreement, there exist the usual joint shop stewards committees and convenors of shop stewards in the bigger plants.) A Joint Works Committee (J.W.C.) is established with up to eight company respresentatives and eight shop stewards, rules for the election of the

---

[27] Turner, *Motor Industry*, p. 253.

[28] Report by A. J. Scamp on Motor Industry Joint Labour Council (H.M.S.O., 1966), p. 9.

[29] Figures calculated from evidence on behalf of the Austin Works Committee. July 1966.

[30] Information and documents kindly supplied by the company.

latter being outlined in the agreement. The J.W.C. acts as a consultative body; as a body to consider the application and interpretation of wage agreements which are "a domestic issue capable of settlement within the factory"; and as part of the procedure.

Stage 1(a) of the procedure requires that the employee raise the matter in question with his foreman; and then if no satisfaction results, that he may (b) bring in the shop steward to discuss it with the foreman. In 1962 the operation of this part of the agreement was transformed by a much clearer definition of a foreman's duties; and the company insists upon the strict operation of stage 1(a) of the procedure. The foreman will not go on to stage 1 (b) unless he has discharged his duties under stage 1 (a). (It may be mentioned also that in some works there is a general foreman interposed between the foreman and superintendent stages.) Stage 2 states that, in the event of failure, worker and shop steward approach their appropriate superintendent, who must, if he cannot solve the matter, report it "without delay" to the personnel manager. Stage 3 says that the matter may then be referred *either* to a J.W.C. *or* to the district officials of the union and the personnel manager. (Also a party may refer to district officials where a J.W.C. cannot agree.) Stage 4 entails reference from district officials to the national officials of the union for discussion with the Director of Labour Relations; or a reference from stage 3 to the National Joint Negotiating Committee (N.J.N.C.). This committee consists of not more than one executive official from *each* of the unions party to the agreement and an equal number of company officials. It meets not less than three times a year, and usually more frequently.

This agreement, to which subsequent minor additions have been made, may be said to combine at lower levels the notion of "employer conciliation" with that of joint decision-making as the issue climbs higher in the machinery. There seems no doubt that it is speedy. Average time for recent issues to go through the whole procedure was one month. Urgent cases have been processed in one week. It also

TABLE 10

	1967	1966			
Issues carried to:	1st qtr.	4th qtr.	3rd qtr.	2nd qtr.	1st qtr.
Superintendent level	301 }	433	234	298	412
Personnel manager.	181 }				
J.W.C. or district official	40	24	22	27	30
National officials or N.J.N.C. . . .	4	3	—	9	3
Total	526	460	256	334	445

SOURCE: Company's records.

seems clear that the disposal rate at lower levels is very high, leaving few matters to be dealt with at national level. The figures in Table 10 represent the five quarters up to January-March 1967.

In the 779 issues arising in the first half of 1966, the records also disclosed a total of 42 stoppages of work involving 313,631 hours lost, plus 26 "overtime bans" (505,543 hours lost). As for causes, 16 incidents were attributable to pay issues, 30 to working hours and conditions, 10 to discipline, 4 to mobility, and 8 to other causes. It goes without saying that there is no separate procedure for dismissals, which are taken up within the normal machinery. The flavor of those of the disputes which caused short stoppages in 1966 may be judged from the following short descriptions by the company (which might not, of course, be wholly acceptable to the unions concerned, but which will be very recognizable to all students of labor relations in operation):

(1) A dispute arose as a result of line speeds being increased following the change from 5-day to 4-day work scheduling. Management's explanation that this would ease and not aggravate the problem of surplus labor was not accepted. Seventy-five employees on the van assembly line stopped work and walked out. On the next day these employees were handed warning letters, but later in the day 49 van assembly workers stopped work early and went home. Consequential layoffs took place. Management dispatched letters to employees concerned making their return to work conditional on signing their agreement to comply in future with their terms and conditions of employment. (Issue was taken to district official level.)

(2) Fourteen men were transferred temporarily to another section to speed up urgent orders that had been delayed through a computer breakdown. As a result, 70 men stopped for 20 minutes, protesting that they should have overtime rather than additional labor. Management acknowledged that the transfer was not preceded by an explanation, and the stewards accepted that the protest should not have occurred; payment during the stoppage was, as a result, allowed. (Issue went to personnel manager.)

(3) An issue arose from the amount of work contracted out when only limited overtime was being worked. The stoppages were intended to highlight lack of response by local management to previous approaches. Management agreed to examine further the economics of overtime working compared to contracting out. (Issue to personnel manager.)

Although, judged in terms of days lost, the above picture does not represent, by any means, the perfect procedure, a comparison with the general situation in the motor car industry as presented by Turner[31] suggests that certain features of this procedure, in particular its clarity and speed, are to be accounted an improvement on general engineering procedure.

CHEMICAL INDUSTRY

Association of Chemical and Allied Employers

The Association of Chemical and Allied Employers,[32] with some 270 firms and a manual labor force of over 90,000, operates various procedures via three National Joint Councils (one termed a Joint Conference). Three main unions are involved for process workers; five craft unions have a separate agreement in certain sectors. (A complicating factor is the existence of a Chemical Workers Union, which originated as a breakaway union and still operates outside normal machinery with its own procedures.) Taking the main Joint Council (Drug and Fine Chemical) Procedure as typical of the industry, we find that it can deal with both the interpretation of agreements, and all other grievances with the consent of the parties (which is never withheld). It has four formal stages: Stage 1 consists of a discussion between the worker, or his shop steward, and the immediate management representative. The shop steward can come in immediately in this procedure; and there is less effort to formalize the workplace procedure than in engineering. At stage 2, the question is discussed between union officials and management with, if the company wishes, an official of the employers' association present. Unlike engineering, joint settlement between employers and unions is less possible without involving the association. Stage 3 involves the reference of the issue to trade union headquarters and the employers' association for a "Headquarters Conference." Despite their name, these conferences are so called only because of the status of their members and are often held at local or plant level, so that to other industries they might be seen as more in the nature of strengthened Works Conferences. Stage 4 takes the question, if necessary, to the council itself, which appoints a Disputes Committee of two employers and two union leaders (usually one from each side not concerned in the dispute). These Disputes

---

31 See especially H. Turner, *Motor Industry,* chaps. viii and ix where the detailed picture for the car firms is persented.

32 See C.B.I. Evidence, Appendix 3, Annexure A; and Marsh and McCarthy, *op. cit.* chap. 4. A new agreement of December 1967 contains a certain division between procedures for "rights" and "interest" disputes.

Committees frequently sit at the place of the dispute, a practice that dates from their origin under an agreement of 1919. The usual prohibition on industrial action before exhaustion of procedure is included, together, in this instance, with an obligation not to call strikes or lockouts at factories other than those where the dispute originates.

The other two Joint Council agreements provide for a fifth stage— one by way of reference to the Ministry of Labour, the other for a more general submission to arbitration—if the parties in their discretion so desire.

The number of issues dealt with in the lower levels of procedure is very high. The Confederation of British Industry reported 42 cases dealt with at national council level in 1964, with a settlement in all but three cases, which were subsequently settled in a Disputes Committee. Recent figures are given in Table 11.

TABLE 11

Year	Number of issues dealth with	
	By headquarters conferences	By disputes committees
1962	22	5
1963	29	3
1964	43	3
1965	46	3
1966	36	7

SOURCE: A. Marsh and W. McCarthy, *Disputes Procedures in Britain*, Research Paper No. 2 (Part 2) for the Royal Commission on Trade Unions and Employers' Associations (1968), p. 45.

The procedure appears to operate speedily, though no exact figures are available on the time required at lower levels, or on the issues taken up. Marsh has estimated that the Headquarters Conference usually takes place within two weeks of the failure to agree at the previous stage. The more intractable issues taken to Disputes Committee level saw an average delay between Headquarters Conference and Disputes Committee of seven weeks and three days between 1960 and 1965. In general, the chemical industry procedure may be accounted a successful joint procedure, and its problems are often those created by a complicated trade union structure including the presence of a major breakaway union not associated with the normal machinery. Marsh and McCarthy attribute this success to the "high sense of mutual responsibility" engendered by the Joint Disputes Committees, and add, "Inducement towards compromise and agreement is such that disagreement is made extremely difficult . . . the weight of custom and practice is very much in the direction of a concession by one side which is met by a similar accommodation on the part of the other." They dismiss any suggestion that this procedure is more specific and formalized than other procedures.[33]

Imperial Chemical Industries

Although associated with the main employers' association, Imperial Chemical Industries[34] operates its own procedures for its labor force, other than "staff," of some 60,000 workers. In the 74 works of all ten divisions of the company, Works Councils are established. Their functions appear to differ from place to place, and in some areas there is clear union resistance to such "joint consultation." A certain number of issues which might elsewhere find their way into negotiating procedure may be discussed here in the Works Council structure (which includes divisional and central levels); for example, dismissals (other than an individual case) might be discussed in either. The negotiating procedure based on a 1937 agreement and introduced in 1952 (amended 1960) is, however, of greater relevance here. It provides first for the election, functions, and operation of shop stewards, and then proceeds to distinguish *factory* and *union* negotiating procedure.

Factory procedure requires the worker to raise an issue with his foreman; then consult with his shop steward and approach the foreman again, who, if he fails to reach a settlement, reports to the relevant manager, and the latter "without undue delay" discusses the matter "with the shop steward and the member of the Union concerned." (The company "encourages" union membership.) If the matter is not cleared up within three days, the shop steward may report the matter to the local officer of the union who makes representation to the company. Some of these stages can sometimes be omitted. For example, if a group under more than one foreman is involved, a shop steward can approach a manager directly. If the matter involves more than one department, stewards may approach the works manager directly and proceed at once to report to local officials.

Union procedure begins from this base. Local officials may apply for a Local Conference to be held within fourteen days. If either side wishes, the matter can be referred higher to an Intermediate Conference, "if possible" to be held within twenty-one days of the reference, when the members of Local Conference (local union officer with representatives of members if they desire and factory management) are reinforced by a headquarters union official and someone from the

---

[33] Marsh and McCarthy, *op. cit.* pp. 43, 44, paras. 15, 17.
[34] Information kindly supplied by the company.

company's central personnel department. If a settlement is not reached, either side may refer the matter to a Headquarters Conference, again to be held within twenty-one days, where the chairman is a member of the personnel department not so far concerned with the matters in dispute. Should this fail, "it shall not be competent for notice of a strike or lockout to be tendered by the respective parties unless and until the question as to whether arbitration on the particular issue is mutually acceptable has been discussed between them" (Negotiating Procedure, Sec. III, clause 10). This clause is supplementary to the 1937 Agreement which provided that no lockout or strike should take place "except in pursuance of a dispute in which the company and the workers concerned by this Agreement are directly concerned" and "there shall be no stoppage of work unless and until a final failure to agree has been formally recorded . . . and then only after the customary legal notice has been tendered. A stoppage of work taking place after compliance with this procedure shall be deemed to be constitutional action."[35]

A few available figures indicate the operation of this procedure, but at higher levels only. For example, the number of Intermediate Conferences, Headquarters Conferences, and Arbitrations were in 1964, 29, 10 (4), and 1; in 1965, 27, 21 (9), and 0; and in 1966, 34, 13 (6), and 0. (The number of Headquarters Conferences where no Intermediate Conference was held, as can happen, for example, under a similar procedure for "staff" workers, is given in parentheses.) For earlier years, the company provided the figures given in Table 12.

TABLE 12

Year	Intermediate conferences		Headquarters conferences	
	Failure to agree (number to headquarters level)	Compromise settlement	Failure to agree (number to arbitration)	Compromise settlement
1961	28(19)*	20	11(2)	8
1962	11(9)	13	7(1)	2
1963	9(9)	18	3(1)	6

*The number of Headquarters Conferences where no Intermediate Conference was held is given in parentheses.

SOURCE: Company records.

Although it was not possible to analyze the precise content of the issues recorded here, it seemed clear that almost all of those that

---

[35] It seems clear that the meaning of this clause must be that constitutional action is possible only when notice *to terminate* employment is given.

proceeded to a higher level were concerned with "economic" claims and that those that might be said to include a "rights" element were settled at the lower levels of the procedure.

COAL MINING

Procedure is inevitably of high importance in British coal mining,[36] which, like its sister industries elsewhere, experiences a high incidence of strikes. On nationalization in 1946 the National Coal Board was required to enter into consultation with appropriate trade unions (which has meant mainly the National Union of Mineworkers) with a view to establishing consultation and bargaining machinery, in the latter case "with provisions for reference to arbitration in default of such settlement in such cases as may be determined by or under the agreements."[37] A National Conciliation plan had, in fact, existed since 1942, and was continued after 1946. There have emerged *three* levels of machinery.

First, national questions are dealt with in a Joint National Negotiating Committee with 16 members from each side and alternating chairmen. Voting is by sides; and if agreement is not reached, the question is, within five weeks, referred to the National Reference Tribunal, provided (since 1961) neither side objects. The tribunal's three members are appointed from persons outside the industry by the Master of the Rolls (who presides over the ordinary Court of Appeal) after consultation with the parties. They sit with assessors, one appointed by each party, who take no part in the award. The tribunal appears to deal mainly with economic claims and interpretations of previous awards, and has dealt with a total of 50 cases in the last 20 years (36 of them concerned with coal miners, i.e., other than staff and management or workers in the coke section).[38] The union's attitude toward the tribunal is reserved, partly no doubt because it is composed of "outsiders," but partly, too, because of the nature of some of its decisions, which have gone against the union. In 1944, for example, the tribunal, presided over by a judge, decided that those sitting on the tribunal would "be guided in coming to a conclusion [on the interpretation of a district and a national award] by the same considerations as

---

[36] See Evidence of National Coal Board, R.C.M.E., vol. 4, especially Appendices A and B; Marsh and McCarthy, *op. cit.* chap. 6.

[37] Coal Industry Nationalisation Act, 1946, sec. 46.

[38] For the detailed figures, we are indebted to I. F. Patterson, "Arbitration in Great Britain," unpublished Ph.D. thesis, Leeds University.

would influence a Court of Law in dealing with the Award of an Arbitrator" (12th "Porter" Award).

At district level a District Conciliation Board is established in the seventeen wage districts, with membership from both sides. If a settlement is not reached, the matter is referred to a district referee, normally within three weeks.

A rather more complicated system operates at pit level. At stage 1, the workmen concerned discuss the matter with the "immediate official" of the pit. If they do not reach a settlement within three days, stage 2 calls for the workmen to go to the manager. Stage 3 consists of a report made to the appropriate union official. Within three days, however, the issue moves to stage 4 and is formally referred to a pit meeting, representative of management and union. This group must meet within five days of request for a meeting and must *complete* its work within fourteen days. If a settlement is not reached, the matter is referred to a Disputes Committee (stage 5) established in each district by the District Conciliation Board, and this committee is given another fourteen days to discuss the dispute. Should no settlement emerge, the issue is referred to an umpire (stage 6), whose decision on a pit question is final. Umpires are appointed in each district.

Thus each level, national, district, and pit has, horizontally so to speak, its own appropriate machinery for settlement of disputes. For grievances, the pit machinery is plainly the most important. It is in this machinery that we find the disputes over piecework payments, the source of many coal-mining disputes.[39] We may notice, too, that a special agreement was entered into in 1947 on "Wrongful and Unreasonable Dismissal of Workmen," whereby the umpire is empowered to give "a definite decision whether or not the dismissal was wrongful or unreasonable" and may "couple with his decision (if it was) a recommendation that the workman be reinstated in his former work." This appears to be a *special* procedure; and indeed the National Coal Board representatives told the Royal Commission that it "is scarcely ever used."[40] But on inspection we find that the agreement provides for a dismissal case to be taken through the *normal* pit machinery *except* that the Disputes Committee stage be omitted. (It is still true, however, that discipline and dismissal may be more often dealt with outside procedure altogether; below p. 147.)

---

[39] Marsh and McCarthy (*op. cit.* p. 82, para. 40) estimate that over 90 percent of the strikes in the industry involve face workers on piecework, who constitute only 40 percent of the labor force.

[40] R.C.M.E. vol. 4, p. 169, para. 800. The agreement is on pp. 157–158.

Persons chosen to serve as umpires represent varied backgrounds. Usually they are former union officials or managers who have retired from industry; but district referees are usually lawyers or academics. In one area, umpires have been lawyers; in some areas, the parties agree on an umpire; at other times, alternate appointments are used, or the cases are referred in rotation to names on a panel.[41] The use of umpires varies considerably from one part of the country to another; but overall it has declined, and they are now involved in only 1 percent of the cases in the Pit Conciliation Procedure.[42] Umpires do not, in the manner of British arbitrators, give reasons for their awards. Marsh has analyzed a sample of 79 umpires' awards mainly concerned with wages and piecework (excluding dismissal cases, which numbered 8) and found that 28 were decided in favor of the board and 21 for the union; in another 28, a direct compromise was reached; one was transferred to another level; and in one the ruling directed the parties to negotiate a new contract![43]

The remarkably frequent use of the Pit Conciliation Procedure is indicated by the figures in Table 13.[44]

TABLE 13

Matters Dealt with through Pit Conciliation

Year	Cases settled by pit meetings	Cases settled by disputes committees	Cases settled by umpires	Total
1961	9,712	410	83	10,205
1962	8,977	383	150	9,510
1963	10,197	293	65	10,555
1964	9,931	252	73	10,256

SOURCE: National Coal Board Evidence, *R.C.M.E.*, vol. 4, p. 149.

In construing these figures, it must be remembered first that no mention is made of discussions *before* the formal pit meeting; and second that the total of cases is being maintained despite a rapidly shrinking work force (from 564,500 in 1965 to 517,900 in 1966, for example). Furthermore the board states: "In practice the machinery operates more rapidly than is indicated in an account of its provisions since in a large proportion of its cases dealt with under the machinery settlements are reached at an early stage in the procedure thus avoiding the necessity of entering into the later stages." Also, Marsh and

[41] *Ibid.*, p. 166, paras. 762–770.
[42] Marsh and McCarthy, *op. cit.* p. 83, para. 45.
[43] *Ibid.*, p. 84.
[44] Pit level settlements in 1959 through 1964 were just under 97 percent of all settlements achieved by the industry's machineries: *ibid.*, p. 77, para. 21.

McCarthy found that the timetable laid down in the Pit Conciliation Procedure was adhered to in four-fifths of the cases. However, it is also well known that even this elaborate machinery does not prevent stoppages on a large scale. The board reported that in 1962 the number of disputes (with tonnage of coal lost) was 2,009 (1,123,381); 1963, 1,640 (1,319,098); and 1964, 1,770 (1,330,413).[45] Marsh's analysis of the causes of such disputes is given in Table 14.

TABLE 14

Distribution of Disputes by Cause, 1947–1952 and 1964–1965

Cause	Percentage of disputes attributable to each cause	
	1947–1952	*1964–1965*
Wages and piecework price lists..................	42.9	44.4
Objections to methods of working, etc.	25.6	18.8
Dissatisfaction with allowances, etc.	5.4	5.9
Sympathy with men dismissed, suspended, etc.......	2.4	3.6
Refusal to accept alternative work	6.9	7.1
All other causes	16.8	20.2

SOURCE: A. Marsh and W. McCarthy, *Disputes Procedures in Britain*, Research Paper No. 2 (Part 2) for the Royal Commission on Trade Unions and Employers' Associations (1968), p. 82.

Such figures as those in Table 14 can serve, in the absence of other information, as a general guide to the sort of disputes likely to reach a pit meeting. However, one important new factor emerges from the National Powerloading Agreement made by the parties in 1966; this factor relates mainly to replacement of piecework by day wages for a gradually increasing number of workers. Furthermore, a procedural clause declares that, in the event of a pit dispute arising over manning, a special four-man group with knowledge of power-loading systems (two appointed by each side) shall decide it and report their findings at district level, while disputes on other matters are to be treated as national questions. The 1966 Agreement, therefore, breaks through the horizontal structuring of coal-mining procedures. On pay and manning questions, the Pit Conciliation Procedure and its arbitration provisions will not be used, while on manning questions, the established, formal machinery is displaced entirely and there has

[45] Marsh and McCarthy point out that coal mining has been traditionally a strike-prone industry and so neither side regards the complete avoidance of strikes as a test for procedural adequacy, and that workers involved in unconstitutional strikes "consider themselves less to be breaking procedure than establishing their claim to make it operate" (*Ibid.*, pp. 79 and 85, paras. 31 and 49).

been substituted an informal procedure containing no arbitration clauses.[46] At a time when new plans for pit closures and running down the industry are being initiated by the government, it must remain uncertain just what the effect will be of an agreement that tries to remove wage disputes from this traditional pit level machinery.

RAILWAYS

The British Railways Board (which now runs the British railway network and used to operate under the former "British Transport Commission") operates a complicated series of procedures with the three unions in its industry (National Union of Railwaymen, Transport and Salaried Staffs Association, and Association of Locomotive Engine Drivers and Firemen).[47] There has been a statutory base for the machinery since 1921; but voluntary agreements had existed in many companies despite turbulent labor relations since 1907. On nationalization under the British Transport Commission (B.T.C.) in 1945, previous machinery was continued until replaced by the modern structure in 1956. The modern structure, however, owes much to its history.

For example, members of the staff are divided into five categories. What is described below is the machinery for some 260,000 "Conciliation and Salaried" staff, the main bulk of employees. For other groups, the arrangements are quite different. For example, for three groups (workshop, workshop supervisors, and electrical staff), the procedures end with the possibility of reference to the Industrial Court, after coming up via local committees, "line" committees, regional conferences, and regional councils. The arrangements for conciliation and salaried staff are much more complicated and are summarized in Table 15.

During the operation of the complicated procedures outlined in Table 15, there should be no withdrawal of labor or "any attempt on the part of the staff to hamper the proper working of the railway."

---

[46] See generally *ibid.*, pp. 76–79.

[47] Information on the railways is mainly derived from *Machinery of Negotiation for Railway Staff* (British Transport Commission, 1956); Evidence of British Railways Board, R.C.M.E., vol. 14, and Evidence of National Union of Railwaymen, R.C.M.E., vol. 17;*Pay and Conditions of Service of British Railways Staff*, Report No. 8 for the National Board for Price and Incomes (CMND. 2873; 1966), Appendix A; Report of a Court of Inquiry under Professor D. J. Robertson (CMND. 3426; 1967); and documents kindly supplied by the British Railways Board to whom we are greatly indebted. On the history, see Sharp, *Industrial Conciliation and Arbitration in Great Britain* (1950), chap. viii.

TABLE 15

Body	Level of operation	Composition	Functions	Procedure
1. Local representatives	Each station or depot with less than 50 employees	Two appointed from their numbers by all regularly employed staff	Discussion with local officials. Negotiation and settlement of local problems. Questions not covered by national agreements.	Not formally regulated
2. Local departmental committees	Each station or depot with more than 50 employees	Four members from either side. Trade union members elected by all staff over 18. Only trade unionists eligible for election. Each side elects one of its members as secretary.	Discussion with local officials. Negotiation and settlement of local problems. Questions not covered by national agreements.	Matters must be submitted to management before being placed on agenda. Meetings as and when necessary. Meetings within 7 days of agenda being agreed on.
3. Sectional councils	Regional	Five sectional councils in each region to each of which are allotted specific grades of workers. Each council has 7-12 representatives on either side. elected by all staff over 18 in the grades in question. Only trade unionists eligible. Each side elects a chairman from its members and a secretary.	Application of national agreements. Appeals where failure-to-agree at local level. Application of agreed promotion and redundancy arrangements. Questions of regrading of posts.	Must meet at least twice annually. Previous reference to management required. Decision by agreement between two sides.
4. Negotiations between regional staff headquarters and railway trade unions	Regional	Not regulated	Any sectional council matter on which there has been a failure-to-agree	Not formally regulated

103

TABLE 15—*Continued*

Body	Level of operation	Composition	Functions	Procedure
5. Railway Staff Joint Council (R.S.J.C.)	National (first formal stage of national machinery)	Council consists of 4 sections (salaried, locomotive, traffic, and general). Each section consists of representatives of B.R.B. and appropriate unions. Union members appointed, not elected.	Any failure-to-agree from sectional council or regional negotiations. Any proposal to vary a national agreement, which has been referred to the other side and not accepted. Application of national agreements that involve only "minor" issues (that do not involve differences of "principle") must not go beyond this level.	Decision by agreement between both sides
6. Railway Staff National Council (R.S.N.C.)	National	Eight B.R.B. and eight trade union representatives with a secretary elected by the council as a whole	Proposals to vary national agreements not accepted by R.S.J.C. Application questions agreed by R.S.J.C. to be of "major" importance, and not settled by R.S.J.C. "Minor" application questions involving issues of principle. Whether an application question is of "major" importance if R.S.J.C. cannot agree on this.	Decision by agreement between two sides, or by a majority.
7. Railway Staff National Tribunal (R.S.N.T.)	National	Three members: one selected from time to time by B.R.B. and one by union, from panel previously nominated; plus the	Proposals to vary national agreements where failure-to-agree at R.S.J.C. and R.S.N.C. Application questions agreed by R.S.N.C. to be of "major"	Assessors, one from either side, may be appointed. Claim and defense to be made in writing before oral hearing, which is in public or private as parties agree.

TABLE 15—*Continued*

Body	Level of operation	Composition	Functions	Procedure
		chairman (see below). Panel members cannot be members or officials of B.R.B. or of trade unions.	importance where R.S.N.C. has failed-to-agree. In latter case consent of parties, "which shall not be unreasonably withheld," needed.	Decision must set out the facts and arguments and be published. Expenses of tribunal shared equally by parties. There is no specific provision making the awards of this tribunal binding on the parties. They are usually, though not always, accepted (see *R.C.M.E.*, vol. 14, para. 2140).
8. Chairman of Railway Staff National Tribunal (Chairman R.S.N.T.)	National	Chairman appointed by B.T.C. and trade unions jointly, or by Minister of Labour after consultation with them if they cannot agree.	Interpretation of national agreements not settled at R.S.J.C. may be referred directly. Also, issues not involving such interpretation, if discussed at R.S.J.C. without agreement, *provided* they are not of "major" importance, in which case they are discussed on R.S.N.C. (In effect, issues that are neither "minor" nor "major"; and decisions whether or not an issue is "minor" or "major.")	Application to chairman, oral or in writing, in public or private, as the parties agree. Except in interpretation cases, chairman should give a decision that is "equitable and reasonable on the merits of the case . . . having regard to the terms of the agreements cited by the parties as relevant."

The unions agree not to support members who contravene this provision and to do their best to induce such individuals to conform to this agreement. In many ways, the procedures, if well adapted to negotiation of new terms, serve somewhat less well as grievance procedures. It must be mentioned at once that questions relating to discipline and dismissals do not fall within them. (The special disciplinary machinery is discussed on p. 148.) On the other hand, ordinary disputes of the "quarrel-with-the-foreman" kind are taken into the machinery, though how quickly is not clear. The Railways Board told the Royal Commission "a lot depends on the calibre of the local manager concerned and of course on the calibre of the staff representatives; but theoretically the answer is that there and then it goes to the local departmental committee or the works committee could be summoned almost immediately."[48]

Through the kindness of the Railways Board, we were able to study the decisions and minutes of the stages numbered 5 to 8 in Table 15 (all of which are recorded and printed). The salient features relevant here seemed to be as follows:

8. *The Chairman's Decisions: Nos. 87 (June 2, 1961) to 102 (August 6, 1965).* All of these decision involved claims by the unions. Fourteen of them involved issues which, by the form of their presentation, fell "for decision by me upon [the] merits and not as an issue involving interpretation." One claim involved the interpretation of national agreements. One was a claim on which the R.S.J.C. had failed to reach agreement concerning eligibility for its own agenda (another case in which direct reference to the chairman is possible). True to the tradition of most British arbitration, the chairman gives no reasons for his awards; but they are rendered quickly, the average of these sixteen awards being fifteen days from the date of presentation. On the other hand, they related to issues that had arisen many years before, often patiently argued through procedure by the parties more than once. Of thirteen awards open to such analysis, the issues had first arisen less than three years before in three cases; between three and five years before in seven cases; and more than five years before in three cases.

7. *Railway Staff National Tribunal: Decisions 24 (July 20, 1961) to 39 (July 15, 1965).* These decisions all involved economic claims, for example, "That the existing annual leave entitlement of Railway Salaried Staff be increased by three additional days." In this respect the tribunal is a typical British arbitration body, dealing preeminently with conflicts of "interests." Six of the hearings were in public and nine were in private, as the parties can request.

6. *Railway Staff National Council: Minutes 420 (October 23, 1959) to 509 (August 13, 1965).* Once again this body scarcely ever deals with grievances, but is devoted to claims: "505: Application for a 40-hour week—Conciliation Staff"; "506: Application for increased annual leave—Conciliation Staff"; and so on. All of the minutes fell into that category except one or two minor administrative minutes and four that concerned the jurisdiction of the R.S.N.C. itself.

---

[48] R.C.M.E., vol. 14, p. 538, para. 2142.

5. *Railway Staff Joint Council: Minutes (1961 to 1965).* Here the picture is very different. First the weight of business is much greater. The number of minutes in the four sections during these four years was: Salaried Section, 159; Traffic Section, 460; Locomotive Section, 169; General Section, 49. The volume containing these minutes is a perfect illustration of the flexibility and multipurpose use of British procedures. So various were the issues and arguments that they defied analysis. What can be shown very easily is that ordinary economic "claims" were followed by disputes involving employees' rights, often the rights of *individuals*. Selecting, for instance, almost at random, from the Locomotive Section one found *Minute L267*: "The representatives of A.S.L.E.F. submitted an application for mileage payment to Driver C. H. G—— and Fireman D. M—— of Copley Hill in respect of mileage whilst travelling home passenger on 17 October 1960." They argued that the men were unable to take up their return working through a late arrival and as they had been deprived of that "through no fault of their own they should receive mileage payment" to make up for their normal work. The railway representatives "reiterated the view expressed previously that there was no prescriptive right to mileage payment regardless of whether or not the mileage had been worked . . . . The claim must therefore be declined." *Minute L268:* "The representatives of the A.S.L.E.F. submitted a claim that Footplate Staff should not suffer a loss of pay or of mileage as a result of adverse weather conditions or other occurrences outside their control. The Railway representatives said that they had examined the claim but were unable to concede it." Similarly in *Minute L275*, the National Union of Railwaymen (N.U.R.) raised the question of who was responsible for the cleaning of cabs in diesel locomotives. The employers "undertook to examine the question" further. In *Minute L276*, the Association of Locomotive Engine Drivers and Firemen (A.S.L.E.F.) applied for payment for "a full turn of duty on 23 December 1960" for Driver K. A. D—— who, having signed on duty, was told that there was not sufficient work for him as a driver, and was asked instead to do work which, the union pointed out, was not appropriate for his grade. The railway representatives held to their view that it had been "reasonable" to ask the appellant to undertake that work and said the "application could not be conceded." In general, an inspection of the cases in the Traffic and Locomotive sections showed that very few of the applications on behalf of named employees resulted in anything other than a refusal by the employers to concede the claim. Nor can it be said that the procedure is here particularly speedy. The case of Driver C. H. G—— and Fireman D. M——, arising

in October 1960, was heard in January 1963; and the time lag for Driver K. A. D—— was December 1960 to January 1963. Most of the individual claims involved a delay of over a year, in which time many of them had no doubt been through the lower levels of procedure.

Slow procedures are, of course, likely to cause particular difficulties when an industry is contracting, and that has been the case with British railways. A series of disputes has broken out in recent years between the unions concerned about members' jobs, and the employers who were making every effort to ease the redundancies they felt it necessary, or were forced, to create.[49] In such a situation it is hardly surprising that there have been a number of inquiries into particular situations (including the Robertson Court of Inquiry of 1967), or that the parties have turned aside from their own procedures to try to settle differences at particular points. An example of the latter occurred in 1965. An agreement had been negotiated in that year between the Railways Board and A.S.L.E.F. and the N.U.R., paragraph D(4) of which made a promise to retain redundant staff for certain periods. Paragraph E stated that negotiations were to be resumed immediately for bonus plans for freight train crews. British railways argued that paragraph E excluded certain footplate staff from the protection of D(4); the unions disagreed. The parties decided to submit their dispute to the ad hoc arbitration of a well-known "trouble shooter" in British industrial disputes, A. J. Scamp, and to abide by his interpretation. He awarded for the unions and decided to give his reasons. The following passages from them are excellent illustrations of the kind of approach British industrial parties would expect of such an arbitrator called in when they could not use their ordinary machinery to resolve a dispute:

> I have not attempted to make a legal interpretation of the agreement. It was not conceived, drafted or to be implemented by lawyers. It attempted to record the understanding of each of the parties as to what was contemplated. I have therefore directed my attention to what I conceive to be the spirit and intention of the agreement.
>
> Section E which looked forward to resumed negotiations on incentive bonus schemes neither specifically includes nor excludes any undertaking as to possible redundancy arrangements. In fact, the wording of the agreement as a whole does not substantiate either the contention of the British Railways Board or the Unions.
>
> The Unions have told me that if they had thought that there was any possibility that the arrangements for redundancy in the agreement were

---

49 On the advanced character of British railway's redundancy plan before the Act of 1965, see Dorothy Wedderburn, *Redundancy and the Railwaymen* (1965).

not to be applied to staff covered by negotiations on incentive schemes, they would not have been parties to it. I accept this contention.

For their part, the British Railways Board have told me that they regarded the negotiations which were to follow as being on a distinct and separate issue and that in signing the agreement their representatives in no way contemplated that similar redundancy arrangements would necessarily be provided . . . . I believe that the British Railways Board contemplated considering the whole question of redundancy in the negotiations which were to follow. But these negotiations were explicitly foreshadowed in the agreement. In the view of the Unions, they were an integral part of the "package deal" which would not be finally established until the negotiations had been successfully concluded.

As I have indicated, it is very likely that the agreement would not have been possible if the British Railways Board had made clear their understanding to the Unions. This is not to say that the Board representatives were in any way remiss for not having done so. I can accept that they believed, and did not question, that their understanding was also that of the Unions.

This was clearly, however, not the case. The agreement was reached and has been implemented only because the Unions thought they had the assurance they sought. This is the present position. In the Unions' view one of the essential foundations of the agreement is now in question. Unless it is maintained, there will be widespread discontent among their members. Mutual trust is essential also for the negotiations on other matters to produce greater efficiency to the benefit of the British Railways Board and their employees.

For all these reasons, I have concluded in interpreting the Agreement that the arrangements in Section D(4) must be held to apply to the staff to be covered in the negotiations referred to in Section E of the agreement.

I hope that negotiations on incentive bonus schemes can be resumed quickly. If it is the wish of the parties, I am willing to give such assistance as I can in the process of such negotiations.

GENERAL POST OFFICE

The General Post Office (G.P.O.) is at present part of the civil service, but in 1969 it will become a commercial public corporation.[50] Therefore, although the position of civil servants has been placed largely outside the scope of this study, a few brief comments will be made on certain features of industrial relations within the Post Office.

First, the department falls under the system of Whitley Councils. The National Whitley Council of fifty-four members, half from the official and half from the staff side, includes on the staff side six mem-

---

[50] The forthcoming Post Office Act, 1969.

bers of the Union of Post Office Workers (U.P.W.) and two from the Post Office Engineering Union (P.O.E.U.), the unions for manipulative and engineering grades, respectively.[51] Departmental and Local Whitley Councils are smaller. At a Whitley Council, the official side takes the chair; each side speaks formally as a whole; and no decision can be reached in the event of disagreement other than the maintenance of the official side's view. Much work is done through standing committees. Since 1925, there has existed an agreement to arbitrate certain issues in the event of deadlock. Since 1936 the arbitration body has been the Civil Service Arbitration Tribunal. Arbitrable issues are claims "affecting the emoluments, weekly hours of work and leave of classes of civil servants." Individual cases are excluded; but there has been considerable controversy about just what is included. Of the 607 cases arbitrated at national level between 1925 and 1959, 113 concerned Post Office staff. Of the same total, 444 concerned salary scales and were mainly in the nature of economic claims.[52] If these figures seem small, Professor S. J. Frankel suggests that "perhaps the best measure of the success of arbitration is the infrequency of its use in relation to the number of issues that are settled by consultation or negotiation." The P.O.E.U. has said: "Through the Whitley System members of the Post Office staff have an opportunity to play a part in the determination of almost every aspect of their conditions. The Whitley machinery of negotiations is no substitute for trade unions and the viability of the Whitley system depends entirely upon the existence of trade unions which are strong, independent and effectively democratic."[53] The problem of dismissals in the Post Office is discussed on p. 151. One other aspect of the Whitley system which has made the Post Office of special interest is the Promotion Procedure. In other industries, customs and practices crystallize within procedures to regulate promotion; and in some (as on the railways), the rules become formal and precise. But in the Post Office formalization of procedures regulating promotion has reached perhaps a high point,[54] which may be the mark of an old, public service industry.[55] It will be interesting to see whether these highly formalized procedures survive commercialization.

---

[51] See H.M. Treasury Evidence, R.C.M.E. vol. 10; *Staff Relations in the Civil Service* (H.M.S.O., 1965); and "Evidence of National Whitley Council Staff Side to Royal Commission," in S. J. Hayward, *Whitley Councils in the U.K. Civil Service.*

[52] See S. J. Frankel, "Arbitration in the British Civil Service" (1960) 38 *Public Administration*, p. 197. The quotation is from p. 208.

[53] Evidence to Royal Commission, para. 30.

[54] We are grateful to the G.P.O., U.P.W., and P.O.E.U. for information about the working of these procedures.

[55] [Post Office Promotion Procedures: For engineering workers, reports are prepared biennially on each officer (1) on *Qualifications for Promotion* and (2) on *Assessment of Performance of Duties*. These are used by the Promotion Board, consisting of management representatives. The *Promotion Board* selects candidates for a Promotion Panel, from which officers are appointed to vacancies as they arise. At various stages appeals can be made in writing, generally within fourteen days of the event giving rise to the appeal: against nonselection for interview (to the *Promotion Board*); against exclusion from, restriction within, or removal from a Promotion Panel (to an *Appeal Board*, also consisting of management representatives); against nonselection for a particular vacancy (to the *Appeal Board*). Also, when a promotion is announced, any officer senior to the officer promoted may appeal to the Postmaster General or Director General, whether he has exercised the appeal machinery or not.

For manipulative grades there are two processes. An *Acting List Board* (consisting of management representatives) appoints officers to an Acting List which guarantees a certain period of time each year on higher duties; and if an officer is not placed on this list, he can ask for a period of trial in higher duties. Second, a *Promotion Board*, also consisting of management representatives, appoints to vacancies as they arise, usually but not necessarily from the Acting List. Nominations for consideration by both boards are made not only by supervisors but by the staff unions, although the latter take no responsibility for the board's decisions. An officer can appeal to the Regional Director against a refusal of trial in higher duties, against exclusion from the Acting List after trial, and against omission from the list if he has been included in the previous year. An officer can also appeal to the Head Postmaster and Regional Director against a proposed promotion and, if the proposal is nevertheless confirmed, to the Postmaster General.]

6.

STOPPAGES OF WORK
AND NEW PROCEDURES

Despite the use of voluntary procedures, however, it is well known that Britain still suffers from work stoppages. This book is not a study of strikes, but there is a special reason for describing certain features of strikes in Britain: in some areas of industry, despite procedure, one regular method of processing some employment disputes is the strike, usually a sudden and short strike. Figures for recent strike incidence nationally are shown in Table 16, and the Ministry of Labour Evidence remarked that

> the great majority of strikes in this country in recent years have been unofficial—i.e., not called or recognized by a trade union. No separate figures for unofficial strikes are published but it is estimated that in the five years 1960–1964 nearly 95 per cent of strikes were unofficial and that these accounted for nearly 60 per cent of days lost. Most unofficial strikes are short and practically all are local. To a large extent they are in breach of the procedure for settling disputes in the industry concerned.[1]

The ministry produced figures relating to the location and causes of strikes. Their main conclusions were that "it is noteworthy that whereas many industry groups consistently lose very few days through

---

[1] Ministry of Labour Evidence, pp. 37–40, paras. 127, 129, and 134.

strikes, the five or six industry groups losing most days per thousand employees have included motor vehicles, shipbuilding and port transport every year from 1960 [to 1965] and coal mining every year except 1962."

Marsh and McCarthy[2] have produced the following figures for 1965:

Days lost per 1,000 workers employed	Official	Unofficial	All
Motor vehicles and cycles	551	1,099	1,650
Port and inland water transport	–	762	762
Shipbuilding and marine engineering	115	642	757
Coal mining	–	737	737

As for causes, the Ministry of Labour added:

The main causes in terms of days lost are wage disputes (claims for wage increases and other wage disputes), disputes over the employment or discharge of workers and disputes over other working arrangements including rules and discipline. . . . Wage disputes over these five years (1960–1964) accounted for about two-thirds of all days lost and nearly half of all stoppages. Other working arrangements, rules and discipline gave rise to nearly a third of all stoppages but less than 10 per cent of days lost, whereas the employment and discharge of workers caused between 10 and 11 per cent of both numbers of stoppages and days lost. It may be noted that all other causes—including demarcation disputes—were comparatively insignificant. The great majority of "other wage disputes" and two fifths of the days lost through them, are in coal mining. Disputes over the employment or discharge of workers as measured by the number of stoppages are concentrated in metals and engineering and in construction, but most days are lost from this cause in motor vehicles. Most strikes over other working arrangements, rules and discipline occur in coal mining and most days are lost there; next come transport (reflecting stoppages of this kind in the docks) motor vehicles and metals.

There has been a trend in recent decades for stoppages over issues other than wage claims to become relatively more important. There can be little doubt that many British trade unionists see their right to take industrial action as an integral part of the "processing" of such disputes, and McCarthy and Parker[3] have recently confirmed this.

The Ministry of Labour's analysis in the *Gazette*, from which Table 16 was taken, further listed fifty-three principal stoppages in various

---

[2] Marsh and McCarthy, *op. cit.* p. 81, para. 35.

[3] McCarthy and Parker, *op. cit.* para. 191. There is also evidence to suggest that an increase in the use of procedure is often accompanied by the occasional use of unconstitutional strikes. In other words, the use of procedure and strikes in breach of procedure may be complementary rather than contradictory activities.

TABLE 16

Analysis of Stoppages Beginning in 1966 by Cause

Principal cause	Mining		Metals and engineering		Vehicles		Construction		Transport		All industries and services	
All wage disputes	230*	(65)†	219	(265)	113	(240)	118	(52)	65	(903)	883	(1,642)
Claims for increases	2	(9)	155	(155)	77	(191)	70	(28)	31	(890)	431	(1,364)
Other disputes	228	(57)	64	(110)	36	(48)	48	(24)	34	(13)	452	(278)
Hours of labour	–	–	6	(3)	6	(5)	2	(1)	2	(2)	26	(14)
Demarcation disputes	2	–	7	(5)	4	(3)	10	(3)	13	(50)	57	(84)
Disputes concerning employment or discharge (including redundancy)	7	(5)	73	(111)	35	(47)	86	(59)	15	(33)	282	(289)
Other disputes on personnel questions	14	(5)	6	(5)	11	(12)	8	(7)	10	(3)	58	(39)
Other working arrangements, rules, and discipline	301	(41)	68	(36)	35	(70)	31	(11)	64	(57)	556	(234)
Trade union status (including refusal to work with nonunionists)	–	–	24	(32)	10	(5)	7	(7)	5	(15)	59	(74)
Sympathetic action	2	(1)	2	(3)	–		3	(1)	4	(8)	16	(18)
Totals												
Stoppages	556		405		214		265		178		1,937	
Thousands of working days lost		(118)		(458)		(382)		(141)		(1,072)		(2,395)

*First figure in column represents number of stoppages.
†Second figure in column, given in parentheses, represents thousands of working days lost.

SOURCE: *Ministry of Labour Gazette*, May 1967, p. 385.

industries during 1966. Thirteen of these concerned discharge, redundancy, and other layoffs. Three included mention of victimization of shop stewards or were dismissals related to union recognition or similar problems. Seven touched on workers' objections to work changes made without consultation. As for dismissal, the category in 1966 of "Disputes concerning employment or discharge of workers" made up some 14 percent of the total number of stoppages. If one takes out wage disputes, the total rises to 27 percent. Meyers[4] calculated the equivalent numbers for stoppages and days lost in 1960 to be about 10 percent (and more than 20 percent when wage disputes were eliminated). He also found, on examining strike records, a number of disputes in construction and building, where short, sharp stoppages by large numbers of men had secured the reinstatement of persons, including shop stewards, dismissed for acts of misconduct or for "unsuitability."

As for the motor industry, where there is much unofficial strike action, Turner has analyzed the issues in strike disputes (*excluding* general engineering stoppages, which would concern wages and hours), and his findings are summarized in Table 17.

TABLE 17

Percentage attributable to	1921–1939		1940–1945		1946–1964	
	Strikes	Striker days	Strikes	Striker days	Strikes	Striker days
(1) Straight wage increase demands or wage reductions	12	36	3	½	13	14
(2) Wage structure and work loads	47½	46½	64	69	39	30
(3) Working hours and conditions	5	½	2	1½	9	3
(4) Individual dismissals ..	8	2	8	4	9	8
(5) Redundancy, short time, etc.	10	8	3	½	12	18
(6) Management questions .	1½	3	6	12	6	6
(7) Trade union relations ..	16	4½	14	12½	12	21½
Total	100	100	100	100	100	100

SOURCE: H. Turner, G. Clack, and G. Roberts, *Labour Relations in the Motor Industry* (1967), p. 65.

The figures in Table 17 show an increase in trade union relations problems and in dismissal cases. Further, the proportion of stoppages

---

[4] Meyers, *Ownership of Jobs,* pp. 28–29.

under the Ministry of Labour heading "other working arrangements, rules, and discipline" had seldom constituted more than 15 percent of strikes recorded in *all* industries annually up to the 1940's; but Turner points out that they now begin to account for about a third of all stoppages. Another analysis of the metalworking industries showed that less than 10 strikes every year were reported on an average as due to these causes in the interwar period. By the early 1950's, some 25 were reported annually; but in the 1960's, more than 80 such strikes were reported in each year.[5] Meyers in 1964 wrote that "Disciplinary dismissals are a major cause of 'unofficial' strikes." If the evidence does not take us quite that far, it certainly shows that discipline and "working arrangements" generally appear to be a significant cause of stoppages.

A report of the National Joint Advisory Council in 1967 gave some information concerning stoppages of work due to dismissals in 1964–1966.[6] These show that stoppages arising from dismissals alleged to be direct victimization for trade union activity are probably not very numerous (though, of course, even a few can be qualitatively important) accounting for only some 4 percent of all stoppages due to

TABLE 18

Analysis of Stoppages Attributable to Dismissal
(other than redundancies, and other than trade union activity dismissals)

	Yearly Average, 1964–1966		
Reason for dismissal	Number of stoppages	Number of workers directly involved (nearest 100)	Working days lost by all workers involved (nearest 1,000)
1. Bad timekeeping and related faults	20	2,900	11,000
2. Time card irregularities....	3	300	1,000
3. Refusal to undertake a particular job	18	3,800	15,000
4. Refusal of another type of foreman's or supervisor's orders	18	2,800	18,000
5. Other disciplinary cause ...	44	11,000	59,000
6. Alleged incompetence	30	5,200	28,000
7. Cause not known	71	13,800	46,000
Total°	203	39,700	178,000

°Rounding of averages sometimes makes sum of items differ from total.

SOURCE: *Dismissals Procedures*, N.J.A.C. Report (1967), Appendix 2.

---

[5] Turner, Motor Industry, pp. 335–336.
[6] *Dismissals Procedures*, N.J.A.C. Report (1967), Appendices 2 and 3.

dismissals in circumstances other than redundancy (8 percent of days lost). Omitting dismissals known to be due to trade union activity (and few employers, of course, will ever admit to such a reason) the report produced the analysis of stoppages given in Table 18.

Two general points may be added. First, the stoppage of work is only one end of a spectrum of sanctions that can be applied (by both sides) at the workplace. We have already observed that the status of a "go slow" or "work to rule" can pose difficult legal problems. McCarthy[7] distinguished in his study four types of sanctions which he found were used by workers (often despite, rather than because of, shop stewards' influence) or by stewards: (1) Withdrawal of forms of cooperation. Stewards withhold their customary help in dealing with problems such as loitering or absenteeism. (2) Insistence on formal rights and customs. If stewards "put the pressure" on management they may revive demands for customary or other rights that have fallen into abeyance, for example, the regular retiming of all disputed piece rates. (3) Restrictions on output or hours. McCarthy found "spasmodic 'go slows' and restrictions occurring, for the most part, among relatively small groups," and often found it difficult to distinguish between "the planned control of output by a work group for the purpose of stabilizing earnings or qualifying for overtime and the deliberate use of output restrictions as a bargaining weapon." But use of such restrictions was common, especially by way of a reluctance to work overtime. This ranges from a spontaneous reaction to disagreeable management decisions to the practice in a chemical firm he studied where "growing dissatisfaction with all kinds of grievance settlements led to a seven month long plant-wide ban on all overtime." (4) Withdrawal of labor, which is "only the most extreme and immediate form of workshop sanction in the hands of shop stewards and their members."

Second, both Clack[8] and Marsh have noted that it must not be assumed that strikes are necessarily on balance harmful to industry. In general terms, Marsh has commented:

It may be that in some circumstances, and in order to achieve appropriate change in means or methods of production, or in order to clarify situations, overt conflict between workers and management is positively beneficial. It is perhaps, as has already been observed, not without significance that in some of the most rapidly developing economies in the

---

[7] McCarthy, *Shop Stewards*, pp. 19–22.
[8] "How Unofficial Strikes Help Industry," *Business* (July 1965); and *Industrial Relations in a British Car Factory* (Cambridge, 1966).

world, losses of working time by strike action are greater than they are in this country.[9]

But by this test of *time* lost, Britain is not, of course, at the head of the league. With twice as many stoppages per 100,000 employees as the United States, the United Kingdom lost less than a third as many days per worker in the major industries as the United States in the years 1955 to 1964.

In some industries or firms, the point may be reached when there is what McCarthy has termed an "endemic strike situation." For example, he studied an engineering establishment that had been well known as a place of industrial unrest. This culminated in 83 unconstitutional and unofficial strikes during one year among 1,250 manual workers, including a three month strike of 1,000 men, in the course of which management discharged 27 of the 29 stewards. Negotiations on almost all matters took place under constant threat of walkouts.

> Elsewhere, in the plants we studied, the strike was very much a weapon of last resort, employed on the rare occasions when frustrations, or a sense of immediate injustice, appeared to demand a sudden demonstration, or when it was thought to be strategically necessary to apply maximum pressure as fast as possible. Here, on the contrary, disputes tended to reach the point at which the strike threat was made or carried out much sooner, and much more readily. In effect the strike had become a part of the normal custom and practice of industrial relations in the firm, an endemic feature of factory life accepted by both sides as being largely inevitable.[10]

A report by the Motor Industry Joint Labour Council Chairman, A. J. Scamp, on the situation in the car industry in 1967 disclosed a similar pattern. Of 600 stoppages that took place in eight firms in the first six months of 1966, all but five were unofficial. Moreover, in many of these procedure had either never been used or had been abandoned early. In one works an endemic strike situation had arisen for

> in 1965, 256 out of 297 stoppages of work had occurred before the senior shop steward had even had a chance to put the grievance into procedure. In the first half of 1966, again 128 stoppages out of 142 took place before the senior shop steward had had time to act on them in spite of special efforts made by the company to provide facilities for the bringing in of senior shop stewards as soon as a problem was known to exist. A closer examination of 445 stoppages of work which took place in

---

[9] Marsh and McCarthy, *Disputes Procedures*, p. 26.
[10] McCarthy, *Shop Stewards*, p. 23.

five motor manufacturing firms in the first half of 1966 shows that over two thirds of them lasted for short periods ranging up to four hours and over 80 per cent lasted for no more than one working day.[11]

Turner confirms that in many car firm stoppages the procedure is not given the chance to work, partly by reason of the workers' reactions to engineering employers' insistence on the sanctity of management functions. In 1964 over 40 percent of recorded strikes occurred on questions of redundancy, dismissal, discipline, allocation of work, and other managerial decisions; but only 20 percent of references to Works and Local Conferences from car firms dealt with such issues.[12] A similar picture is suggested in the coal industry, where there are indications that workers turn more quickly to an unofficial stoppage on certain matters than to the machinery.[13]

Of course, even if formal procedure is not being operated in such a situation, one of the jobs of the shop steward will be to argue the case with management to secure a return to work. In such discussions some arguments will be regarded by both sides as valid and some not. Even where the working relationship has been ruptured, there will not be a complete absence of consensus about which arguments are relevant and which are not. McCarthy, for example, cites a case which he and Coker found:

> There a departmental manager sacked a worker for throwing a sponge at a foreman although in fact it missed him. A five-day strike secured the reinstatement of the man concerned, and the basis of the steward's case was that three years earlier another man threw a sponge at a foreman which hit him. On that occasion the culprit was only suspended.[14]

But it would be foolish to conclude that such a situation is necessarily caused by poor procedures. As Professor Clegg put it to one company, which found that its factories in Britain compared badly with its enterprises in the United States, there is an exceptional concentration of strikes in Britain in a few industries, such as motor vehicles. Said Professor Clegg,

I do not know of any other country in the world where there is a

11 Report by A. J. Scamp on Motor Industry Joint Labour Council (H.M.S.O., 1966), p. 10.
12 Turner, *Motor Industry*, pp. 256–257.
13 N.C.B. Evidence, R.C.M.E., vol. 4, e.g., para. 809.
14 McCarthy, *Shop Stewards*, p. 18.

heavy concentration of strikes in such a few industries. So if one finds a bad comparison between your factories here and your factories in the U.S., does this necessarily prove anything? Taking the rubber manufacturing industry, would it not be the case that a comparison between Britain and the United States would show a good record for Britain and a bad one for the United States and then we might say: "Isn't the British system wonderful?"[15]

This concentration in coal, docks, and above all motor vehicle firms makes it interesting to note in which direction new developments appeared to be turning in Britain in 1966. There were some indications of an increase in legal action. Cases like *Stratford, Ltd.* v. *Lindley* arising from disputes in the London docks were matched by employers in the Midlands who obtained injunctions against striking car delivery workers.[16] An injunction was obtained *ex parte* in the same year against unions sympathetically supporting striking airline pilots.[17] Also, a number of actions for the new tort of "intimidation" came to trial, though these were mainly actions by other workers in a position similar to Rookes.[18] The Trade Disputes Act, 1965, stopped the flow of the latter (although its operation was suspended for a six month period during which a number of such actions were begun). Furthermore, the very existence of the Royal Commission probably curbed the eagerness of any employers who wished to turn to legal remedies. Some employers (notably the Motor Employers, Engineering Employers Federation, and London Transport) have urged new strong legal sanctions against unofficial or unconstitutional strikes. But it remains doubtful whether most employers would use such weapons in Britain even if effective means of enforcement were ever discovered. Events in 1966 suggested a rather different development, an extension of the methods of inquiry to supplement "procedure" where it had not worked to prevent stoppages.

---

[15] Question to Massey Ferguson, Ltd., R.C.M.E., vol. 25, p. 1007, para. 3680.

[16] *Progressive Deliveries* v. *Birmingham* (1966), *The Times*, June 29, 1966.

[17] *Olympic Airways S.A.* v. *International Transport Workers Fedn.* (1966), reported only as news in *The Times*, August 25, 26, and 31.

[18] For example, *Morgan* v. *Fry* [1967] 2 All E.R. 386; and *Hughes* v. *McKinley* (1966), news report in *The Times*, November 14, 1967. [In 1968 the process was continued in *Torquay Hotels, Ltd.* v. *Cousins* [1968] 3 W.L.R. 506 (C.A.), where the High Court granted an injunction against union officials who "interfered" with commercial contracts by industrial action when seeking recognition of the union, even though no breach of the contracts was caused. An appeal in *Morgan* v. *Fry* succeeded: [1968] 2 Q.B. 710 (C.A.).]

THE MOTOR INDUSTRY JOINT LABOUR COUNCIL

There is a power in the Industrial Courts Act, 1919, whereby the Minister of Labour can refer for the advice of the Industrial Court any matter arising out of a trade dispute, or trade disputes in general, or "any other matter which in his opinion ought to be so referred" (section 3). But the Industrial Court does not provide for special panels that include members expert in the problems of particular industries. It was therefore thought advisable to try to promote some more specialized method of inquiry which could suggest solutions to particular problems. Such a method could make use of committees or Courts of Inquiry. But an even more flexible weapon was found after meetings between employers and trade unionists in the motor car industry under the chairmanship of the Prime Minister and Minister of Labour in September and October 1965. It was agreed to set up on a voluntary basis the Motor Industry Joint Labour Council[19] with Mr. Scamp as unpaid chairman, a panel of six employers and six trade union representatives, and a secretary provided by the ministry. The functions of the council were to include inquiry into particular disputes leading to serious unofficial strikes or lockouts in breach of procedure; the review of industrial relations in particular firms; and the maintenance of a review of the general state of relations in the industry. Fourteen inquiries were held in the period up to July 1967, of which three were inquiries into industrial relations at an enterprise, and eleven were regarding wage or similar claims which had led to disputes where stoppages had occurred or were threatened. In the first inquiry virtually the whole council participated in the inquiry. (This was based upon the precedent of an earlier attempt by motor industry employers and trade unionists between 1961 and 1964 to use ten of their leading members to investigate difficult strike cases by means of a Joint Study Group which may be regarded as the forerunner of the council.[20]) But this method proved unwieldy, and in later investigations the numbers have been much smaller. In many only the chairman and two "wingmen" sat; though in the eighth inquiry eight members participated. In three inquiries, the Minister of Labour gave Mr. Scamp the powers of a formal "Court of Inquiry"; in two, because the firms involved were outside the strict ambit of the council's juris-

---

[19] Information from the published and unpublished reports of the council and other information kindly supplied by Mr. Scamp and the council's secretariat. The work of the council ceased in 1968, and talks began between motor employers and trade unions for the establishment of a new joint council for the industry.

[20] See Motor Industry Employers Evidence, R.C.M.E., vol. 23, p. 835.

diction (car *delivery* firms), in the other, because both parties did not give their consent to the inquiry so that an appointment under the Industrial Courts Act, 1919, as a "Court of Inquiry" had advantages. But in another case it was possible to get the agreement of the parties to an inquiry (No. 5) in a component manufacturing firm which lay just beyond the frontiers of the council's jurisdiction strictly construed; and Mr. Scamp has said: "I believe it is better to allow the Council's position in these two fields (manufacturing and component firms) to continue to develop empirically rather than attempt a formal extension of its scope and terms of reference at this stage" (General Report, para. 5).

The method used has always been that of inquiry and not that of judicial hearings. The council team has usually gone to the premises of the company in question so that the men on the job can see them in action. Both parties to the dispute are in the room at the same time, but questions are put from the council. There is no cross fire or cross-examination between the parties, although, since it hears the case of the other side, each is able to advance arguments in rebuttal, but through the chair. This insistence by Mr. Scamp upon the method of committee meeting rather than a judicial hearing has been of the utmost importance. It is noteworthy, too, that the parties are represented by company representatives on the one hand and, on the union side, by national and local officers *together* with the relevant shop stewards. It will be recalled that under the York engineering procedure, national officials present the case at Central Conference without the presence in the same room of the local officials or shop stewards.

Mr. Scamp's General Report states that it is implicit in his terms of reference

> that the Council was not authorized to act in respect of official strikes but was expected to investigate serious unofficial strikes. It was, however, necessary from the outset to avoid situations in which interventions by the Council might come to be regarded as an alternative to the full use of the normal procedure for the resolution of disputes. . . .
>
> Experience has shown, however, that in certain circumstances (notably in cases where the normal procedure has been exhausted without a settlement being reached) the parties to an official dispute may wish the Council to intervene as it has done successfully at the Ford Motor Company Dagenham (Inquiry 4) and in the Pressed Steel Co. Ltd. Swindon (Inquiry 6) [General Report, 1966, para. 4].

To these examples we may now add Inquiry 14, July 1967, where a dispute between the Draughtsmen's Trade Union and Pressed Steel

Fisher Co. allowed for an inquiry after failure to agree at Central Conference, and despite the fact that the union maintained its workplace sanctions during the course of the inquiry (which the council "deplored"). The findings of this inquiry were generally favorable to management's undertsanding of a previous agreement between the parties and to an offer of a wage increase made by management as a reasonable solution of the dispute. What is perhaps remarkable is the degree of responsible cooperation achieved with the union in the inquiry itself despite all these factors.

With the exception of Inquiries 12 and 14, in all other instances there has been a return to work or withdrawal of strike threats before the inquiry began. The council has instituted a regular research program to follow up the recommendations made in its reports; and by the end of 1966 it had been found that the recommendations had all been accepted and largely implemented (with one rather serious exception in the case of Inquiry 1, where the reform of the Works Committee structure was hampered by trade unions being unable to agree about representation). Such successes must be measured against the fact that in many of the inquiries, either normal procedure had been used and exhausted or the parties had shown that they were unable or unwilling to use it. In these cases the council was breaking a deadlock. As Mr. Scamp has remarked: "Every time I produce a report I am at risk. I'm amazed I've lasted this long."[21] Naturally, in view of the different character of the problems investigated, temporal delays have varied widely. The time between the emergence of the original dispute (taken as the date of the first formal claim) to the council hearing has ranged between eleven months and more in four cases to less than six weeks in three others. (The hearing has always taken place within one to six days from the decision to inquire.) In three of the long-delay cases, the parties themselves had taken the matter through procedure to Central Conference in, respectively, twelve and one-half, eight, and five and one-fourth months.

A glance at some salient features of major reports by the council gives the flavor of its activities. In Inquiry 2,[22] Scamp, armed with Court of Inquiry powers, faced a dispute over a claim for a bonus by car-ferry drivers. Neither side had been willing to take the case through its special procedure, contained in an agreement renewed only on a year-to-year basis. Thus, if there was ever a failure to agree on a new annual agreement, there was "no longer an agreement in

---

[21] *Sunday Times*, April 2, 1967.
[22] Court of Inquiry into dispute at Longbridge Group of Delivery Agents (CMND. 2905; H.M.S.O., 1966).

force even for the procedure for the avoidance of disputes." (This comment shows the distress felt when the much-maligned procedure is *not* present in British practice.) Also the parties said they did not agree about the meaning of the arbitration clause—"either party may ask for an Arbitrator to be appointed by the Ministry of Labour Conciliation Department." The union had banned work in breach of procedure; but Scamp's general conclusion showed an overall immaturity of labor relations to be the cause of the breakdown, and he made a series of recommendations accordingly. In Inquiry 3 the union members had taken unconstitutional action before exhaustion of procedure.[23] But on a complicated question of interpretation of their entitlement to payment for public holidays that fell on a Saturday under the collective agreements in force (which bore a relation to the order made under a Wages Council for certain types of drivers), the inquiry upheld the union interpretation. In both, the advantages of an inquisitional method over a quasi-judicial hearing, which would inevitably have concentrated more upon the merits of "unconstitutional" actions under the procedure clauses, were readily apparent.

In Inquiry 4, the Ford Motor Company encountered a strike when management attempted to initiate work changes after a union claim for increased allowances for unpleasant conditions had not been met. The report was critical of both parties for not fully utilizing the procedure, and not referring the matter for a second time to the National Joint Negotiating Council (N.J.N.C.); partly of the unions for refusing to negotiate on an offer from the company; partly of the company for refusing to take a more positive approach to certain problems. Recommendations included an increase in allowances in return for a reduction in work breaks. Inquiries 5 and 12 both involved disputes at Birmingham Aluminium Castings, Ltd., over claims for increased pay for dirty working conditions and of a general kind. (The second was a Court of Inquiry and is discussed below, p. 230.) For the present we may merely note the chronology of the dispute. The claim was first made in the autumn of 1965 when the union came to the conclusion that the company's efforts to clean up the shops would be unavailing. A Works Conference was held on November 9, at which the employers offered a one-shilling-per-hour increase to workers when engaged on certain, specific tasks. The union rejected this offer because it regarded the conditions as bad overall. A Local Conference was held on December 2 and a Central Conference on January 13 and

---

[23] Also a Court of Inquiry: Motor Vehicle Collections, Ltd., and Avon Car Transporters, Ltd., Solihull (CMND. 2935; 1966).

14. The Central Conference decided to delay any conclusion pending an inspection of the shops by the employers' panel. This inspection took place on February 22, and the panel took the view that the conditions were by no means abnormal. Consequently, the company withdrew its offer and at a Central Conference on March 11 a formal failure-to-agree was recorded. The union then suggested arbitration to the company, but the company's reply was that any such suggestion could only be considered by the Engineering Employers' Federation. On March 16 thirty-two men in the shops went on strike. On March 21 the union and the company agreed to an investigation by the Motor Industry Joint Labour Council (M.I.J.L.C.), and on the following day the strikers agreed to return to work.

Two passages from the complex recommendations illustrate the manner in which Scamp's conclusions tend delicately to interweave the techniques of the adjudicator concerned with the parties' existing relationships with those of the investigator looking to the future:

> We do not, however, recommend that an allowance should be given specifically in respect of dirty conditions. This would introduce a new and, in our view, undesirable principle into the present wages structure, and might well lead to unwarranted reprecussions in other parts of the factory. We would suggest, instead, that the position could best be met by redefining each grade in such a way as to take explicit account of other factors besides skill. [para. 40]

> Although little direct evidence was presented regarding the wider question of industrial relations generally within the firm, this was evidently causing some concern, and we recommend that a discussion should be arranged between the parties on this subject, possibly in the form of a special conference, in the near future. [para. 42]

In Inquiry 6 (wage rates of welding maintenance fitters at Pressed Steel, Ltd., Swindon), a union claim had been heard formally at a Works Conference on July 28, 1964, and adjourned for inspection of the plant. After recording failure-to-agree on November 23, Local Conference met on December 16. After adjournments and inspections, failure-to-agree was recorded only on April 30, 1965. Central Conference first took the matter up on June 11 but did not record failure to arrive at recommendations until August 13, more than a year from the first formal meeting. A threat to strike made in February was withdrawn when the M.I.J.L.C. agreed to investigate on March 11. The council's report is here largely against the union's claim, and in this case, as in Inquiry 14, it is perhaps worthy of notice that the union (Transport and General Workers Union) was willing, after a fierce struggle for an increase, to accept and abide by the report of Mr.

Scamp's council. Mr. Scamp himself has been heard to say that such successes are related to his having an easily remembered monosyllabic name! As important no doubt are the methods, personality, and background he brings to bear upon the problem. After leaving school he was a railway clerk, served in the Army, became personnel manager in a car firm and later a variety of other companies, and is currently Personnel Director of General Electric Co., Ltd.

Inquiry 9 (Morris Bodies Coventry) finds the council making detailed proposals concerning the wage structure of a car firm. The issues had been taken to Central Conference which had "retained" them, but adjourned *sine die!* Similarly in Inquiry 10 (Standard Triumph Motor Co.), where engineering procedure could have been used but had not been, there are a series of detailed proposals relating to bonus and piece rates. As for the procedure:

> It is by no means the case that all procedural references must emanate from the unions; the company has suffered considerably from the effects of the dispute and management itself could have put the matter into Procedure. Their reasons for not doing so are not entirely convincing. In particular, the existence of discussions between the Federation and the A.E.U. Executive does not seem a valid reason, in the light of the seriousness of the situation, for holding back from using Procedure. The discussions have not, in any case, served to resolve the problem.

The dispute itself had arisen from alleged changes in the rates for timed work, over the calculation of which the shop stewards appeared to have gained control. The Report accepted that the "disputed times have in fact been operated by custom and practice over a period of years."

> We fully understand the Company's concern over rising costs and their wish to take positive action. Clearly, increases in earnings must be related to increases in productivity. Nevertheless, the problem facing the Company cannot be solved by one party acting alone; there must be a joint approach carried out in an atmosphere of mutual confidence . . . . The establishment of this kind of understanding will take time and it must be based on something more than discussion at two or three meetings.

Similarly, Inquiry 11 (Austin Motor Co.) may be summarized as follows:

> Claims for wages increases were made by three groups of workers: pyrometry section workers, electronic maintenance workers and maintenance electricians. The pyrometry section workers, who control and

maintain equipment used to regulate heat treatment processes, claimed parity with the electrical maintenance workers on the basis that the skills required in their job had increased since the previous settlement in 1962. The claim was presented at a Works Conference on 7 July 1965, at a Local Conference on 20 August and at a Central Conference on 11 March 1966. Throughout, the company took the position that no increase in skill was required to perform the job and argued that the electrical maintenance workers were differently qualified so that no basis existed for the claim for parity. The electronics maintenance workers, on the other hand, claimed an increase in their differential over the maintenance electricians on the basis that the skill required for *their* job had increased. This claim was considered at a Works Conference on 2 July 1965 and thereafter on the same dates as the pyrometry section workers' claim. Here, management denied the claim on the basis that the skill required by the maintenance electricians had increased also. The third claim was made by the maintenance electricians who claimed their wages should be related to those of the production workers because of the intimate relationship between the work of the electricians and the output of the factory. The company denied the existence of this relationship in the form claimed. The claim was heard at a Works Conference on 28 February 1966, at a Local Conference on 16 March and at Central Conference on 13 May.

The report said that these questions show "the difficulties in ensuring that, within a complex wage structure, pre-existing differentials are maintained continuously to the satisfaction of all concerned." The union's claim was also based upon the effect of technological change upon the work of the three categories, but the report argued that sectional claims could not be considered in isolation because they raised issues of relativities across the whole range of the company's rates for day workers. "Without a full up-to-date technical description of the job requirements in each category at the present time, however, we find it impossible to give a considered view as to whether the various groups of electricians are correctly remunerated (a) in relation to each other or (b) in relation to other workers in the plant." Some steps must be taken, however, to eliminate the present sense of grievance. Thus there should be a "complete review of day workers' wages structure on the basis of modern job evaluation technique" (para. 60). There should be a meeting between the company and representatives of all day workers to this end. Such a meeting was held.

Report 13 dealt with a dispute between drivers of the Transport and General Workers Union (T.G.W.U.) and Pressed Steel-Fisher, Ltd. (which had been Morris Bodies, Ltd.). The inquiry was held, as usual, in private on the company's premises and resolved a complicated conflict. In the course of the inquiry, the men concerned agreed to return to work. There had been some delay in applying the new wage measurement methods (brought in after Inquiry 9) and this had contributed to the discontent of the drivers; but there had also been redundancies at the factory, and the drivers claimed that their "work load became increasingly frustrating; they were frequently switched from one job to another." The one-page report manages to deal with all three aspects of the dispute: the manning of the vehicles, mobility within the factory, and the wage structure.

The other inquiries have been into "general industrial relations," and their main value has been to elucidate the facts on which some solution may be sought to the problem of short unofficial stoppages in the motor industry. The most important of these was No. 8 (Morris Motors Cowley), from which some of the essential figures on strikes, as quoted in the first General Report, have already been cited. As the General Report suggests (paras. 24–27), no simple explanation either in terms of shop stewards' conspiracies, work frustrations, or managerial weakness seems adequate to explain this phenomenon.

Some details have been given about the work of what may be only a transitional body, the Motor Industry Joint Labour Council. The council is of primary importance because it represents the form taken by the nonlegalistic response to problems created in one of the most strike-prone sectors of British industry. Its methods are those of inquiry, where possible also of mediation and conciliation. It comes not to bury the old procedures, but to supplement them; not to praise them, but to suggest improved ways of using them or even of changing them. In these respects the council represents an extension of the methods of investigation and inquiry as ways of processing employment disputes. Such methods have been in prominence in Britain at least since 1919 and have been used increasingly of late in difficult areas, sometimes operating through machinery provided by law. To this we return in Part III. Whatever its future, the Motor Industry Joint Labour Council will remain in the records as a bold attempt to get (and where necessary knock) heads together round a table as a way out of apparently insoluble disputes.

7.

DISMISSALS, DISCIPLINE, AND
GRIEVANCE PROCEDURES

W e have already noted that problems of dismissal can be discussed in the ordinary procedures and that the legal weakness of the
union employee, able to demand no reason for his dismissal and protected only by his right to notice for the infringement of which his remedy is slender, may be transformed into an industrial strength whereby
his union official can even demand and secure his reinstatement. This
chapter takes up that problem in greater detail in the light both of the
information collected in our own research and of the valuable study
produced in October 1967 by a Committee of the National Joint Advisory Council on Dismissals Procedures (N.J.A.C.).[1] The N.J.A.C. estimate of 3,000,000 dismissals per year (of which some 333,000 to
500,000 are for misconduct), and their figures on stoppages of work
have already been quoted. We shall adopt their three headings for
discussion: (1) Private Industries' Ordinary Procedures ("External
Procedures" in the N.J.A.C. Report); (2) Private Sector "Internal"
Procedures and (3) The Public Sector.

ORDINARY PROCEDURES IN PRIVATE INDUSTRIES

From its general review based especially upon a Confederation of
British Industry survey of 34 member employers' associations, the

---

[1] *Dismissals Procedures*, N.J.A.C. Report (H.M.S.O., 1967). The council contains one official of the Ministry of Labour (with another as secretary), three
representatives of the Trades Union Congress, three of the Confederation of
British Industry, and one from the nationalized public corporations.

N.J.A.C. was able to state that "almost all regarded the industry's disputes procedure as the appropriate machinery for handling dismissal questions . . . . Dismissal cases generally form a small proportion of all disputes handled under procedures particularly at national level. Often those dealt with are mainly cases of dismissal of trade union representatives" (paras. 62–63). The awards resulting from procedure are "almost invariably" observed.

As to the number of cases handled, the figures already given (above, p. 80) confirm the picture in the building industry presented by the N.J.A.C. in (para. 63). Of 127 cases dealt with regionally and 26 cases nationally in 1965 by "joint machinery" (presumably of either type), 68 and 12, respectively, arose from dismissals "in one way or another." Later they say that "roughly half of the cases under both procedures" in building arise from dismissals (para. 138). In civil engineering between April 1964 and February 1967, of 57 cases heard by the National Conciliation Board (the final stage; but in this industry there are no regional boards), 20 were dismissal cases. Also in engineering the figures given for 1966 are: 155 cases considered at Works Conference (the total number of cases of all kinds being 5,273), of which 79 were settled. Forty-seven went on to Local Conference where 17 were settled, and 14 to Central Conference where 5 were settled.

The N.J.A.C. adds the significant comment that 59 other dismissal cases were dealt with "informally" and 32 of them settled, out of some 2,000 cases dealt with in this way in the industry. It will be noted that the figure for 1966 at Central Conference is smaller than the total recorded by Marsh and Jones in 1959 (above, p. 86). In the engineering agreements, as has been noted earlier, management prerogative to dismiss is enshrined in the words protecting "the usual practice in connection with the termination of employment of individual workpeople." This section is mainly concerned with individual rather than mass dismissals; but it may be noticed that the employers have always resisted the demands for a national agreement regulating redundancies (though in other industries these have now become common).[2] On the other hand, as well as a rudimentary agreement on termination by notice (which does not improve on the Contracts of Employment Act, 1963), there is also a clause under which management has to give "consideration" to "any *class* of workpeople displaced by any act of management" with a view to affording them suitable work in the same establishment in preference to dismissal. Complaints about a failure to observe this obligation would go through the normal procedure.

---

[2] See Marsh, *Industrial Relations*, Appendix D.

One important point not discussed by the N.J.A.C. is the standing of a worker whose notice expires while his case is going through procedure. Practice clearly varies between and within industries; but there are certainly some cases in which by custom the dismissal is not made final until procedure is exhausted. We found that in the furniture industry, for example, the procedure was applied with an agreement that the status quo be preserved so that a worker would be suspended from work during the procedure. Although he would be paid if the decision eventually went in his favor, this practice might mean a loss of pay during the considerable period needed for the procedure to operate. Plainly it would be more satisfactory if the worker remained paid during the discussions. We were not able to obtain figures indicating the extent of any such practice under ordinary procedure; but we shall observe the view of the Industrial Court that suspension is unusual.

In some industries, dismissal cases cause either a slightly special use of ordinary procedures or the operation of a special procedure. In the iron and steel industry, there are ten employers' associations with separate procedures, many of them unwritten; but most provide for a Works Conference; a Local Joint District Committee; a Joint Board above that which may appoint a "neutral committee" with two members from each side (none from the relevant works); above that, a National Joint Conference; and in some agreements, arbitration. These procedures are used for dismissals but mainly by the use of the stages that precede, and not through the use of the "neutral committees" that have plenary powers. "In practice however, it is understood that neutral committees are little used, as differences are almost always settled within the works" (para. 139). The boot and shoe industry uses informal Joint Committees of Inquiry to deal with dismissal disputes (which "almost always reach agreement"), and not, it seems, interestingly enough, the system of reference to arbitrators and umpires which is built into the time-honored procedural agreement. The N.J.A.C. also found a "very few cases" of quite special procedures for dismissal. In flat glass manufacturing, for example, an agreement demands that dismissals have the approval of a works' manager and that the employee receive one week's notice except in emergencies such as gross misconduct. But even then the notice of dismissal is not to be issued until the shop steward is informed so that he may make representations and, if the case is not settled, so that the local union official can discuss it with the works manager. Similarly in chemicals, a special agreement gives a worker or his union a right of appeal against summary dismissal or suspension.

Without being able to offer proof, we have the impression that, below the national level, there may be a gradual increase in such special agreements. For example, one regional agreement discovered by us serendipitously was that between a regional employers' association in ship repairing and the Amalgamated Engineering Union. After stating that "all employees are entitled to justice and have an established right of appeal through successive stages of executive authority up to the Managing Director" of each member company, the agreement goes on to set out the conditions for warning (for minor offenses), suspension, and dismissal. In cases of a serious character, the employee is to be informed of the complaint in writing, may reply in writing, and may be represented and call witnesses in a hearing before the manager. The actual procedure resembles that in many of the "internal procedures" discussed below. What is important is that these rudimentary rules for natural justice in dismissal and discipline cases were negotiated between a regional employers' association and a union in 1966. The N.J. A.C. concentrated on national arrangements, and more agreements of this kind may well exist now at lower levels as companies' internal procedures established by management become the subject of bargaining.

One special procedure that has existed for a long time concerns the docks. We have noticed that a dock worker has had since 1946 statutory status under his dock labor board, as well as an employment relationship with the employer. If not employed by an employer, he has been able to draw full back pay. Only removal from the register of the board is equivalent to dismissal, and in such a case the dock worker has the right to appeal to a tribunal with (usually) an independent chairman and two wingmen. Between 1963 and 1966 local boards dismissed an average 765 men a year (17.4 percent of all disciplinary cases); and of these, 214 workers were reinstated on average every year. The dock labor scheme has recently been revised so as to create as far as possible conditions of permanent employment with a single employer, but the system of appeal tribunals is retained and a "permanent worker" can appeal against his dismissal by his employer from permanent employment and against his dismissal or suspension from the plan by the local board.[3]

The N.J.A.C. Report adds little to our knowledge in regard to the delays of procedures. Three employers' federations are quoted as saying, respectively: (1) that three cases of dismissal had gone to national level in six years (one involving 38 men) and one went on to

---

[3] The Dock Workers (Regulation of Employment) (Amendment). Order 1967, S.I. 1252, clauses 14A, 17, 18.

arbitration, and the gap between dismissal and final settlement was six to eight weeks; (2) that cases could be discussed at national level by a conciliation board which met once a month (concluding that the delay would usually be less than a month, which seems unduly sanguine); and (3) that the three cases that had gone to national level between 1962 and 1965 took an average of six months from the date of dismissal, and in each case a failure-to-agree resulted (para. 66). Marsh, it will be recalled, estimated that dismissal cases went through engineering procedure in between eight and ten weeks.[4]

As the N.J.A.C. remarks, it is axiomatic that the "individual cannot, of course, himself take his case through the disputes procedure; that can only be done by a trade union which is party to the procedure" (para. 63). That will invariably be true, though in instances where a *special* procedure has been negotiated which speaks in wide terms about *workers'* rights (such as the ship repairers' agreement cited above), there would be nothing in principle to stop any employee from demanding to be given access to the steps set out. If such a worker had a contract of employment that purported to incorporate the collectively agreed terms, the question whether such procedure clauses were appropriate for incorporation would acquire new importance in judging his legal position. Where those terms set up a procedure to be followed in individual dismissals, there would seem to be little reason for denying them incorporation into individual employment contracts. [His industrial power to enforce his demand would, however, clearly be much weaker.] Moreover a few procedures "can only deal with certain types [of dispute], e.g. where notice has not yet expired" (para. 72). This practice might be thought to be that used in engineering; but actually, shop stewards take into procedure not merely cases of workers under notice but also, on occasion, cases where the worker has already been dismissed. As Marsh puts it:

> In fact considerations of this kind are not allowed to stand in the way of procedural handling of dismissal cases even if this means turning a blind eye to some of the technicalities of procedure. A common expedient is for employers' associations to agree, as a starting point, to informal conferences between the parties at works level; another is to allow dismissal issues to be raised initially at Local Conference stage. . . . But other associations would normally allow formal Works Conference as the first step.

The technical problem of whether a dismissed employee counts as

---

[4] Marsh, *Industrial Relations,* p. 130.

an employee capable of being claimant, which has so easily encouraged litigation under legal structures such as the Contracts of Employment Act, 1963,[5] has little place in the operation of procedure.

The N.J.A.C. in discussing the problem of the individual nonunionist counterposes the argument that he should have an equal protection against dismissal with the view

> that a worker who chooses not to be a member of a trade union naturally forfeits this protection, just as he forfeits other forms of protection which the union can provide (e.g. against failure to observe agreed wage rates); if he subsequently regrets this it is his own responsibility, and in any case he can remedy his lack of protection by joining the union. We think there is a good deal of force in this argument, and we believe that unions would normally adopt a generous attitude towards taking up dismissal questions on behalf of newly-joined members, even if the incident complained of took place before membership. But it has to be remembered that some workers are non-members not because they choose to be but because it is not easy for them to join a union—principally workers in less highly organised sectors of employment and in small firms where there is no union representative; in such circumstances it may be far from easy for a worker to join a union and maintain membership.
>
> We do not wish to exaggerate the problem of non-members, whether of trade unions or of employers' associations. It is a problem of external procedures; there is no reason in principle why internal procedures should not generally be available to union members and non-members alike, though naturally the non-member cannot enjoy the support and assistance of a union representative. As we have already said, external procedures cannot take the place of adequate procedures within the firm. Again, none of the evidence we have had indicates that dismissal problems are particularly serious for non-unionists [paras. 143–144].

They add later: "While not disputing the need for every worker to have the right of appeal against dismissal, we think it not unreasonable that as far as voluntary external procedures are concerned, a worker who chooses not to be a trade union member should forfeit their protection as regards dismissal just as he forfeits other forms of protection by the union. We recognise, however, that special problems arise in the less highly organised sectors of employment where it may not be easy to obtain trade union protection" (para. 189).

In all these procedures a flexible variety of remedies was available, ranging from reinstatement to (in some cases) even compensation. (As

---

[5] See the line of cases referred to above, p. 25, on whether an ex-employee could bring a complaint to the Industrial Tribunals relating to written particulars of employment: See Wedderburn, *Cases*, p. 68 n.

the N.J.A.C. points out, "reinstatement" should mean reemployment without any loss of status or rights; but there, as here, it also includes *reengagement*, even if there has been some loss of rights or seniority of some kind.) Meyers noted a case in the cooperative retail trade where a woman in Wales was dismissed when she married during her employment. Under the procedure the matter went to an arbitrator who decided that the method of the dismissal was improper and awarded back pay up to the date of his award; but he determined that the dismissal itself must be upheld, though he directed the society to make it clear that single women would be dismissed if they married.[6]

On the other hand, Meyers' conclusion that in building the awards merely order back pay and the worker is "not reinstated" does not seem to be correct. The N.J.A.C. records that reinstatement was recommended in 15 of the 69 cases dealt with at regional level and 3 of the 12 cases dealt with at national level in building. On the other hand, our examination suggests that Meyers' view is largely correct in regard to the National Joint Council Conciliation Panel cases, where what is normally asked for and awarded is money in lieu of notice, which should have been given under the National Working Rules (N.W.R.). Even so, the awards go beyond mere mechanical interpretation of the N.W.R. In February 1965, for instance, the panel was asked to adjudicate on a case of summary dismissal for alleged misconduct. In view of a "conflict of evidence" about the operative's part in a disturbance on the shop floor, the panel was "unable to make an award but considers and so recommends that the firm should make an *ex-gratia* payment to Mr. B—— equivalent to one day's pay." Similarly in the case of Mr. McG—— in 1966 the panel confirmed a Regional Panel discussion that he had not been guilty of misconduct within the N.W.R.; but concluded that since he had within a week of his improper summary dismissal secured another job at a less favorable rate, he should be paid the difference between his old and his new rate for four weeks, that being his entitlement as a period of notice. On the other hand, the Emergency Disputes Commissions in this industry have regularly recommended reinstatement where this is proper (though the great majority of dismissal appeals are rejected, as the N.J.A.C. figures confirm). The flavor of Disputes Commissions' awards may be gathered, without giving the details of the cases, from the following examples chosen from the decisions between 1961 and 1966:

1961: Having considered the evidence, the commission finds that during an altercation on the site on September 12, certain remarks

---

[6] Meyers, *Ownership of Jobs*, p. 27.

were made by the scaffolders' steward which could be construed as threats, leading the firm to take disciplinary action in accordance with rule. In view, however, of the man's previous satisfactory record with the firm, the commission recommends that they offer him alternative employment.

1963: 1. From the evidence the commission does not consider victimization has taken place. 2. Due to misunderstanding on both sides there appears to be some justification for the union's attitude. 3. In all the circumstances, the commission recommends that the firm offer re-employment to Mr. S—— and consider making an *ex gratia* payment in the order of one week's wages.

1964: 1. The evidence in this case was conflicting, but it appears that on this job where relations had been good and the federation steward had carried out his duties satisfactorily over a period of months, a minor incident had become very much exaggerated. 2. In all the circumstances, it is the view of the commission that the steward should be reinstated.

1966: 1. The commission notes and endorses the findings of the Regional Joint Emergency Disputes Commission, held on April 22, 1966, that the case for summary dismissal was not established. They find that, in these circumstances the three joiners concerned should be paid one day's pay in lieu of notice. 2. The commission also notes that the contract is now proceeding smoothly and endorses the intention of the second paragraph of the Regional Findings that in the event additional carpenters and joiners are required, the matter should be discussed between the management and the Amalgamated Society of Woodworkers (A.S.W.) official concerned.

Unless it be thought that trade unionists are wholly satisfied with these procedures, it is worth recalling that the leader of the building workers trade union told the Royal Commission:

> One of the greatest causes of unofficial strikes in my industry for instance is the dismissal of workers' representatives. This is one of the biggest causes of unofficial disputes, the sacking of a shop steward although there is a procedure agreement—that is the green book procedure in the industry's agreement. The men argue that they will not strike if the firm will restore the status quo, so that the man will remain in employment until the dispute is looked at by the machinery. But then the employers will never agree that the status quo shall remain. They always argue their right to manage, to sack the man and the man can be on the street a month. By the time you have got through the procedure and you have maybe won the case and the man should be reinstated, he is not going back because he has found another job.[7]

---

[7] Mr. Lowthian, T.U.C. Oral Evidence, R.C.M.E., vol. 61, para. 9876.

No figures are available to prove that this is truly the typical case in building; but plainly in an economy where full employment is taken less for granted than it was, such cases are bound to disturb trade unionists.

In general, it may be concluded that for many workers, probably the majority, the ordinary procedure of their industry as operated by their trade union forms their effective machinery for processing grievances relative to discipline or dismissal. The "almost invariable acceptance" of the awards given, especially the ready acceptance of such awards as reinstatement "which is not a remedy provided to employees in the courts" (N.J.A.C. Report, para. 130) mark their value. But N.J.A.C. comments on the problems that use of ordinary procedure can pro- duce. There may be undue delay, which is a serious matter in a dis- missal case, especially if the usual practice is followed and the dis- missal takes effect at once. There can be difficulties for nonunionists. There is also the special difficulty of the nonfederated firm that does not adhere to the industry's procedure. At higher levels in procedure, the problem may be discussed "without that close knowledge of the particular circumstances which can often contribute most to a sensible solution" (an approach that is "not consistent with the need for im- partiality"). The council commends "special arrangements" for pro- cedures to deal with dismissals though they do not think they can "lay down general rules applicable to all industries" (paras. 130–144). Be- cause of the attendant problems, the council concluded that ordinary procedures "cannot take the place of adequate procedures within the firm," the so-called "internal procedures."

INTERNAL PROCEDURES IN PRIVATE INDUSTRIES

General

"Internal procedures" within the firm overlap with ordinary proce- dures in that the latter invariably commence with an approach to a foreman and steps up to a Works Conference. Further than that, most firms would claim that ordinary workers can appeal to higher manage- ment: "The managing director's door is always open." But, the N.A.J.C. comments, "Unless this right forms part of a definite and known dismis- sal procedure, it often means little in practice." A formal procedure is needed to encourage workers to use it and to prevent the appeal to higher management from being pointless.

It seems that firms operating any internal procedures whatever in

Britain are in the minority. Information is largely limited to the inquiries of M. Plumridge and of the N.J.A.C.[8] The former investigated 50 organizations by questionnaire and another 14 in greater depth, but his sample "consisted almost entirely of organisations which might commonly be referred to as 'progressive' and which possessed an established personnel department." The N.J.A.C. results stem from three samples: (1) 373 firms visited by ministry officials; (2) 38 firms, covered by a questionnaire, which were believed to have "good personnel records"; and (3) 45 member firms, mainly large in size, of the Engineering Employers' Federation. These small samples all suggested that formal internal procedures are "the exception rather than the rule." The percentages of firms possessing them were, respectively, (1) 27, (2) 18, and (3) 33. The N.J.A.C. estimate is that firms with internal formal procedures are well below 20 percent of the national total;[9] that these include many of the larger firms employing 1,000 workers or more; that they are rare in the smaller firms which still make up the "vast majority" of enterprises in Britain. It may be remarked that these smaller firms will include also many of the places not yet organized by unions so that they will not be covered by an "ordinary" external procedure either.

Even in firms with procedures, the rules sometimes were restricted to particular types of case, such as bad timekeeping. Plumridge found in his sample that "in private industry, rules and punishable offences were outlined but specific penalties were seldom referred to," and many of the rules were "vaguely worded" (though he regarded this as often desirable since they could be supplemented by "precedents"). The N.J.A.C. supplied the following concrete example:

> A *textile firm* employing about 30,000 has issued the following statement of Company policy on disciplinary procedure:
> 1. The prime objective is to build up a relationship on a departmental basis as between supervision, operatives and Shop Stewards in order to maintain discipline by means that are both fair and reasonable to both management and workpeople.

---

[8] Plumridge, unpublished thesis on "Disciplinary Practices in Industry," which he most kindly made available to us; some parts of the results were described in his article in *Personnel Management* (September 1966), p 138. Quotations are from the article unless otherwise specified. The N.J.A.C. inquiries are described on p. 5 of their report.

[9] In their brief remarks on this matter, the Government Social Survey reports that in two-thirds of the firms that imposed penalties on employees, there was "a special procedure by which workers could appeal against dismissal and other punishments" (McCarthy and Parker, *op. cit.*, para. 166). It is not made clear what constitutes a "special procedure."

2. If and when discipline falls down, depending upon the degree of indiscipline, a man will be talked to or reprimanded by his supervisor in the department.

3. Where the degree of indiscipline is such that it is considered that it cannot be handled on a departmental basis, the man concerned will attend at the Labour Office (as will also the supervisor concerned) and the Labour Officer will hear the full facts of the case from both the supervisor and the man. Due consideration will then be given to the case by management and a decision by them will be taken as to what action is deemed necessary.

4. Depending upon the circumstances, such action could be:
  (i) Case dismissed
  (ii) Verbal reprimand
  (iii) An officially recorded warning, or final warning
  (iv) Suspension from work of up to three days
  (v) Discharge with appropriate notice
  (vi) Summary dismissal

5. Depending on the nature of the alleged offence, the appropriate Shop Steward or Works Secretary may be brought into the investigation if he has any pertinent evidence he wishes to offer as a witness.

6. In any event, where a "charge" is going to be pressed in respect of an officially recorded final warning, a suspension, or a discharge, the defendant concerned will have the right to have his appropriate Shop Steward or Works Secretary present unless he desires otherwise (for example for personal reasons).

7. In the case of an officially recorded final warning, a suspension or a discharge, the appropriate Shop Steward or Works Secretary (whether or not he has been present during the investigation) will be advised of the decision and all the known circumstances that led up to it.

8. The Shop Steward or Works Secretary is in no way asked to be a consenting party to the action to be taken and, if Management's decision is regarded as unjust or unreasonable, he will be entitled to pursue the question under the negotiating procedure.

9. The whole emphasis of this procedure is on the positive rather than the negative approach, whereby the aim is to prevent indiscipline occurring by having good departmental relationships, but where indiscipline does occur, to deal with the situation with as much care and fairness as such situations deserve [Appendix 4].

Some firms list penalties in this manner and some attach penalties to particular offenses, such as absenteeism, as in engineering firms. Not unnaturally, firms use a system of warnings, sometimes having such warnings recorded and expunged after a certain period if the worker shows improvement. After warning, the penalties used are dismissal or disciplinary suspension. Only in a few firms did the N.J.A.C. find that a worker was put on "precautionary suspension," with or without pay, during the period of the hearings until determination of the case. It seems clear that management prerogatives to fire first and listen afterward are still closely guarded even in these firms. The right to dismiss was found by both the N.J.A.C. and Plumridge rarely to exist at foreman level and had often been transferred to the personnel department; but in many cases the latter's role was to make a recommendation to a higher line manager with whom the final decision would rest.

Plumridge found that disciplinary suspension without pay was used in 29 of the 50 firms he surveyed, in 20 of which the maximum was three days, though in others examples of up to four weeks could be found. We have seen that the right to suspend in this way must be found in the worker's contract of employment. There is no unilateral right to use the weapon; but it is often provided for in Works Rules.

TABLE 19

Penalties Awarded in Sample of Firms, 1961 to 1963

Reason for dismissal or suspension	Number of workers dismissed (50 factories)	Number of workers suspended (28 factories)*
Bad timekeeping	319	698
Absenteeism	1,316	145
Leaving job without permission	93	165
Incompetence or unsuitability	958	53
Negligence	32	210
Intoxication	23	20
Theft from employer	104	94
Theft from fellow employees	21	7
Insubordination	151	60
Safety violation	23	60
Fighting or using violence	72	69
Falsifying clock cards	51	5
Smoking in forbidden areas	8	135
Gambling	1	1
Criminal offense outside firm	57	—
Other offenses	56	244
Total	3,285	1,966

*Of the 698 suspensions for bad timekeeping, 629 occurred in the two factories where suspenion was widely used. The same factories accounted for 1,375 of the total. These factories for example operated a schedule of punishments and if an employee was late more than eight times in a year suspension followed automatically. The established labor force for the 50 factories in 1963 is given as 90,979. The figure for the 26 factories (omitting the two that accounted for all but 591 of the suspensions) was "almost 63,000."

SOURCE: Plumridge, "Disciplinary Practices" (supplementing the figures given in *Personnel Management*, p. 139).

The practice seems to have been given a boost during the war when employers' powers to dismiss many categories of workers were restricted by Essential Works Orders; and the courts had some difficulties in certain cases in deciding whether there was a contractual right of disciplinary suspension or whether the employer was, in law, dismissing with an offer to reengage after the time specified.[10] Plumridge found differing attitudes among both management and trade unions to this penalty in modern conditions. Some firms had recently reintroduced it for such reasons as the need to have a substantial penalty for offenses (e.g., insubordination and fighting) where dismissal was too severe; or the need to have something left to negotiate with a union without having to climb down from a dismissal already awarded. The figures for the use of suspension and dismissal Plumridge obtained in his sample are given in Table 19.

The part played by trade union representatives varies. Some rules made specific reference to such representation, while talks with shop stewards about dismissals are in practice "fairly common" (N.J.A.C. Report, para. 24). Naturally, the majority of the engineering firms in N.J.A.C. sample (3) replied that they allowed a workplace representative to be present at an early stage in their procedures; but the N.J.A.C. appears to underestimate the operation of ordinary procedure here, for federated *engineering* firms would of course devise their "internal" procedures as far as possible to fit in with the operation of the ordinary procedure agreement. Even so, the N.J.A.C. surveys as a whole showed that "comparatively *few* of the procedures covered specifically provide that the worker should have the opportunity to state his side of the case to a representative of management before any decision is taken (though we have little doubt that this is the general practice)" (para. 23).

A Special Case

There do exist a few examples in British practice of "participative structures," as Plumridge terms them. The N.J.A.C. found "three or four" firms in its surveys (of 456 firms) in which the decision whether or not to dismiss is a "joint one by management and union representatives." One of these exceptional firms was kind enough to allow us further access to its detailed results.[11] The company is a member of the Rubber Manufacturing Employers Association and covered, there-

---

[10] As in *Marshall* v. *English Electric Co., Ltd.* [1945] 1 All E.R. 653; *Cases,* p. 144.

[11] We are most grateful for the information provided for analysis about this

fore, by the National Joint Industrial Council procedures for the industry (with the usual steps through foreman, managers, joint works committees, a National Joint Council Executive committee with a conciliation panel, and a "tribunal" above that with two members from each side and an independent chairman, appointed by the Minister of Labour, who may give a decision in case of deadlock). But quite apart from this, the 2,400 production workers (all members of the T.G.W.U. under a closed shop agreement) are covered by an internal Misconduct Committee. This committee was set up first in 1941 to deal with all misconduct questions other than absenteeism and timekeeping. More recently, cases of theft were also excluded from its jurisdiction (though one such case was heard by agreement in 1964). Between 1941 and 1966, the committee heard 1,034 cases, but the rate of hearings has dropped consistently since the war to a level of, now, about 10 a year. (This decrease perhaps supports the N.J.A.C. contention that an effective internal procedure has as its most valuable feature a preventive effect.) An analysis of the cases between 1962 and 1966 (55 in number) showed that bad workmanship was the most frequently alleged offense (in 22 cases), followed by being off the job without permission (11), clocking offenses (8), and insubordination (6). In 22 cases the offender was dismissed, in 16 warned, and in 11 suspended (for up to three days). In all cases some punishment was imposed.

The procedure was speedy. Of 46 cases in which the dates were clear between 1962 and 1965, 5 were dealt with on the *same* day as the alleged offense; 23, in two days or less; 15, in 5 days or less; and only 3 took a longer time.

Most important, however, are the composition and procedure of the committee. The members are the manager of the department concerned,[12] three shop stewards, and a chairman who is from the industrial relations department of the firm but acts as a "neutral." The union shop stewards are elected every two years from among the twelve who represent departments in the enterprise. One of these must be the chief shop steward (the "convenor"). In practice there has been considerable continuity of service of shop stewards on the committee. The decisions of the committee must be unanimous, but once given

---

unusual and interesting experiment at Firestone Tyre and Rubber Co., Ltd. Accounts have been published by the industrial relations manager, I. S. Walton, in *Industrial Society* (1966), p. 23; and in *The Times*, December 29, 1965.

[12] The *Works Handbook* names only him as management representative. Mr. Walton (and *The Times*) in describing the operation of the committee adds "the foreman concerned."

are final. (They are posted on the notice board and state the name, offense, argument in outline, and the decision.) All that an aggrieved employee can do after the decision is complain to his district union official; but this has happened only twice in ten years. Thus the local union stewards have, on the face of it, a decisive voice in matters of dismissal and discipline. Some observers suggest that such a system inevitably compromises the status of union stewards; but this does not appear to be so in this firm. The industrial relations manager has written:

> My personal observation is that they take a highly responsible attitude towards the cases they hear, nearly always recognising where pressures for leniency are justified or where they should stand firm with management in supporting stern penalties. That union representatives share this responsibility with management does not set them up badly in the eyes of the people they represent.

But it has been suggested that what happens on such a joint participative committee is something in the nature of a "judicial" proceeding, and that its decisions come to build up a body of "case law." Such legalistic notions need reconsideration when the operation of the procedure is more closely considered, though no doubt the actual decisions come to be regarded as "precedents," as in the ordinary run of such industrial affairs as the "sponge" negotiation mentioned earlier (p. 119). The manager in question writes a report for the industrial relations department, and this is put before the meeting with "any other relevant information" collected by the neutral chairman. The employee concerned is summoned to appear; but he is not accompanied or represented by a union official. The industrial relations manager has described what happens then as follows:

> In committee, the chairman reads the report on the case and will ask the manager to clarify or substantiate any aspects which are not clear. Union representatives will cross-examine, and in a frank exchange management will answer questions put by the union, and the employee concerned will be questioned by both sides. The chairman is required to be and is accepted as impartial. By common consent the questioning does not stretch to argument while the employee is present. The man is asked to leave, the committee discusses the case and decides the action to be taken. It is the practice for the manager to state the course he wishes to adopt and to seek agreement for such a course. If the manager's recommendation is disputed by the union, as is quite often the case, the discussion must go on until a unanimous decision is reached. Adjournments and side-meetings may take place and the chairman may exercise pressure on either side, depending on circumstances . . . .

In committee there is no question of the union scoring over management or vice versa, and if the union succeeds in getting a penalty reduced the representatives will support the manager in seeing that the reprieve is not seen by the man on the floor as a let-off. The minutes agreed for publication will also make this clear.

Maybe managers will sometimes seek harsher penalties than seem justified, in the belief that they will be pressed to step down the penalty. Maybe there will be some lobbying between chairman and union or between chairman and management before a case is heard. Whatever unorthodox moves are adopted everything is on the table in committee.

From this account emerges the authentic flavor not so much of a quasi-judicial body, but of a negotiating or bargaining body using a preagreed set of principles and procedures invoking some semilegal processes. The bargaining functions of the stewards are translated from the shop floor to a higher level where they have both greater power and greater responsibility. The process is less that of adjudication than of joint bargaining and decision-making. Though these participative committees are still rare in the British experience, it was thought worthwhile to examine the best-known example in some detail to see just what happens at its hearings. Some commentators have used the precedent of such participative bodies to suggest a system of labor courts to deal with discipline. It would be a gross error to see the germ of the latter in the former unless it be remembered that a labor court, as in the French experience, may ordinarily exclude lawyers altogether and concentrate on conciliation and compromise, rather than on the judicial process. Furthermore, the "judges" in this participative system are closely associated with the very parties to the dispute. No labor court tolerates that.

The N.J.A.C. Report

Despite the weaknesses in internal procedures, the N.J.A.C. favored a development of them (together with external procedures) on a *voluntary* basis as the best way ahead. It examined the argument for statutory tribunals to administer a new law on unjust dismissals but decided that there were "strong arguments against the introduction at an early date of legislation to provide for statutory machinery" (for which, in this instance, the T.U.C. had asked). In any event, if introduced, statutory machinery should be only a "fall back" (i.e., it should operate only where there is inadequate voluntary machinery). The Minister of Labour in a foreword remarked that this question of legislation "will need to be considered further after the Royal Commission on Trade Unions and Employers' Associations has reported." The N.J.A.C. was no doubt much affected in its views by the position in the public sector.

THE PUBLIC SECTOR

For employees of the civil service, local authorities, and the commercial public corporations, the dismissal procedure tends to cut across the division between internal and other procedures. This is inevitable where there is only one employer in the industry. In all three sectors, the procedures are highly developed and the N.J.A.C. Report confirms the following T.U.C. statement:

> In the public sector there are usually special procedures covering disciplinary action including dismissals. The principal features of the machinery in the public sector are: (a) written notice of disciplinary action; (b) the right of appeal at successive levels; (c) the opportunity of a personal hearing and the right to be represented by a trade union representative or a fellow employee; (d) final decisions by an executive (or appeals) authority.[13]

The N.J.A.C. Report documents the proof of this in regard to the public corporations (paras. 33 to 48)[14] and most (though not all) of the following examples are given there. In form, the corporations' procedures are, largely, highly developed machineries of the internal kind. All provide for notification to the employee. The British European Airways and British Road Services procedures specify that, when disciplinary action is being considered, the employee must be informed in writing of the alleged offense and have the opportunity to make representations, either in writing or at a disciplinary hearing. The National Coal Board procedure for nonindustrial staff stipulates that the individual will be informed of the grounds on which the proposed measures are based and given the opportunity to make representations. (The 1947 Agreement concerning "workmen" uses, as we have seen, the first stages of the normal pit conciliation machinery.) Written notification is required in British Railways.

Most of the procedures and instructions speak of the gravity of dismissal as a penalty. Summary dismissal is however recognized (except

---

[13] Evidence to Royal Commission, para. 337.
[14] Summarizing the procedures of the National Coal Board, Electricity Council and Gas Council (and their area boards), British European Airways, British Overseas Airways, London Transport, British Road Services, and British Railways. On the last, our own research has provided some detail, below, p. 149.

in British Road Services, where it is never used) as the appropriate penalty in given circumstances. National Coal Board employees can be summarily dismissed only for breaches of the Mines and Quarries Act and for other similar acts of serious misconduct. British European Airways' regulations provide for summary dismissal for misconduct in cases including smuggling, violence, and clocking offenses; but even in such cases, the full procedure is normally used. Except in the case of summary dismissal for exceptional misconduct, extensive use is made of warnings as a penalty. London Transport's procedure covering railway workshop wages staff provides for a graded system of penalties for bad timekeeping and absence without reasonable excuse. An employee who is persistently late or absent receives, on the first occasion, a caution from his foreman; on the second occasion, a severe caution from a senior official; and on the third occasion, a final caution. If he defaults after the final caution, he will be discharged. All penalties are, however, subject to appeal. In British Road Services the least serious penalty, written warning, is entered on the employee's record but is expunged after a further year's service without warning or punishment.

Similarly in most of the procedures provision is made for suspensions. But British Road Services state the "immediate precautionary suspension" (pending the hearing) is to be used only where the alleged misconduct prevents continuance of work. The same employers also set out a range of penalties (from warnings up to dismissal) specifying the level at which each can be awarded. For example, serious offenses may be met by suspension without pay; while major offenses merit sterner measures, including "dismissal" (when the employee is not to be reemployed) or "removal" (when that ban does not apply).

With rare exceptions all employees can appeal formally against disciplinary dismissal to a higher level of management. One such exception is in the case of the coal-mining workers dismissed for breaches of the Mines and Quarries Act, 1954, who are excluded from appealing. Most procedures provide for various stages in the appeal. For example, in British European Airways, a three-stage process ends with a tribunal of the chief executive and two board members advised by the personnel director. In London Transport a disciplinary hearing on any serious case of misconduct is held, which is conducted by a senior management representative or, in some departments, a disciplinary board composed of senior management representatives. These disciplinary boards normally number two or more such representatives. An employee may appeal to higher management against any penalty imposed at the disciplinary hearing. Appeals are normally held before the head of the department. In British Road Services the appeal lies to the next immediate level of management and finally to the managing director, a stage actually used in practice for matters of principle. On occasion, certain groups of workers are excluded from the procedure, as for example in the case of the Model Procedure recommended by the National Joint Council for Local Authorities' manual workers where the right to take the matter through the procedure (which here merges with normal conciliation procedures) attaches to workers only after "six months' probationary Service."[15] Most of the procedures specify time limits for an appeal—in British Road Services, ten days; in British European Airways, seven days; and so on.

The only remaining procedure that allows for appeal to an independent arbitrator is in coal mining. Here, as we have seen on page 99, the normal pit conciliation machinery is used, omitting the Disputes Committee stage, under the Agreement on Alleged Wrongful and Unreasonable Dismissal of 1948. The umpire here has power to order reinstatement, though before doing so he must hear representations and "satisfy himself that the recommendation (for reinstatement) is one which the management and the workman may reasonably be required to implement and that the recommendation or implementation would not undermine the authority with regard to discipline in the pit" (clause 2(e)). It is no accident that, as soon as third party arbitrators were called in, such limitations on the right to reinstate had to be fully spelled out. Also, under this agreement the status of the workman differs according to whether his notice has or has not terminated before appeal. If it has not, his appeal is taken through procedure "on the understanding" that it is to expire on the day following the appeal, and if he wins the board then withdraws it. If it has expired, or he has received wages in lieu of notice, the appeal nevertheless goes forward (another case of an "ex-employee" using procedure) and he may be reinstated with full payments (clause 3). In fact, as we saw in the case of 87 Umpires Awards, of which only 8 related to dismissal (above, pp. 99-100), very few dismissal cases go to umpires. The N.J.A.C. put it as "seldom or never," and Marsh and McCarthy estimate that the umpires dealt with 7 dismissal cases in 1967.[16]

In all instances trade union representation is allowed. Sometimes, the union range is limited (e.g., in British Overseas Airways the union must be one in membership of the National Joint Council). But usually

---

[15] Evidence of Electrical Trades Unions, R.C.M.E., vol. 57, p. 2486.
[16] Marsh and McCarthy, *op. cit.*, p. 76, para. 15, n.1.

the accused employee also has the right to be accompanied by a fellow employee to plead his case. For example, the Gas Council representative describing its informal appeal machinery (in this case, on a wider range of grievances than discipline), when asked by the Royal Commission whether it was the union or the man who processed the grievance through the procedure, said:

> Literally it is the man but he is always in my experience represented by a union official. . . . The appeal machinery is open to anybody. I do not think he could persuade a union official to take it up if he was not a member of a trade union but he would be able to make his appeal.[17]

In one case the appeals procedure can be used only with the agreement of the worker's trade union (being a union recognized in negotiation procedure) that the appeal is justified. This is where British Railways dismiss for "exceptionally grave misconduct in which summary action by the Management is justifiable." This exceptional trade union right arose from circumstances in which the union objected to a worker's utilizing the appeal procedure in such a case; and management took the view that they did not wish to undermine union support for the appeals procedure. The N.J.A.C. reports however that "generally unions seldom refuse to support an appeal," which, if unsupported, goes to the appropriate superior officer of British Railways. The ordinary cases of misconduct in British Railways are governed by the remaining clauses of the 1956 Agreement, which, we have already noted, established a disciplinary procedure separate from the ordinary procedure. Under this agreement, discipline and dismissal are a regional matter. The employee is to be informed of the offense *in writing* "as early as possible." He may be put on "precautionary suspension" for certain types of offenses; and it must be imposed where the alleged offense is "inconsistent with his further employment in any capacity." The employee states his defense *in writing* within three days (or an extended period when agreed). If he desires he may be heard by the appropriate officer of the Railways Board, and at such hearings he may call witnesses and be accompanied "by a spokesman who shall either be a fellow employee employed in the same Region . . . or a representative of a Trade Union recognised . . . for negotiating purposes." If adjudged guilty, he is informed in writing. The main types of "recordable" punishments are: reprimand, severe reprimand, suspension, reduction in grade, and dismissal. He has the right to appeal to the

---

[17] Evidence of Gas Council, R.C.M.E., vol. II, p. 408, para. 1804.

appropriate superior officer in the region, which appeal he must make in writing within seven days. The appeal is to be heard and decided "as early as possible." The agreement has attached to it 41 regulations detailing points related to the procedure. The last regulation, for example, sets out the employee's right to be paid as if on duty when appearing as the accused or as a witness, though his rights to payment are extinguished if he is "not found free from blame" and the hearing was outside ordinary duty hours.

TABLE 20

Charges and Punishments in One Region of British Railways, Central Division, between March 1965 and March 1967

	Commercial staff*	Motive Power staff†	Operating staff‡	Totals
Number of Cases........	61	84	238	383
Charges				
Dishonesty	22	5	38	65
Damage to property ...	12	—	—	12
Lateness/absence	17	17	149	183
Aggression/foul language	9	1	28	38
Insubordination	6	3	22	31
Breach of operating regulations	3	59	81	143
Failure to report	2	1	12	15
Total	71	86	330	487
Punishments				
Reprimand	17	33	115	165
Severe reprimand......	13	35	21	69
Final warning	2	2	4	8
Withdrawal of travel facilities	—	—	4	4
Suspension	9	10	41	60
Transfer	5	—	4	9
Demotion	3	1	12	16
Dismissal	15	2	37	54
Total	64	83	238	385
Appeals	2	8	20	30
(Successful)	(1)	(5)	(5)	(11)

*Commercial staff (goods handlers), approximately 1,000.
†Motive power staff (drivers, firemen, engine cleaners), approximately 1,150.
‡Operating staff (porters, signalmen, guards, shunters), approximately 2,800. (The clerical staff consisted of approximately 1,000 workers until the 1967 split between commercial and operating staffs.)

SOURCE: British Railways Board.

We are able to describe the actual operation of this machinery in one division of a region of British Railways.[18] Between March 1965 and March 1967, a work force of about 6,000 gave rise to some 386 discipline cases, made up as shown in Table 20.

It was also possible to analyze further the cases that gave rise to 64 hearings in this division between January 1 and May 31, 1967. The average time taken, for example, between the issue of "Form 1" (the first written information of a charge) to the actual hearing was 18 days. (Twenty-three issues were heard within a fortnight, 28 within three weeks, and only 13 took longer than 21 days.) There were only three appeals (which took, respectively, only 4, 5 and 2 days to reach the appeal hearing) of which two were successful. A surprising feature discovered was that in only 21 cases was the worker accompanied or represented. In 43 cases he had no spokesman and put his own case. Out of the 21 cases, 9 were instances in which he was represented by a union official from headquarters, and 9 others were instances in which his spokesman was a "fellow employee" who was also a union official of some kind. The other 3 cases appeared to involve ordinary fellow workers as spokesmen. Lastly, we came across 5 cases of appeals with union agreement by staff who had been *summarily* dismissed in this period (this being also the total number of summary dismissals in the period). None of the 5 was successful.

The formality that is occasionally introduced into the public sector procedures (such as the insistence upon *written* charges and answers which appear in many procedures apart from the railways) is probably not unrelated to the influence of the procedures agreed by the Civil Service National Whitley Council. In serious charges, the civil servant is given a written statement of the charge and of the facts supporting it. He makes a written reply. In the event of conflict of evidence he may support his case orally before an appropriate officer in his department *other* than his immediate superior officer. In some oral hearings he may have a friend of colleague (who may be a union representative) present to assist him. In certain cases the department may set up a board to advise the head of department; and in exceptional cases a formal board of inquiry can be set up by the minister to ascertain the facts and make recommendations. The procedure in the civil service is not further explained here for the reasons already given;[19] but the formality of the civil service style comes out well in the procedures

---

[18] We are most grateful to the Railways Board for providing these divisional figures.

[19] See N.J.A.C. Report, paras. 53–59, for a short account.

used in the General Post Office, which will probably be subject to some modification when that department changes its status. Briefly it operates as follows:[20]

Disciplinary offenses may be either irregularities or offenses. Irregularities are faults in the performance of an officer's duties caused by carelessnss or negligence rather than by deliberate intention. Irregularities may be minor ("isolated slips or omissions"), major ("breach of an important rule"), or serious ("grave or persistent carelessness or negligence"). Offenses are faults of personal conduct. These may be lesser or serious. Minor irregularities should be dealt with orally and should not be made the subject of a formal written explanation. Major irregularities and lesser offenses must be dealt with in writing (see below), but normally action is not necessary beyond drawing the officer's attention to them. These are not entered on a permanent record and after twelve months the papers connected with the misconduct are destroyed, unless another offense of the same nature occurs within the twelve months, in which case both sets of papers are kept for twelve months from the date of the second offense. Repeated offenses may lead to a warning that any further offenses may involve deferment of increment or other disciplinary action.

Serious irregularities and serious offenses are recorded and must invariably be dealt with formally in writing. A form is issued by the supervising officer directly concerned to the alleged offender seeking an explanation why the incident occurred; a written reply is given to the inquiry; the management decides what action to take, and if this action involves a punishment, the officer is asked if he has any reasons why this punishment should not be imposed; a reply is submitted in writing; management notifies the officer of its disciplinary decision. Branch officials can assist the officer in the preparation of replies to official forms. In grave cases where the penalty may be very serious and there is a "conflict of evidence" between the charge and the officer's written reply, the officer, if he wishes, may represent his case orally to a suitable officer of rank not lesser than area engineer. This officer must not be his immediate supervisor. In presenting his case the officer may have present with him a friend, who may be a union representative. (There appears to be no uniform practice on the friend's functions, i.e., whether he can act as counsel or, at the other extreme,

---

[20] We are grateful for information supplied by the General Post Office, the Post Office Workers' Union, and the Post Office Engineering Union. The present summary cannot do justice to the niceties of Post Office procedure, but it is hoped that it does not do them violence.

is confined to silent observation.) On written application the local manager may give the officer permission to submit the papers of the case to union headquarters for advice.

Local managers (i.e., the telephone manager or head postmaster) can deal with most cases, but certain types must be referred to the regional director, for example, dismissal, compulsory transfer, reduction in rank or pay of established officers, cases relating to political matters, cases against officers in their capacities as branch secretaries. Punishments include: reprimand, deprivation of pay for one or more days, deferment of an increment, reduction in pay, compulsory transfer, reduction in rank, and dismissal either with or without notice. *Appeals* may be personal or through the union. (1) Personal appeals: Notice of intention to appeal must be given in writing within three days and the appeal itself submitted within a week of the expiry of the three days. Appeals after the three day period are allowed if the officer can produce evidence not available during the three days. Punishment is not to be inflicted until the appeal is rejected. If the punishment was inflicted at local management level, no appeal is allowed beyond the local manager. Otherwise the case may go to the regional director. In the exceptional cases of dismissal, reduction in rank and pay, withdrawal of supervising allowance, or compulsory transfer, there may be a personal appeal to Post Office Headquarters or the Postmaster General. (2) Appeal through the union: Strictly this is allowed only for serious irregularities and serious offenses, but the unions have been known to take up with regional directors cases of major irregularities involving a monetary penalty. Where an officer wishes to appeal through his union after rejection of his personal appeal, he must give notice within three days of the rejection, and the union must announce its intention to appeal within a further two weeks and actually appeal within a further week. The officer first approaches his branch and if the branch committee decides the appeal should be supported the papers are sent to the union headquarters. If the union headquarters is also in favor of supporting the appeal, it will take up the question with Post Office Headquarters or perhaps the regional director. This does not involve an oral hearing of the officer, and at no stage of the appeal procedure does an interview appear to be mandatory or even usual. The Post Office Engineering Union receives about twelve appeals a year at headquarters and supports about eight. (The union represents about 76,000 workers.)

In addition, three other features may be noted: (1) For the branch secretary (in Post Office Workers, at least) no punishment can be inflicted for misconduct committeed as a branch secretary (necessarily usually offenses) without prior consultation between Post Office and union headquarters. (2) For late attendance (again in Post Office Workers, at least) there is an agreed automatic procedure whereby certain numbers of unexcused latenesses of more than 5 minutes entail a certain penalty, viz: 16 to 20 instances of late attendance in one year, one day's pay lost; 21 to 25, two days' pay lost; 26 to 29, three days' pay lost. (3) Suspension is not used as a punishment as such, but officers may be suspended from duty pending proceedings if the "public interest" demands it (e.g., if accused of theft by police). Remuneration is withheld during suspension, but in cases of severe hardship interim payment can be made. If no disciplinary measures are subsequently taken, reinstatement is accompanied by back pay. Even if disciplinary measures are taken, these may not necessarily involve dismissal.

Part Three

MACHINERY PROVIDED BY LAW TO ASSIST IN RESOLUTION OF DISPUTES

8.

THE STATUTORY STRUCTURE

IN GENERAL

The machinery provided by the law to assist in processing employment disputes falls under three headings: (1) arbitration, (2) conciliation; and (3) inquiry. Under all three, the Minister of Labour has power provided by the Conciliation Act, 1896, and the Industrial Courts Act, 1919. Briefly, the powers allow for the following processes:

(1) The reference to the Industrial Court, or an ad hoc Board of Arbitration, or a Single Arbitrator of a dispute, when the parties consent after having exhausted ordinary procedures and the minister thinks fit. There is also provision for the minister to refer any industrial problem to the Industrial Court for its advice, but "in practice this provision has been rarely used and not at all since 1946."[1] (There are also certain special jurisdictions of the Industrial Court which in different ways do not wholly rest on the consent of the parties; these will be dealt with conveniently under the same heading in chapter 9.)

(2) The conciliation services provided by the ministry stem from the same acts. These do not need the express "consent" of the parties; but they are "voluntary" in the sense that the ministry has a "general policy to avoid intervening in a dispute until the agreed procedure in the industry has been exhausted. Even if in a particular instance there is no agreed procedure the parties are generally expected to try and settle the differences themselves before seeking conciliation. When conciliation does take place it is in effect a continuation of the process of collective bargaining with outside assistance."[2]

(3) The powers of inquiry and investigation do not depend upon

---

[1] Ministry of Labour Evidence, p. 101.
[2] *Ibid.*, p. 95.

TABLE 21

Use of Statutory Arbitration and Inquiry Machinery, 1946–1966*

Year	Voluntary arbitration: Industrial Court (voluntary jurisdiction)	Single arbitrators: Appointed under Act of 1919 similar functions	Single arbitrators: Persons appointed under 1896 Act with similar functions	Boards of arbitration	Special jurisdictions: Section 8 of Terms and Conditions of Employment Act, 1959	Special jurisdictions: Other jurisdiction of Industrial Court‡	Inquiry: Courts of inquiry	Inquiry: Committees of inquiry	Inquiry: Committees of investigation
1946	32 (7)†	37	(7)	—		—	4	—	—
1947	34 (8)	22	(6)	1		1	5	1	3
1948	56 (11)	24	(5)	1		6	2	2	1
1949	35 (6)	47	(1)	4		7	—	1	2
1950	34 (4)	23	(2)	2		5	1	1	2
1951	59 (5)	42	(1)	1		4	2	2	1
1952	60 (5)	25	(5)	4		6	1	—	3
1953	60	23	(4)	3		4	3	—	1
1954	54	18	(5)	—		5	4	—	1
1955	40	12	(1)	5		—	2	—	1
1956	43	14	(5)	1		3	2	1	—
1957	35	14	(1)	4		5	4	1	—
1958	34	15	(10)	1		2	2	1	1
1959	36	24	(1)	6	6	4	—	—	—
1960	36	26	(1)	3	15	7	—	1	1
1961	52	18	(3)	4	20	3	—	—	—
1962	36	23	(–)	1	13	4	—	—	—
1963	42	30	(2)	—	13	—	1	2	—
1964	38	23	(1)	7	10	5	1	3	1
1965	21	38	(2)	3	9	1	2	2	1
1966	20	49	(–)	—	22	—	5	1	—
Total	857 (46)	547	(63)§	51	108	72	41	19	19

the consent of the parties. The minister has powers to set up a Court of Inquiry under the 1919 Act or a Committee of Investigation or of Inquiry under the 1896 Act, or under his "general powers." Such powers are used sparingly; and the recommendations of such bodies do not bind the parties to a dispute.

None of these headings includes anything, it can be noted, in the nature of compulsory arbitration. (The one possible exception is certain, rare, "special" jurisdictions of the Industrial Court, the main example being a bequest of wartime compulsory arbitration in existence from 1940 to 1951, modified but continued between 1951 and 1958, an experience analyzed later at p. 210.) This omission does not imply that proposals were lacking half a century ago—or now—for compulsory

NOTES TO TABLE 21: USE OF STATUTORY ARBITRATION AND INQUIRY MACHINERY 1946-1966

°The source for the figures relating to the Industrial Court and the Courts of Inquiry is the published reports of these bodies. The source for the Single Arbitrators, Boards of Arbitration, Committees of Inquiry and Investigation is the files of the Ministry of Labour. Some minor discrepancies between these and the figures published in the Ministry of Labour Evidence, p. 111, are to be explained by the fact that the above are figures for *awards*, whereas the Ministry's figures are of *refererce*, in any year. As will be seen, p. 190, we were able to inspect all the awards of Boards of Arbitration. Our figures for boards and Single Arbitrators do *not* include decisions that were mere interpretations of their own earlier awards.

†he figures in parentheses are not included in the totals for the voluntary jurisdiction of the Industrial Court. They relate to cases referred to the court under the Conditions of Employment and National Arbitration Order, 1940, article 2, and the Industrial Disputes Order, 1951, article 4. Under these provisions the Minister of Labour might, before resorting to a compulsory reference of the cases to the Industrial Disputes Tribunal or the National Arbitration Tribunal, "take any steps which seem to him expedient to promote a settlement of that dispute or issue" (art. 4). A reference to the Industrial Court was one possible step. In theory such a reference was still voluntary in that the consent of the parties was required, but there was in the background the possibility of the minister's exercising his compulsory powers if the parties did not consent. Under the 1940 order, an award by the Industrial Court was binding on the parties in the same way as a decision of the National Arbitration Tribunal. Concerning the 1951 order, see below, pp. 210 ff.

‡In practice this has meant: under the Fair Wages Resolution; Road Haulage Wages Act, 1938; Civil Aviation Acts, 1946 and 1949; Road Traffic Act 1930; and Road and Rail Traffic Act, 1933. Also in 1959 three cases were referred by virtue of the provisions of the Air Corporations Act, 1949.

§The column of "persons appointed under the 1896 Act" relates to such persons as chairmen appointed by the ministry either to bodies established by the parties on which they could exercise powers of an umpire, or chairmen who would sit in some other way with arbitral powers in case of disagreement. We are grateful to I. F. Patterson of Leeds University for discussion about the categorization of such persons. Mr. Patterson's figures in his Ph.D. thesis on "Arbitration in Great Britain" differ slightly from ours, both in respect of Single Arbitrators and similar persons and of Boards of Arbitration, largely because he includes interpretation decisions in his totals. After discussion with him, we consulted the original awards again to ensure accuracy.

159

arbitration. On the contrary, many bills were introduced to that purpose.[3] But both the basic statutes of 1896 and 1919 were passed at that formative era of British labor law and practice when, on the one hand, trade union pressure was able to induce the legislature to exclude legal sanction from trade disputes where it would have prohibited collective workers' action, and, on the other, the emergence after the war of a nationwide collective bargaining structure encouraged the notion that the best way to proceed was by voluntary action, a concept behind which the influential Whitley Committee, appointed in 1916, threw its full support. The legal machinery is therefore aimed at making collective bargaining effective, not at supplanting it.

To some extent, therefore, the success of British legal machineries is to be measured by the *infrequency* with which they are used. Table 21 gives the complete figures for annual use of all types of statutory arbitration and inquiry machinery between 1946 and 1966.[4] These figures show the comparative paucity of occasions in the postwar era on which the industrial parties or the minister have found it necessary to use such machinery. The total of the number of cases taken voluntarily to the Industrial Court in twenty years (857), for example, may be compared with the thousands of hearings in engineering or coal-mining procedures in one year alone at workplace level and above. Also, in the postwar era there has been a marked shift in the incidence of the use of different types of voluntary arbitration. For example, Sharp[5] reported that between 1919 and the end of 1938, the total number of references to the Industrial Court was 1,669; to Single Arbitrators, 224; and to ad hoc boards, 91. Between 1946 and 1966, the figures were: Industrial Court, 857; Single Arbitrators, 547 (or 610, if persons appointed under the 1896 Act are included); boards, 51. The increased use of Single Arbitrators no doubt marks the growth in the importance of local grievances, with which they usually deal. The decline in the Industrial Court average, however, does not mean quite

---

[3] On the history before 1896, see Sharp, *Industrial Conciliation and Arbitration in Great Britain*, Part Two, chap. i.

[4] We are most grateful to the Ministry of Labour for allowing us to make an analysis of these figures and also for the provision of other information which made possible the compilation of this part of this report. It must be again emphasized, of course, that the ministry is in no way responsible for any interpretative remarks that have inserted themselves into the interstices of information given in the present text.

[5] *Op. cit.*, pp. 359, 366. By 1929 the references dropped to under 50 a year where it remained. But in 1936, cases concerning the civil services were deflected from the court to the Civil Service Arbitration Tribunal; and Sharp comments that "but for this separation the number of cases brought to the court in 1938 would have exceeded that for any year since 1927" (p. 359 n.).

what it seems to mean, for of the 1,669 cases between 1919 and 1938, a very large number was heard in the first five years of the court's existence (539 in 1920 alone). Certainly any dissatisfaction with the court—and criticism is sometimes heard in trade union circles—cannot be based upon fears that the president is being influenced by a government "incomes policy," for he has insisted to the Royal Commission that "arbitration should be entirely independent of and free from the advice and influence of the Government or any Government Department. I believe this to be the correct and universal view."[6]

Even if the number of instances be small, however, it is worth examining with care the operation of these arbitration machineries. The actual cases emerge with the authentic flavor of British industrial practice. The research for this project was, therefore, much concerned with a study of these cases, and some detailed examples are given below. Since we shall show that the court now draws no distinction between issues of "rights" and "interests," it is parenthetically interesting to note that the 1919 Act and emergency legislation at the end of World War I did, at the outset, transfer the two types of issue at *different* dates, nine months apart, to the court; but no distinction flowed from this historical accident.[7]

---

[6] Sir Roy Wilson, Q.C., R.C.M.E., vol. 45, p. 1937. But in a more general sense, he thought arbitrators kept in mind the "national interest" (p. 1936). On the relationship between voluntary arbitration and "incomes policy," which cannot be discussed in this chapter, see the Ministry of Labour Evidence, p. 109.

[7] The explanation briefly is that compulsory arbitration had existed under the Munitions of War Acts, 1915 to 1917, applying to "differences." The definition of "difference" (sec. 3, 1915 act; sec. 9, 1916 act) clearly related to "interest" disputes about what employment conditions ought to be. From November 1918 to September 30, 1920, a Wages (Temporary Legislation) Act, 1918, gave temporary *compulsory* legal effect to certain collectively agreed or customary terms, and differences over "rights" and "interests" were treated together (sec. 2). The Schedule of the Industrial Courts Act separated the two types of issue, leaving the 1918 Act in force on "rights" until September 30, 1920, but transferring disputes over "interests" to the Industrial Court on a voluntary basis from November 21, 1919.

9.

ARBITRATION

VOLUNTARY ARBITRATION POWERS[1]

The Industrial Courts Act, 1919, was passed as a result of the Fourth Report of the Whitley Committee[2] which was itself set up to consider *inter alia* the experience that had been gained with compulsory arbitration during World War I. The report, however, was opposed to the imposition of compulsory arbitration and stressed the need to give full support to the parties' own voluntary machinery. State intervention in arbitration should be confined to the provision of standing arbitral machinery, to which the parties could resort if they so wished upon the exhaustion of their own procedures.

> We desire to emphasise the advisability of a continuance, as far as possible, of the present system whereby industries make their own agreements and settle their differences themselves . . . .
> We are opposed to any system of Compulsory Arbitration; there is no reason to believe that such a system is generally desired by employers and employed, and in the absence of such general acceptance, it is obvious that its imposition would lead to unrest . . . .
> We further recommend that there should be established a Standing Arbitration Council for cases where the parties wish to refer any dispute

---

[1] The Arbitration Act, 1950, governing commercial and similar arbitrations does not apply to the industrial statutes: Conciliation Act, 1896, sec. 3; Industrial Courts Act, 1919, sec. 3(3).
[2] (CMD. 9099; 1918). •

to arbitration, though it is desirable that suitable single arbitrators should be available, where the parties so desire. . . .

The act followed this guidance, and section 2 provides:

1. Any trade dispute as defined by this Act, whether existing or apprehended, may be reported to the Minister by or on behalf of either of the parties to the dispute, and the Minister shall thereupon take the matter into his consideration and take such steps as seem to him expedient for promoting a settlement thereof.

2. Where a trade dispute exists or is apprehended, the Minister may, subject as hereinafter provided, if he thinks fit and if both parties consent, either:

a. refer the matter for settlement to the Industrial Court; or

b. refer the matter for settlement to the arbitration of one or more persons appointed by him; or

c. refer the matter for settlement to a board of arbitration consisting of one or more persons nominated by or on behalf of the employers concerned and an equal number of persons nominated by or on behalf of the workmen concerned, and an independent chairman nominated by the Minister, and, for the purpose of facilitating the nomination of persons to act as members of a board of arbitration, the Minister of Labour shall constitute panels of persons appearing to him suitable so to act, and women shall be included in the panels. . . .

4. If there are existing in any trade or industry any arrangements for settlement by conciliation or arbitration of disputes in such trade or industry, or any branch thereof, made in pursuance of an agreement between organisations of employers and organisations of workmen representative respectively of substantial proportions of the employers and workmen engaged in that trade or industry, the Minister shall not, unless with the consent of both parties to the dispute, and unless and until there has been a failure to obtain a settlement by means of those arrangements, refer the matter for settlement or advice in accordance with the foregoing provisions of this section.

Thus the minister alone refers a case to arbitration when he thinks fit. The parties do not go directly to the arbitrator or the Industrial Court. On the other hand, the minister is under the obligation to see that two conditions are satisfied before he refers the case: First, the consent of the parties must be obtained.[3] (This consent need not be in any particular form but is usually required to be in writing to avoid

---

[3] The consent of the parties may be given in advance, e.g., in a collective agreement between them. The ministry thinks that "a high proportion" of the voluntary cases are of this nature, but has no exact figures, and makes no distinction between voluntary and compulsory arbitration clauses.

subsequent dispute on the point.)[4] Second, the parties' own machinery, insofar as it falls within the definition of (4), notably the requirement that the parties be substantially representative organizations in both sides, must be exhausted. In this way it was hoped to prevent the court or arbitration from in any way replacing the functions of collective bargaining. However, Sharp,[5] quoting Lord Amulree, the first president of the court, suggests that in practice the Ministry of Labour infers the exhaustion of the parties' machinery from their request to refer the case, and that this condition is not the subject of a separate inquiry. Sir Harold Morris, K.C. (second president of the court), writing in 1939, suggested[6] that the intervention of the Ministry of Labour was a waste of time and that the parties should be able to refer a question directly provided both consented; but the Ministry of Labour in its Evidence to the Royal Commission says: "This provision is one which is always observed by the Ministry before cases are referred to arbitration" although it adds that a decision by one party not to pursue the matter through the negotiated machinery would constitute a failure of that machinery.[7]

There are only two situations in the "voluntary" jurisdiction when it is possible for parties to go to the Industrial Court without going through the minister. Subsequent interpretation of the court's awards is provided for under Rule of Procedure 7. This provides that "the Minister or any party to the award may apply for a decision on such question." The theory is presumably that the consent given at the time of the original submission enures to later questions of interpretation. The position of the minister is more difficult to justify on theoretical grounds. Also on occasion details of the settlement are left to subsequent negotiation and the parties given the option of returning to the court if they cannot agree: "Either Party shall be at liberty to report

---

[4] Mackenzie, *Industrial Court: Practice and Procedure* (1923), p. 7.

[5] Sharp, *Industrial Conciliation and Arbitration in Great Britain* (1950), p. 350; Mackenzie, *op. cit.*, p. 8: "If in order to obtain a speedy settlement both parties agree to refer the matter to the Industrial Court for settlement without the Minister making previous inquiry as to whether there has been a formal failure to agree, it is apprehended that the Minister would not oppose; as after all the object of the statute is to promote settlements, and if the parties wish a settlement in a particular way there is no sound reason why the Minister should say that it shall be in another way; and the agreement to refer implies a failure to settle."

[6] In Garnett and Catherwood, *Indutrial and Labour Relations in Great Britain: A Symposium* (1939), pp. 48–49.

[7] Ministry of Labour Evidence, p. 101. It seems that even if the parties chose to ignore their own procedure, a case might still be referred if the minister saw fit.

such failure to the Court; and the Court will, after hearing the Parties, determine the matter in point" (Award 3062).

Even when the two conditions are satisfied, the minister is under no obligation to refer the case; he may do so "if he thinks fit." Thus the minister may not only attempt conciliation before referring the case (as is usual), but can also enforce a resumption of work pending the hearing (which was once also usual)[8] by threatening to refuse to refer the case or bring pressure to bear on the parties in respect of their terms of reference. Normally the ministry is concerned only that the terms of reference should clearly state the issue the arbitrator must decide; but during the "Pay Pause" of 1961, the ministry required that all the terms of reference of wage claims going to the court should contain a provision that the arbitration was to deal with the question only after a certain date (e.g., Industrial Court Award Number 2939, Trade Union and Official Side of Shipbuilding Trades' Joint Council, claim for a reduction in the working week, November 1962, where the terms of reference contain the statement: "Having regard to the Government Economic Policy, it is agreed between the parties that the question of an operative date earlier than 1 April 1962 is not before the court").[9]

There is, of course, one further restriction on the minister's power to refer. There must be an existing or apprehended "trade dispute." This is defined by section 8 to mean "any dispute or difference between employers and workmen, or between workmen and workmen connected with the employment or non-employment, or the terms of employment or with the conditions of labour of any persons." That is very similar to the definition under the Trade Disputes Act, 1906 (above, p. 11) with the addition of the words "or difference" which may very slightly widen the ambit of the phrase.[10] "Workman" is, however, defined widely, and very differently from the manner of the 1906 Act:

The expression "workman" means any person who has entered into

---

[8] Mackenzie, *op. cit.*, p. 11. Today this would not be a universal requirement, although the consent of the parties usually means that normal working has been resumed by agreement in references to the Industrial Court at least.

[9] It may be said that this is one method whereby the minister can protect government "incomes policy" (apart from his greater power under the Prices and Incomes Acts, 1966 and 1967). Sir Roy Wilson told the Royal Commission in 1961 that he knew of no case where the minister had *refused* to refer a case to arbitration when the parties had so requested that: Oral Evidence, R.C.M.E., vol. 45, para. 7237.

[10] See *Beetham* v. *Trinidad Cement Co., Ltd.* [1960] A.C. 132; *Cases*, p. 394, where Lord Denning remarks that a "difference can exist long before the parties become locked in combat." But so, it is thought, can "a dispute."

or works under a contract with an employer whether the contract be by way of manual labour, clerical work, or otherwise, be expressed or implied, oral or in writing, and whether it be a contract of service or of apprenticeship or a contract personally to execute any work or labour. [Under section 10, "persons in the naval, military or air services of the Crown" are excluded.]

These definitions at least do not seem to have prevented the court or an arbitrator from hearing any case that they wanted to hear. The definition of "workman," it will be noticed, is wide enough to include "self-employed" persons or "independent contractors."

THE INDUSTRIAL COURT

The Court

The Industrial Court is established by section 1(1) of the Industrial Courts Act, 1919: "For the purpose of the settlement of trade disputes in manner provided by this Act, there shall be a standing Industrial Court, consisting of persons to be appointed by the Minister of Labour . . . , of whom some shall be independent persons, some shall be persons representing employers, and some shall be persons representing workmen, and in addition one or more women." It is not a "court" in the sense of a court of law. Its president has, however, defended the use of what might be thought a misleading title on the ground that the word suggests "a permanent body" which "will not be subject to Government influence except insofar as Government policy may become embodied in an Act of Parliament."[11] The court is maintained at state expense and provides therefore a public service as a standing arbitral body (though, as we shall see, in some "special" jurisdictions it seems to act as a "private" body). When the court is acting under one of the jurisdictions provided for by the Industrial Courts Act, 1919, or other statutes, it is probably subject to the prerogative orders (mandamus, for example) though the *dicta* are not wholly clear on the point as far as its purely "voluntary" jurisdiction is concerned.[12]

The persons appointed to the court are chosen by the Ministry of Labour from persons among whom the ministry can make its choice

---

[11] Supplementary Evidence, R.C.M.E., vol. 45, p. 1965. In oral evidence he had agreed that the court might as well be called a "tribunal" (p. 1955, para. 7211).

[12] Compare the *dicta* in R. v. *Industrial Court ex parte A.S.S.E.T.* [1965], 1 Q.B. 333 with those in R. v. *N.J.C. for Crafts of Dental Technicians* [1953] 1 Q.B. 704.

whenever it needs outsiders to help it fulfill its functions (e.g., on advisory committees, courts of inquiry, committees of investigation). The list is compiled informally. A person may not necessarily know he is on the ministry's list until such time as he is asked to undertake a specific task. At present, the president of the Industrial Court (appointed by the minister under section 1(4) of the act) is Sir Roy Wilson, Q.C., a lawyer called to the bar in 1931 and a Bencher of Gray's Inn, who has industrial experience dating from the chairmanship of the Committee of Inquiry into Smithfield Market in 1958. He is appointed on a full-time basis at a salary of £6,875, "during good behaviour" (like a County Court judge) and retires at the age of 70. He is the only full-time member with power to act as chairman and usually fulfills that function. In addition to the president there are panels of independent persons, and of employers' and employees' representatives, and a single Women's Panel Member, Barbara L. Napier, M.A., J.P., whose normal occupation is that of general adviser to women students at Glasgow University. She sits in practice as an additional member to the court when only women workers are involved in a case. There are ten people on the employers' panel, and all of them are appointed on a part-time basis. Typically they are managing directors of firms with experience on the councils of employers' organizations. There has evidently been an attempt to obtain a wide spread of experience, and industries represented range from jute to insurance, from shipping to printing. There are seven people on the employees' panel, and these are all past or present general secretaries of trade unions. Dame Anne Godwin, an ex-trade unionist of high repute, is a permanent member of the court and usually sits as the employees' representative. Thus, the court is typically constituted by Sir Roy Wilson, Dame Anne Godwin, and an employers' representative. The president has a discretion in the matter of its constitution, however (sec. 1(3)); and the minister has given all the independent members the power to act as chairman under section 1(4). The independent members, all part-time, include one Queen's Counsel, one academic lawyer, and one professor of economics with long experience in arbitration. The court has power to sit in divisions, but this power is rarely needed or exercised.

Procedure.

As for the procedure up to the hearing, the reference to the Ministry of Labour is made of course by the parties themselves or by someone acting on their behalf (sec. 2(1)). This seems to indicate that where a union takes up a case involving a group of workers, it is strictly the workers, and not the union, that are the parties; and certainly there is no *statutory* ban upon an individual or small group of employees bringing a case without the assistance of, or even in opposition to, a trade union. However, as far as the court's consensual jurisdiction is concerned, the point must be very largely academic in that an employer is unlikely to agree to a reference except as the result of union pressure. We analyzed for the purposes of this chapter the 449 awards given between 1958 and 1966, including the 315 based on the court's voluntary jurisdiction. In none of these cases did we find as a party to a voluntary arbitration an individual employee or group of employees not organized in a trade union.[13]

The notification to the minister need take no particular form but must give him sufficient information to fulfill his statutory duties.[14] Once the minister's consent to the reference has been obtained, the parties must, with the minister's help, try to draw up agreed terms of reference. Examples of such terms of reference are:

(3111) To determine a difference between the Federation and the Union as to the interpretation of Clause 3(b), relating to overtime worked outside the factory, in the Working Rules Agreement for the Organ Building Industry.

(2996) To determine whether the professional ballroom dancers appearing in the Granada T.V. Network Ltd. programme series "Let's Dance," come within the terms of the Agreement dated 1 March 1962 between that Company and the Variety Artistes' Federation.

(2986) To determine whether, in view of the nature of the work performed in the Mintex Division of British Belting and Asbestos Ltd., the conditions of workers employed in the Mintex Division should be governed by Agreements in the Engineering Industry.

(2722) To determine a difference between the Parties concerning the grading of posts of Divisional Education Officer in 11 divisions in Kent.

(3057) To determine the Union's claim for an improvement in the annual holiday entitlement of workpeople covered by the Road Transport Workers' Agreement between the parties.

(2982) To determine the claim of the Trade Unions representing the Workshop Supervising Staff employed by the London Transport

---

[13] Contrast the position under some special jurisdictions, e.g., Road Haulage Wages Act, 1938, below, p. 201.

[14] Turner Samuels, *Industrial Negotiation and Arbitration* (1951), p. 269.

Board that the standard hours of the Workshop Supervisory Staff should be 40 per week on the same basis as British Railways Workshop Supervisors controlling Railway Shopmen.

Alternative formulations of the terms of reference are acceptable if they both put the same issue before the court, but not if they formulate different issues. If even this measure of agreement cannot be obtained, the claimant can send a document to the court setting out its case and the defendant the reply, and the court will deduce the terms of reference from these. But in none of the cases studied did this become necessary. In practice, the parties are requested to send to the court and to each other written summaries of their cases at least one week before the hearing.[15] This is all that is necessary by way of "pleading." If all runs according to course, the hearing will take place about three weeks after the reference by the minister of the case to the court, and this will be true all the year round since the court has no vacations.[16] The hearing will be in London unless one party would be seriously disadvantaged by the fact. In practice the only hardship the court usually recognizes is that of a small employer who runs his own business. Thus the court rarely sits outside London. Among the cases examined, we found only 44 where the court had sat outside London. On only nine occasions had the court felt the need to view the "locus in quo." Practice here is quite different from that of Single Arbitrators by reason of the nature of the cases heard by the two types of body.

The procedure and hearing are governed by the Industrial Court (Procedure) Rules, 1920; but these ten Rules provide a mere skeleton for procedure which is largely determined as the court proceeds and is always informal. For example, the rules provide:

5. The court may with the consent of the parties act notwithstanding any vacancy in their number and no act, proceeding, or determination of the Court shall be called in question or invalidated by reason of any such vacancy, provided such consent has first been obtained.
6. The Court may correct in any award any clerical mistake or error arising from an accidental slip or omission. . . .
8. Persons may appear by counsel or solicitor on proceedings before the Court with the permission of the Court.

---

[15] We are indebted to the president and secretary of the court for information on the practice in this and other respects.

[16] The gap between receipt by the ministry of a request for arbitration and its reference to the court seems to be from four to ten days. Cases under the Act of 1959 take longer because the ministry exercises some general check on whether the case has a chance of succeeding (below, p. 204).

9. Subject to these rules the Court may regulate their own procedure as they think fit.

Representation by lawyers is thus at the discretion of the court (though the president in his evidence says he has never refused such a request.)[17] Legal representation is not in practice frequent, and the president takes the view that the parties can present their own evidence best unless difficult issues of interpretation of statutes or documents arise. Representation by a lay person is possible without the consent of the court, and the usual situation will be that the union case is presented by a union official and the employer's case by a company director or an employers' federation official. The party that wishes to alter the status quo will open and amplify its written statement. The other side will reply in like manner, to which the first side rejoins and this process can continue until both sides feel they have exhausted their arguments. During this exchange, the members of the court, especially the president, do not necessarily maintain a neutral silence but will put questions to elicit a complete explanation of the case on either side, and will dominate and control the proceedings to a greater or lesser extent, according as the parties themselves are capable of putting their points. This is, of course, only a description of an "average" case, since the court has a large discretion (Rule 9) in the regulation of its own procedure. Oral evidence is not given on oath, and the court cannot compel the attendance of witnesses. In any event most of the evidence is documentary, but once again the court cannot order the production or discovery of documents. There are no rules as to what may or may not be put in by way of documentary evidence; it is merely a question of what in any particular instance the party can persuade the court to accept when it has heard the counterarguments from the other side.

The court cannot punish for contempt; is not a court of record; and the accepted proposition that statements to the court are absolutely privileged is open to dispute.[18] There is provision under Rule 4 for the court to use assessors on technical points: these would be present at the hearing, ask questions, and deliberate in the discussions afterward, but would take no responsibility for the award. The present president

---

[17] R.C.M.E., vol. 45, para. 28, p. 1943. Figures on this point are not kept, and the published awards do not disclose whether the parties are represented.

[18] The proposition rests upon *Slack* v. *Barr* (1918) 82 J.P. 91 and *Copartnership Farms* v. *Harvey Smith* [1918] 2 K.B. 405. Neither case had the court in mind being decided before it was established. See too Mackenzie, *op. cit.*, p. 14.

takes the view that assessors should not be used since the members of the court themselves must understand the technical issues and the parties are capable of explaining these. He has never used assessors.[19]

Awards

The hearing usually lasts only one day. In the cases examined of 1958 to 1966, it lasted longer on only five occasions, and more than one hearing took place in only twelve cases.[20] The members of the court retire to discuss the matter and also usually reach a decision on the same day, except where the parties have agreed to submit additional written evidence after the hearing because of inadequacies revealed during it. If the court is not *unanimous*, then the chairman decides the case, acting as an umpire by virtue of section 3(4) of the act. He does so even if there is a majority in favor of one side. Thus the award is always one with which the chairman agrees, even if the two wing-members oppose it. In his written evidence, Sir Roy Wilson supported this system (para. 27) *inter alia* on the grounds that there might be three views rather than two, and so a majority opinion would not be arrived at. In none of the cases examined was there a disagreement—in contrast to the Boards of Arbitration. The parties, however, do not receive a typewritten copy of the award until some three weeks later, and the interval seems to be taken up by the secretary to the court in producing the award and obtaining the members' signatures to it. Awards of the court are published; and this typewritten copy is in the same form as the award ultimately officially published, containing the terms of reference, an introduction, the arguments from either side, and the award.

In the vast majority of cases, the court does not give reasons for its awards. For the first few years after its establishment, the court did give reasons; but it found that this was not the better practice. In special cases it will still do so, and the president refers to an increase in such cases in his evidence (there were in 1965, for example, four cases in which detailed reasons were given). But mainly the court has been a major influence in setting its seal upon a regular (though not universal) practice of British industrial arbitration, the refusal to give reasons. This is, of course, not unrelated to the fact that the arbitrators

---

[19] R.C.M.E. vol. 45, p. 1942. Contrast the first president, Lord Amnbrie, who said that "much use" was made of assessors (Mackenzie, *op. cit.*, pp. 14–15.
[20] For his unpublished Ph.D. thesis for Leeds University, "Arbitration in Great Britain," I. F. Patterson, however, discovered thirty cases between 1958 and 1966 in which there appeared to be proceedings on more than one day.

do not make a firm distinction between conflicts over "rights" and over "interests."

Typical awards read:

Having given careful consideration to the evidence and submissions of the Parties the Court find and Award that the true interpretation of Clause 3(b) of the Agreement is that travelling time is not to be taken into account as part of the normal 40 hour working week beyond which overtime is payable. [3111]

. . . find against the claim of the A.U.B.T.W. and Award accordingly. [3055]

. . . find that the professional ballroom dancers appearing in the Granada T.V. Network Limited programme series "Let's Dance" do not in relation to that programme come within the terms of the 1962 Agreement. [2996]

. . . find that the Claim of the Amalgamated Engineering Union that the conditions of workers employed in the Mintex Division of the Company should be governed by agreements in the Engineering Industry has not been established, and Award accordingly. [2986]

In defending the ordinary practice of not giving reasons, Sir Roy Wilson gave the Royal Commission four reasons which may be summarized as:

1. The award is intended to put an end to the dispute and not to prolong and exacerbate the difference. This, it is feared, would be the result if the parties were given the reasons for the award to argue over.
2. The effect of giving reasons would be to build up a body of case law which might lead to a more rigid treatment of disputes.
3. Sometimes the members of the Court come to the same conclusion for different reasons, and the authority of the award would be lessened if this were revealed.
4. The members of the Court prefer not to give reasons because of the practical work in industrial relations which they do outside the Court.[21]

Similar reasons were given in the House of Commons in 1958 by both the then opposition spokesman George Brown, who said:

To Hon. Gentlemen who have recently suggested that one of the great contributions we could make towards improving the situation would be to have the arbitrators publish the reasons for their decisions,

---

[21] R.C.M.E., vol. 45, p. 1935.

let me say, as one who has been nearly twenty-one years in the trade union movement, that, if they want a dispute, nothing would lead to it more quickly than that.

and the then Parliamentary Secretary to the Ministry of Labour, who said:

> It seems to me that with the rapid changes we have experienced in the economic climate since the end of the war, the idea of a stable body of common law in these matters would, in fact, be unattainable in practice.
>
> I am confirmed in that belief by what happened in the early days of the Industrial Court. This experience was tried and elaborate machinery set up, but it had to be abandoned.[22]

Reasons will be given, however, if the parties ask for them or if they are necessary to make the award comprehensible. Award 3054, for example, an arbitration in January 1965 between Amalgamated Union of Building Trade Workers (A.U.B.T.W.) and the Iron and Steel Trades Employers' Association, involved a demarcation dispute of considerable complexity, including claims by three unions (A.U.B.T.W., T.G.W.U., and Iron and Steel Trades Confederation [I.S.T.C.]) and the relationship of a previous award (3028) with a single arbitration carried out by D. T. Jack for the Trades Union Congress. Not surprisingly, the court found it impossible to give a short "yes" or "no," but went into an explanation of its reasoning in 3028 and added its advice about the best method for settling demarcation disputes in the future. The case is also interesting because the court heard evidence from T.G.W.U. and I.S.T.C., although these were not strictly parties to the

---

[22] Hansard, H.C., February 1958, cols. 1459 and 1475. The government spokesman had previously said:

The circumstances of almost every dispute are different. A statement of the factors entering into an award would not necessarily be helpful, but might be positively embarrassing to arbitrators dealing with subsequent disputes. We should remember that one of the features of our arbitration system is that arbitration courts are composed not only of independent persons, but also of representatives of employers and workers. I believe, that the presence of those representatives with their intimate experience of industry, its workings and its atmosphere, has added considerably to the effectiveness of arbitration and its acceptability to both sides. It might make the task which those representatives have to carry out more difficult if they had to set out reasons for their conclusions. Again, arbitration is intended to operate as a clear-cut end to a controversial episode. An award which gave reasons, the validity of which might be challenged by either party, might merely carry on the dispute. That, I think, was the very valid point the right hon. member [Mr. Brown] had in mind.

case. In fact, the court sometimes not merely gives reasons but suggests further courses of action to the parties:

> Having given careful consideration to the evidence and submissions of the Parties the Court find and so Award that the claim contained in the Terms of Reference has not been established, but consider that the Parties should enter into negotiations for increased rates of pay for the workers concerned having regard, inter alia, to the rates now being paid to women workers similarly employed by the Ministry of Aviation at the Royal Radar Establishment, Malvern. [3041]

Again in 3081, T.G.W.U. and Silcock and Colling, Ltd (November 1965), a case to which we return, part of the terms of reference were "to determine and report whether a breach occurred of the procedure for the avoidance of disputes . . . and if so, which of the two parties was responsible." The court considered that they should "set out the main reasons for their conclusion in relation to this item . . ."; and did so in considerable detail, mainly, it would seem, to help the parties in the operation of their procedure on future occasions. In 3080 (T.G. W.U. and Stratford Market Tenants' Association, Ltd., November 1965), a question arose about a previous case (3062) which had recommended a five-day week for a number of London markets and indicated the broad lines along which the award should be implemented. The details were left for negotiation between the union and the various market tenants' associations. These were settled subsequently except in regard to the Stratford Market, but on lines rather different from those recommended in Award 3062. The failure at Stratford was reported to the court, and a complete settlement asked for (as 3062 provided), but there was the additional complicating factor of whether the court should revise its broad guidelines laid down in 3062 in view of the actual settlements made at the other markets. The court decided it should and gave its reasons, no doubt to avoid the charge of having gone back on itself. Award 3062 itself was an example of the court's giving reasons "in view of the somewhat unusual circumstances and background of this case."[23]

The award of the Industrial Court acting as a voluntary arbitration tribunal is not enforceable in the ordinary courts without more. In practice, the awards are usually complied with. Once the award has been acted upon, it may become an implied term in the relevant em-

---

[23] This same question had led to a strike in June 1964, as a result of which a Committee of Inquiry under the chairmanship of D. T. Jack, C.B.E., had been appointed and had reported. It was the failure of the parties to agree upon the recommendations of the inquiry that had resulted in the arbitration.

ployment contracts. Where the parties have previously agreed to abide by the arbitration, or where they customarily do abide, it would be arguable that the award should automatically become such a term. Two poorly reported cases in courts of inferior jurisdiction have been often quoted as establishing this proposition.[24] We have already seen that recent case law has done little to resolve the obscurities surrounding incorporation of terms into such contracts (see above, pp. 45 ff.), and automatic incorporation would seem to be the exception rather than the rule.

Types of Dispute before the Court

In order to see whether any pattern could be established in the direction of a distinction between disputes over "rights" and claims concerning "interests," we analyzed all the 449 awards between 1958

TABLE 22

Result of Analysis of 315 "Voluntary" Industrial Court Awards, 1958-1966

"Interest" Claims	
National claims (wages, hours, holidays)	160*
Regional claims (wages, hours, holidays)	51
Claims at firm level (wages, hours, holidays)	24
Named posts (wages, hours, holidays)	11
Other terms and conditions	15
Piece rates	3
Total	264
Disputes Involving "Rights"	
Interpretation of written agreements	23
Interpretation of oral agreements	3
Regrading cases involving rights	13
Miscellaneous	4
Total	43
Other Cases	
Interpretation of previous award	5
Demarcation cases	3
Total	8

*The national claims came from the following sources: national health service, 54; civil air transport, 33; railway shopmen, 11. The other 62 national claims were divided among 38 other industries.

SOURCE: Published awards of Industrial Court (2677 to 3125, omitting statutory and special jurisdiction cases).

---

[24] Magistrates' Court cases: The Newcastle Case, *Newcastle Daily Chronicle*, August 12, 1927, also reported on in 30 *Lab. Gaz.* 322; and the Kilmarnock Case, *Kilmarnock Standard*, April 2, 1924, commented on by A. J. Walkden, *Daily Herald*, February 26, 1924, p. 6.

175

and 1966, and especially the 315 "voluntary arbitration" awards. A liberal view was taken of anything that could possibly be called a "rights" dispute (e.g., the arbitrations over regrading of workers were allocated to "rights disputes" if they could possibly be regarded as essentially questions of interpretation of existing agreements). Even so only 43 of the cases could be put under this heading. The detailed results of the analysis are shown in Table 22. It goes without saying that there is nothing in the procedure or award of the court which in any way makes this distinction between the types of case. However, some examples of the cases may be suitably given. Cases where we find the Industrial Court perhaps most nearly faced with the sort of problems with which lawyers are familiar are those concerning disputed interpretations of a collective agreement. One example is Award 3111, decided in August 1966, a case brought by National Union of Musical Instrument Makers against the Federation of Master Organ Builders. The question invoked the interpretation of an overtime agreement, which read in part: "Overtime Worked Outside the Factory—applicable after normal weekly hours as provided for in Clause 1. Rates Up To Midnight: Overtime shall be calculated on the basis of the accrued first 10 hours at time and a quarter, thereafter time and a half." The disputed point was whether traveling time was to be included in the "normal weekly hours" for the purposes of determining when overtime began. Yet a close reading of the report suggests that the true position was that the parties either did not have the point in mind at the negotiations or had different intentions in the matter which they did not communicate to each other. At the time of the agreement the point in question was not important, since, as the employer's side stated, these men on outside jobs usually lived on the job so that the amount of traveling time to outside jobs was small. Now that it was more common for outside workers to travel to work (some six years later) the "interpretation" proposed by either side would produce anomalies. Thus on the trade union side it was pointed out that a worker who spent a long time traveling to work might never in any one week work sufficient productive hours to get onto the overtime rate and would in fact be worse off than under the previous agreement whereby overtime rates were payable after ten hours' work above the normal forty hours (in which traveling time was presumably included). The employers for their part indicated that the unions' interpretation placed the factory workers in an unfair position, for they were not allowed any traveling time at all. The court found that the "true interpretation of the Clause" was that of the employers. This problem may be a familiar one to lawyers and judges who, in contract cases, decide the issue by talking about the "objective intention of the parties." The fact, however, remains that the point is one that the parties glossed over originally, but would have negotiated about had it been brought to their minds as sufficiently important, and to this extent an apparent arbitration on a point of "right" is a substitute for negotiation.

A similar case was Award 3070 decided in May 1965 between the Operatives' and Employers' Sides of National Joint Council for the Exhibition Industry. In 1963 the working rules of the industry were renegotiated, and among the provisions altered were those dealing with the period of notice to be given on the termination of the contract of employment, in order that the working rules should conform with the Contracts of Employment Act, 1963. Rule 5, which was the one in question, was not stated to come into effect at any particular date, but the last paragraph of the amended rules reads: "The amendments will operate from the pay week beginning midnight 5 April 1964." The Contracts of Employment Act was to come into effect on 6 July 1964. From which date should Rule 5 be operative? As the employers' side stated, the point had never been discussed between the two sides, but the employers had intended to do no more than comply with the minimum provisions of the act, and the date of July 6 was implicit in their statement, while the employees had thought that in the matter of the date of operation they had obtained a concession from the employers. The court found that "the intention of the Parties must be taken to have been" that the operative date should be April 5.

One particularly important interpretation case already mentioned was Award 3081, between the T.G.W.U. and Silcock and Colling, Ltd., in 1965:

> 1. To determine and report, whether a breach occurred of the procedure for the avoidance of disputes (as provided by Clause 3 of the Agreement governing the wages and conditions of Car Transporter Drivers and Statutory Attendants), and if so, which of the two parties was responsible for such breach.
> 2. To determine whether driver F. Murray should be reinstated in his former employment with Silcock and Colling, Ltd., at Halewood, Lancashire, and the Union's claim that this should be from 17th August, 1965.

The parties were in disagreement about the facts concerning the interviewing and ultimate dismissal of Mr. Murray, a car transporter driver and member of the union. The court on the whole preferred the company's account and decided against reinstatement. The union, it held in an award which gave detailed reasons on the facts, was in breach of the procedure agreement. The grounds for this finding are interesting:

(5) In the event, when the interview was over the district official did not get into telephone communication with the Chairman of the Association or indeed with any of the directors at Dagenham. Instead, he and the senior shop steward had a discussion with the other shop stewards and thereafter called a meeting of the Company's hourly-paid staff then on the site, following which those members of the staff and subsequently the remainder of the hourly-paid staff withdrew their labour. On the 19th August this strike was recognised as official by the General Executive Council of the Union.

(6) It is an express provision of the Procedure (see Clause 3(f) of the Agreement quoted in paragraph 5 above) that "No strike or lock-out will take place while the above procedure is complied with, and both parties will ensure that it is not unncessarily delayed or obstructed." In view particularly of this provision it is plain that, unless the submissions argued before the Court by the Union are correct, the strike mentioned in paragraph (5) above was started, and subsequently approved by the Union, in breach of the procedure. The substance of the Union's argument is that the depot manager's refusal to suspend his dismissal of Mr. Murray until the district official could take the matter up with the directors at Dagenham constituted itself a breach of a non-compliance with the Procedure; that it constituted an "obstruction" of the Procedure within the meaning of the above-quoted Clause 3(f) of the Procedure; that it nullified the operation or application of the Procedure in relation to the dispute in question; and that in consequence the strike did not constitute any breach of the Procedure. The Court are unable to accept this argument as correct. They consider that the true position is as follows. The depot manager has the Company's authority to dismiss a driver, if necessary forthwith, in cases where this course appears to him to be justified by the facts. If in any case a dispute arises as to whether his decision is justified the Procedure comes, or should come, into operation. If at any stage of the Procedure it is agreed (or, in the case of the last stage, awarded) that the manager's decision was unjustified or should for any reason be reversed, the normal and right course is that if the driver has already been dismissed the agreement or award makes proper provision, if necessary, for his reinstatement. This is what commonly happens in industrial disputes. It may possibly, in the circumstances of any given case, be wise for a manager to suspend the dismissal pending the operation of the Procedure, but it is no breach or obstruction of the Procedure for him to adhere to his decision to dismiss the worker and to leave it to the Procedure to rectify that decision if it is wrong. The Court accordingly find that the Union are wrong in contending that by reason of the course taken by the depot manager the strike did not constitute a breach of the Procedure.

(7) In the Court's view the Union are also wrong in contending that the Company were in breach of the Procedure in not acceding to an

invitation by the representative of the Ministry of Labour to meet representatives of the Union for exploratory talks in Liverpool on the 25th August 1965. The Court consider that it would have been reasonable and courteous for the Company to accept that invitation, if only to make clear their point of view; but their attitude cannot be said to have been a breach of the Procedure in view of the fact that at the date of the invitation the Union's members were on strike in contravention of that Procedure.

It is particularly interesting to find the court accepting and upholding managerial prerogative to dismiss within the context of an ordinary procedure agreement, and finding that the manager has authority to dismiss "if necessary forthwith," leaving it for the procedure to come into operation on the basis of a *fait accompli.* If later it is agreed or awarded that his decision should be reversed or was "unjustified," then the award "makes proper provision, if necessary, for (the worker's) reinstatement. *This is what commonly happens in industrial disputes.*" Suspension may be "wise"; but it is not required by the typical procedure in the court's eyes at least.

Closely analogous to, and to be classed with interpretation cases in the 23 listed in Table 22, are questions of the application of agreements to the facts of the particular case. There will be standard cases to which the rule clearly applies, but there will also be debatable cases where the words are neither obviously applicable nor obviously ruled out. Had the particular situation been foreseen at the time of the negotiations, the parties might have been asked to alter the form of wording to make it clear whether the rule was to apply or not, but only at the expense of creating further doubtful areas about the operation of the amended rule. Whatever lawyers may think, or courts do, an industrial arbitrator is bound in such a case to have in mind *both* the strict interpretation of the agreement *and* the future relations of the collective parties, for as Sir Roy Wilson said in another connection: "It is to my mind clear that industrial arbitrators are intended to have and to bring to the performance of their task, an experience of the facts of industrial life extending far beyond the facts of any particular case."[25]

In view of what has been said above, it is not surprising that parties in argument before the court sometimes fail to keep questions of "right" and "interest" separate, even though the facts of the case seem to invite such a distinction. In Award 3036, August 1964, Iron and Steel Trades Confederation and Iron and Steel Trades Employers' As-

---

[25] R.C.M.E., vol. 45, p. 1936.

sociation, the union had agreed with Samuel Fox and Co., Ltd., *inter alia,* a base tonnage bonus rate on the understanding, generally accepted in the industry, that any variation in it should be the subject only of national negotiation except in the case of a local "change of practice." The relevant clause read: "It shall be competent for either party to this Agreement to seek a revision if a change of practice has taken place. . . ." Clearly, then, before one party could demand that the other negotiate with it a new agreement (interest), it would have to prove that a change of practice had taken place (right), within the terms of the existing agreement. However, the terms of reference asked the court not only to decide whether a change of practice had taken place, but to adjudicate upon the company's claim for a 12½ percent reduction in the tonnage bonus rates. This claim was based upon a permanent increase in production brought about by new methods; but in argument the union said that there had been no "change of practice" because improved techniques should benefit employees as well by giving them higher wages and had in any case increased the risks to which the workers were subject and for which they ought to be compensated. The court did not stop to distinguish the character of the two issues. Its award reads: "Having given careful consideration to the evidence and submissions of the parties, the Court find that the claim has not been established and Award accordingly." It would be a lawyer of more than brilliant qualities who could make a precedent out of that.

Connected with cases concerning the application of agreements are some of the regrading cases. Typically, these are in effect claims for wage increases for individual or small groups of white-collar workers employed by local corporations, nationalized industries, and the like, which take this form in a graded wage structure, except when the claim is for an overall increase. Ten of the 23 regrading cases were of this kind. However, a number of regrading cases involve the problem of applying rules to doubtful fact situations, notably a series of national health cases arising from the introduction of a completely new salary structure on July 1, 1958. One example is Award 2802, September 1960, Confederation of Health Service Employees and South Western Regional Hospital Board: "To decide whether the duties attaching to the post occupied by Mr. L. Coller are appropriate to the Senior Administrative or General Administrative Grade with effect from 1 November 1958."

Of a similar nature is the small group of cases dealing with oral agreements or understandings, and the question before the court seems to be whether the conduct of the parties in the past has been such that the "understanding" claimed should be upheld as one of the principles for future negotiation. An example is Award 2846, June 1961, an arbitration between the Clerical and Administrative Workers' Union and the Aluminium Wire and Cable Company, Ltd. The employer was a nonfederated firm, and the question was of the applicability of an agreement between the union and the Engineering and Allied Employers' Federation. The terms of reference from the union side claimed that the increases in that agreement "shall be applied to the Union's members in the Company's employ"; those from the company asked whether the increase "should" be applied. This was because one of the points at issue was whether there was an understanding between the parties that the Engineering Agreements should be followed. The union claimed that this was the basis upon which previous agreements had been negotiated between the company and the union, while the company merely conceded that "it had been their practice to have regard to recommendations of the Engineering Employers' Federation when reviewing salaries towards the end of each year" but said that it "had not specifically agreed and had not given any undertaking to the Union to follow the Engineering Industry." The court found in favor of the union.

Finally, there are the miscellaneous cases. Among these, surprisingly, one must place Award 3081, discussed above, which dealt with a question of dismissal. It is, however, the only dismissal case the court has had since 1952. Even then it was coupled with important questions about the interpretation of the disputes procedure. (The court rejected the claim for reinstatement.) The number of dismissal cases before the Industrial Court has declined. Between 1946 and 1952, its awards include one or two cases of this type each year. This, as we shall see, is in marked contrast to the cases heard by Single Arbitrators. In a number of other cases we found it hard to classify the arguments in any way. For example in Award 2986 the question arose whether the company should apply to certain workers the Engineering Agreements, or the Narrow Fabrics Agreement currently applied. The main argument was directed to the question which agreement was "appropriate" in view of the work carried on in the works division; but the employers also argued that the Engineering Agreement was only slightly more favorable than the Narrow Fabrics Agreement and that the latter, coupled with the company's fringe benefits, provided much more favorable terms and conditions. The court found in favor of the company. Again in Award 2980, July 1963, Hinckley and District Hosiery Warehousemen's and Manufacturers' Associations, the question was whether female labor could be used in the countering of hosiery. The

181

employers based their claim mainly on the need to reduce costs; the employees, on the reduction of male jobs in the town and its consequent likely depopulation. The court allowed the claim subject to an undertaking by the employers that there should be no male redundancy.

Our analysis of the Industrial Court cases has been deliberately close. The result has been to show the variety and complexity of its work and the refusal which it resolutely maintains to become embroiled in any legal categories which could impede its arbitration awards being of assistance to the parties in their future relationships.

SINGLE ARBITRATORS

Appointment and Procedure

The Single Arbitrators find their jurisdiction in Section 2(2)(b) of the Industrial Courts Act (above, p. 163), which gives the Minister of Labour, as an alternative to a reference to the Industrial Court, power to refer the matter to one or more persons appointed by him for settlement. In general, most of what was said about the functions and procedure before, during, and after hearing, with reference to the Industrial Court, is true also of the Single Arbitrators; only the important differences are noted here. First, the Single Arbitrators are appointed ad hoc for each dispute, and there is no special institutional machinery to help them. They are usually paid a small fee plus expenses for the arbitration. An arbitrator is chosen, in theory at least, by the Ministry of Labour from among the people on the maintained list of independent persons. Those appointed in recent years have been mainly academics with social science backgrounds, plus a few lawyers and rather more retired ministry officials. In practice the ministry will probably accede to a request from the parties for an arbitrator with a particular type of background or even for a particular arbitrator. Once the arbitrator has consented to take the case, the Ministry of Labour will act as secretariat in arranging a time and place for the hearing and in inviting the parties to submit and exchange written statements before the hearing. The hearing is invariably held in the area where the dispute occurs, either on the company's premises or in the local Ministry of Labour offices. The arbitrator's report is submitted to the ministry within a few days of the hearing, and the ministry dispatches copies to the parties. Procedure is even more informal than that before the Industrial Court, and counsel are even less frequently used.

Through the good offices of the ministry, we were able to consult on a confidential basis the records of single arbitrations between 1961 to 1965, and we found only one case out of 138 in this period in which a lawyer was used (a solicitor for the employers). It was the only arbitration in which the parties seem to have argued about who should "open" the case.

There is another possible source of appointment under the Conciliation Act, 1896, section 2:

(I)   Where a difference exists or is apprehended between an employer, or any class of employers, and workmen, or between different classes of workmen, the [Board of Trade] may, if they think fit, exercise all or any of the following powers namely,

(a)   inquire into the causes and circumstances of the difference;

(b)   take such steps as to the [Board] may seem expedient for the purpose of enabling the parties to the difference to meet together, by themselves or their representatives, under the presidency of a chairman mutually agreed upon or nominated by the [Board of Trade] or by some other person or body, with a view to the amicable settlement of the difference;

(c)   on the application of employers or workmen interested and after taking into consideration the existence and adequacy of means available for conciliation in the district or trade and the circumstances of the case, appoint a person or persons to act as conciliator or as a board of conciliation;

(d)   on the application of both parties to the difference, appoint an arbitrator.

The powers were transferred from the Board of Trade to the Minister of Labour in 1916. If the minister wished, and the parties desire, he could appoint under both (b) or (c) *and* (d), so that the person appointed would be in effect a conciliator with power to become an arbitrator. The 1896 act supplies no definitions of "difference" or "workmen." Nor does it exactly demand that the parties' own machinery be *exhausted*, though the minister would not today normally appoint where it was not. The arbitrator's methods of conciliation in such a case will, of course, be personal (see chapter 10); but normally he will see the parties separately, or attempt conciliation from the chair at a meeting, or both. If he fails, he gives a "chairman's award." The number of occasions in the last five years on which such arbitration with powers under section 2(1)(b) or (c) *and* (d) of the 1896 act have been appointed has been small, the figures being:

1966	1965	1964	1963	1962
nil	2(1)	2	3(1)	1(1)

(The figures in parentheses represent successful conciliations where there was no chairman's award.) This same method has in the past been used on an informal basis in a more continuing form. For example, in 1959 Lord Birkett was appointed by the Minister of Labour at the request of the parties in dispute in the printing industry. There were a series of questions in dispute. The method adopted was to empower Birkett to act as a conciliating chairman until everyone agreed that deadlock had been reached on a point, and then allow him to give a binding ruling on that, so that the parties could continue from there. A settlement was ultimately reached by this method, which may be called "rolling conciliation" with pauses for arbitral breath. This method has not been used often; although some of the Courts and Committees of Inquiry held recently disclose analogies to the method (below, p. 224).

Awards

The awards of Single Arbitrators are not published. On the whole, Single Arbitrators follow the Industrial Court practice of not giving reasons for their decisions; but of the 138 cases between 1961 and 1965, we found a slightly larger number which departed from the simple formula of a bare award for either one side or the other. Many of the awards, it is true, followed the stock Industrial Court pattern: terms of reference, arguments of claimant, arguments of defendent, award. But in some, the arbitrator states the arguments and facts in his own narrative, a form that inevitably indicates gradually his line of thinking, and in some the narrative includes evaluations much more in the nature of judgments. Occasionally we found that the reasons were indicated in the award itself. The arbitrator, like the Industrial Court, sometimes feels that he must add suggestions to his award, as in one case in 1961 where, after upholding a suspension as justified, he ended by saying that the company might reexamine its practice of having men interviewed by the department or personnel manager through a window, clarify its procedures for complaint, and make less arbitrary the occasions on which sick men returning to work were forced to undergo a medical examination.

The Single Arbitrator deals with essentially local issues. This appeared from our analysis of 131 of the 138 arbitrations between 1961 and 1965. Here we found that the average time between appointment and report was 21 days. Seventy-six cases were completed within this period, 34 of them within two weeks; whereas 15, 13, and 10 cases took an extra one, two, and three weeks, respectively, and only 3 cases, a further period. We found that 27 concerned disciplinary matters, all of them dismissals except for 1 demotion and 4 suspensions. The arbitrator was always able to say whether the management's decision was or was not "justifiable," though the precise reasoning behind this concept of industrial jurisprudence is never explained. Most of the dismissal cases seemed to be ad hoc arbitrations; but in a few there was evidence of their being the last stage in a formal internal procedure in a firm. The N.J.A.C. Report confirms that the ministry's arbitrators are occasionally used under such procedures and says instances have "averaged four to five cases a year in recent years."[26] In our sample, all but four of the discipline cases involved an allegation that the employee had broken some company works rule. The union's reply was usually either that he did not do the acts alleged or that the penalty imposed by the employer was too severe. The arbitrators consistently heard evidence of what had been done in similar cases in the firm—another example of the weight given to precedent in regard to punishments—but often written evidence of what had previously happened was missing, and the evidence of the two sides conflicted. (It is often objected that new *laws* protecting workers from unjustifiable dismissals would require too much paper work on the part of management and make both sides "barrack room lawyers."[27] The present situation perhaps suffers from the opposite vice of records inadequate for a system that does, in practice, take past precedent very seriously.)

Of the ten dismissal cases the union won, reinstatement was granted in seven. Indeed (in contrast to the legal position in the British courts), reinstatement is so easily accepted as the *normal* remedy that it is not always necessary to ask for it specifically and certainly not to mention it in the terms of reference. In a 1962 case the arbitrator was merely asked to "determine the dispute" that had arisen over the dismissal of an employee for being in the canteen when he should have been working. He found that the management's reasons for the dismissal were not convincing and ordered reinstatement. Consequently, one cannot even be sure in the three cases where the arbitrator merely declared that the dismissal was not justified that this was not taken by the parties as equivalent to an order to reinstate. Contrary to some assertions that a union will sponsor discipline cases only when victimization for trade union activity is involved, only half the cases in this period contained any such allegation. In only five cases was it clearly indicated that the employee was suspended pending a decision on the

---

[26] N.J.A.C. Report, p. 19 n.
[27] See questions to K. W. Wedderburn in R.C.M.E., vol. 31, paras. 4736–4739, in response to his proposals to enact such laws.

dismissal. In others his status during the procedure is obscure; but in most his dismissal plainly took effect (as in the normal industrial practice noted by the Industrial Court; above, p. 179). In a few of the cases where the arbitrator upheld the dismissal, it is interesting to note that the employer had in argument expressed a willingness to reemploy the offending worker after a period of time, an argument that would surely not have been addressed to the arbitrator unless it was likely to weigh with him, though strictly a lawyer might not think it relevant to whether a dismissal is "justifiable" or not.

An example of a dismissal case involving a question of the degree of punishment is a 1965 case. The employee in question was dismissed for smoking in the factory. The union claimed his dismissal was unfair because others committing the same offense had merely been named, and that the foreman and manager had taken the opportunity to satisfy a personal grudge. The works' rules did not say smoking was forbidden. The company said their action was justified because of the high fire risk in the factory and that this was the first time a clear instance of the offense had come up. The arbitrator found in favor of the company. An example of a straight conflict on the facts is a 1961 case, where the company claimed that two employees, aggrieved at the company's failure to extend the time allowed for a particular job, fraudulently overestimated their production figures at the end of one day. The employees asserted they had fulfilled what they claimed and denied any suggestion that they could have inadvertently miscalculated the number of units produced. The arbitrator found in favor of the company.

Although these are the two most common ways of challenging the decision to dismiss (and in all the cases the burden is on the union to act), there are other elements in the cases, notably in insubordination cases. Here the essence of the matter is the refusal of a reasonable order which may, in some cases, however, be justified. The union can thus argue either that the order was not reasonable, or that the refusal was justified on other grounds. Thus in 1964, an employee was dismissed for refusing to stack a third tier of pallets; the works' rules classed failure to carry out an instruction as misconduct. One defense put forward by the union was that the refusal was reasonable because the pallets were too heavy to be stacked in a third tier and such a procedure would be dangerous because the floor was slippery. The arbitrator did not find in support of this argument. In a 1963 arbitration, an employee was dismissed for refusing to obey a normal order, an order to load a lorry. Here one of the defenses put forward by the union was that, by the time of the refusal of which the employer complained, the company's dispute with the employee was no longer on an individual basis but had merged with a general withdrawal of labor of which the employee's refusal was only one aspect, so that his refusal should have been dealt with by the employers on that basis and not singled out for special attention. The arbitrator upheld the argument. Here is a clear case of the arbitrator putting aside the ordinary legal rights of the parties (for the employee, on this basis at least, was in breach of his contract of employment). Even so, the arbitrator awarded that the employee be allowed to continue his employment— but with a warning that he ought to carry out his duties with "more tact and discretion."

The discipline cases were dealt with speedily. The average delay between the offense alleged and the final award was ten weeks in the 22 cases where this information could be reliably acquired. Similarly, out of 23 cases where the dates are given, the average time from *appointment* to award was only 15 days. (Special circumstances in a twenty-fourth case raised that figure to 49 days, and this case was omitted since the average would have been badly distorted.) It seemed clear that arbitrators were anxious to make their award on discipline cases within the shortest possible time. Nevertheless, the man concerned might well have been unemployed for this time.

Some twenty cases deal with interpretation or application of agreements, and here the problems are similar to those with which the Industrial Court has had to deal. The vast majority of the cases are the "penumbral" ones, however: What does short-time working mean? Must it arise from a trade recession, or can it also occur when members of another union in the same factory go on strike? Is there a "stoppage" when employees refuse to do a certain type of work but make themselves available for any others? Does the term "overtime" include hours worked before the normal daily hours? Is there a "lockout" when employees refuse to return to work until a fellow worker has been reinstated? Does a "normal working day" cease to be normal when some of the employees are on strike?

In discussions we had with some arbitrators, we found a certain variation in approach to interpretation questions. The age-old question of how far an arbitrator must keep to his terms of reference is bound to arise, as it does so often in the United States. One, for instance, took the view that his task was to obtain the right answer for the future in order to set the parties' negotiations upon a firm foundation. Another, a lawyer, held himself unable to go beyond these terms even when he clearly thought it desirable to do so. One arbitrator was presented with a case in which a union and a company had an agreement that certain classes of semiskilled workers should be eligible for the rates of pay for merit that skilled craftsmen could obtain, and their agreement stated: "The Merit Grading Scheme will apply as in all other skilled sections." Both sides admitted, however, that there had been an oral understanding at the time that the semiskilled should not be able to achieve the highest grade on the merit scheme. The union claimed the abandonment of this provision on the grounds that originally few craftsmen had achieved that grade either, but now this was much more common, and the semiskilled should be given their chance as well. (To this extent the question might be said to be not one of interpretation at all but a claim for revision of an agreement. As usual the categories are not kept wholly distinct.) When the arbitrator came to hear the case, he found it much more complicated. The parties had already agreed to terminate their merit scheme and had negotiated a new scheme based upon a different rate for each job. The implementation of the new agreement had, however, been frustrated by the government's incomes freeze. The union's present claim was a tactic designed to show that the rates agreed for the semiskilled workers under the new agreement were inadequate. The arbitrator decided that the parties should negotiate the new agreement clear of all considerations of the old. He found against the union's claim, adding a strong recommendation to the parties that they should submit the semiskilled jobs to a proper evaluation. In another case an agreement between the parties provided for the same datal rate for assistant turbine drivers and turbine drivers at a certain plant. This clearly appeared from the working of the agreement; but the company argued that this was the result of a clerical error. They had intended to maintain a differential between the two grades of turbine drivers and, equally, the parity of the assistant turbine drivers with the assistant boiler operators, who were in turn paid less than boiler operators. This had always been the position; but the union's claim would destroy both the differential and the parity. The arbitrator felt that, as a principle of interpretation (and he was asked to interpret), the parties must be bound by the document they had signed, though he clearly felt that the solution contended for by the company was justified as a matter of general policy because he recommended that the differential and the previous parity be reintroduced at the next round of negotiations. What he refused to do was to take the present opportunity of achieving this by supporting the company's argument, because doing so would be going beyond his terms of reference.

The majority of cases (84), however, as with the Industrial Court, deal with claims. What is noticeable about them is that they are nearly all of local importance only. Thus the 48 claims relating to wages, hours, and holidays contained not a single national claim, only 7 extended over a district, and the rest applied only to single factories. The majority applied only to single factories. As such, the intention of the framers of the act that the single arbitrators should be used in small, local cases has been fulfilled. However, except in the area of discipline, it is not true that cases of only local significance do not come before the Industrial Court. The many cases in that court concerning application of the Whitley Council criteria at particular hospitals are examples of this, and the Industrial Court cases exactly parallel a single arbitration of 1965 concerning the distinction between Technicians Grades I and II. This distribution is probably a matter of the likes and dislikes of particular unions. Thus the Transport and General Workers Union, which has a lot of local cases because it has a lot of small agreements, favors single arbitrators, if there has to be an arbitration. This union was party to some 40 of the 131 analyzed references to single arbitrators between 1961 and 1965, whereas its appearances before the Industrial Court are proportionally much fewer. There is, of course, no provision in the act for directing disputes of a particular content or with a particular area of significance to a particular form of arbitration. The parties make this decision themselves, subject to such influence as the ministry is able and willing to bring. What is noticeable is that the particular combination of parties is unlikely to have been before the court or arbitrator before. This is true even of the National Joint Councils if one regards the real parties as being the union on the employees' side and the firm on the employers'. The only possible exception is the National Joint Council for Civil Air Transport, where the constitution has had a compulsory arbitration clause, and the number of employers is small and usually dealt with together. Even in the case of the T.G.W.U., before single arbitrators, one must remember that the initiative comes from the union official handling the dispute in the locality; and executive approval, though needed in the union, is nearly always given, so that the particular official is unlikely to have had experience of many arbitrations before. Of course, the officials of the few unions which go regularly before the Industrial Court, or some similar body, acquire great experience in handling such cases; but in the main it can readily be seen that anything in the nature of processing a grievance through arbitration is a comparatively rare event even for the managers, officials, or shop stewards most immediately engaged in industrial disputes.

BOARDS OF ARBITRATION

The Boards of Arbitration[28] may be much more briefly described. Set up by the minister under section 2(2)(c), Industrial Courts Act, 1919 (above, p. 163), they invariably reflect the desire of the parties to adopt this form of arbitration. A board is composed of an independent chairman appointed by the minister and, usually, two other members. The "wingmen" may be nominated either by the minister after consultation with the parties, or by the parties themselves. In the latter case, the state subsidy is withdrawn and the parties pay the fees and expenses of the nominated members. We were able to inspect the 33 reports of boards held between 1946 and 1965, but no indication was there given as to whether the wingmen were partisan representatives or not. If the minister appoints, he always appoints persons who are not connected with either the industry concerned or similar disputes in other industries. The ministry always makes arrangements for the hearings. (Exceptionally, the minister may appoint two wingmen on each side. This happened in 3 of the 33 cases.) Only in 6 of the 33 cases were the hearings outside London. In these the dispute could be called a "local" dispute; but there were other local, or at least regional, disputes in which the board sat in London. In a few cases, Boards of Arbitration are referred to as "courts of arbitration," usually to satisfy some requirement of the parties' own machinery (as in the case of the Constitution of the National Joint Council of the Quarrying Industry, which provides for such "courts" as the final stage of procedure).

The procedure of the boards was apparently as informal as the preceding forms of arbitration; for in only 2 cases did it appear that counsel had been engaged for the two sides. The temporal calculations could, in 29 of these 33 cases, be precise in view of dates made available in their reports. Average time from the appointment to report was 28 days, only 7 cases taking longer than five weeks. On average this was made up of 18 days from appointment to hearing, and 10 days from hearing to Report. Naturally, in this case, such details tell us nothing about the time that had elapsed *before* appointment of the arbitrator. The subject matter of the 33 cases may be represented as follows: 28 were claims (21 national); 3 were concerned with the interpretation of an agreement; 1 with dismissal; and 1 with the right *not* to join a trade union. From this it can be seen that

---

[28] Information from the Ministry of Labour Evidence, p. 103; and inspection of the unpublished records of Boards of Arbitration, 1946 to 1965.

boards, like the court, are typically a form of arbitration used to resolve disputes about economic claims and not grievances or disputes that involve any "rights" element. The Ministry of Labour Evidence says that the boards are used for "settling important disputes"; but an inspection of the cases left us with the feeling that it was only the individual desires of the parties which prevented them from going to either the Industrial Court or, in local cases, to a Single Arbitrator. Sometimes, one side will claim that a board can be appointed with members of special technical competence. For example, this was one of the contentions of the British Air Line Pilots Association (B.A.L. P.A.) to a Court of Inquiry in 1967 held by Mr. Scamp. He agreed that it was "right that pilots, and indeed any section of employees, should have the *choice* of arbitration facilities mentioned in the Act"; though he went on to point out that the B.A.L.P.A. complaint that their claims were always referred to an incompetent Industrial Court read oddly in the light of the facts that most of the claims were about salaries and that the Industrial Court could always appoint technical assessors if it wished.[29]

In five cases, it may be noted, the parties came back for an interpretation of the board's award. These awards are not normally published and are not normally reasoned decisions. The custom is to adopt the practice of the Industrial Court; but once again, as in the case of the Single Arbitrators, we found greater flexibility of form. Sometimes reasons were given, and on at least one occasion the board added recommendations for the future guidance of the parties. More important, the parties, as the Ministry of Labour Evidence puts it, "are required to agree in advance that should the Board be unable to reach a *unanimous* decision the chairman shall be authorised to make the award acting with the full powers of an umpire" (italics supplied). This is, it will be remembered, the equivalent of the power possessed by the chairman presiding over the Industrial Court by virtue of section 3(4) of the 1919 Act; but here its basis is, in theory, consensual, in practice, a condition of the minister seeing fit to appoint this form of arbitration.

The cases going to boards included proportionately a high number involving white-collar workers—12 out of the 33. Furthermore, 16 cases concerned employees of local government authorities or other public bodies. In this connection mention may be made of the Civil Service Arbitration Tribunal. We have already noted that this body came, from 1936 onward, to be the arbitration tribunal under the Civil Service

---

[29] Report of Court of Inquiry (CMND. 3428; 1967), pp. 90–92.

Whitley Council Agreement originally made in 1925, and ousted the Industrial Court that had for eleven years had that jurisdiction (above, p. 109). Technically, it does not fall under the statutory arrangements; and its similarity to the Industrial Court as a standing body, rather than to ad hoc Boards of Arbitration, is perhaps marked by the fact that its awards, like those of the court, are regularly published. Once again, however, it is concerned almost exclusively with economic claims.

SPECIAL JURISDICTIONS OF THE INDUSTRIAL COURT

There are some situations in which the jurisdiction of the Industrial Court rests upon a quite different base from that of its voluntary jurisdiction.[30] Such situations arise when an administrative or legal sanction is added to the arbitration and when the court is used for the extension of collective agreements. The three procedures described below illustrate the invasion of the law into areas typically suffused with the values of voluntarism. The ensuing subsections deal with (1) the "fair wages" clause inserted into public contracts; (2) the enforcement of "fair wages" in exceptional cases by statute through the court; and (3) the Terms and Conditions of Employment Act, 1959, section 8. These structures are not described, however, because the number of such cases in the Industrial Court is high. Indeed, an investigation of the 177 cases before the court between 1946 and 1966 which were not heard under its "voluntary" jurisdiction produced the analysis shown in Table 23. Only 72 of these cases fell under the first two headings of our present section. It may be said, however, that the presence of the various administrative or legal sanctions described here can be important in the processing of a grievance, if for no other reason than that the employer will particularly wish to avoid a reference to the Industrial Court where an adverse award can carry such sanctions against him. But in view of the number of cases and the character of the subject matter, the account that follows has been restricted to little more than an outline of what are, in many cases, complex procedures.

---

[30] For a general account, see *The Worker and the Law*, chap. 4; and, as it was in 1954, O. Kahn-Freund in *The System of Industrial Relations in Great Britain*, ed. Flanders and Clegg (1954), p. 75. The development of the Resolutions between 1891 and 1946, and of the provisions described below, p. 193, are exhaustively examined by O. Kahn-Freund's articles in (1948) 11 M.L.R. 269 and 429.

TABLE 23

Special Jurisdictions of Industrial Court: Number of Awards, 1946-1966

| Year | Administrative | Statutory fair wages | | | "Extension" |
	Fair Wages resolutions of House of Commons	Civil Aviation Acts, 1946 and 1949 [Air Corporations Act, 1949]	Road Traffic Acts, 1930 and 1933 (now 1960)	Road Haulage Wages Act, 1938 (Part II)	Terms and Conditions of Employment Act, 1959, section 8
1946	—	—	—	—	
1947	—	—	—	—	
1948	2	1	3	—	
1949	2	—	4	1	
1950	2	1	2	—	
1951	2	2	—	—	
1952	1	2	3	—	
1953	1	—	1	2	
1954	3	—	—	2	
1955	—	—	—	—	
1956	2	—	—	1	
1957	4	—	—	1	
1958	1	—	—	1	
1959	—	[3]	—	1	6
1960	3	—	—	4	15
1961	3	—	—	—	20
1962	1	—	—	3	13
1963	—	—	—	—	13
1964	2	1	—	2	10
1965	1	—	—	—	9
1966	—	—	—	—	22
Total	30	10	13	19	108

SOURCE: Published awards of Industrial Court. (Awards 2724, 2725, and 2746 arose under a special agreement under the Air Corporations Act, 1949, and are included under the third column.

Fair Wages Resolution, 1946

For over half a century public authorities, both local and national, have insisted that those who contract with them should observe "fair wages" and conditions of work. The House of Commons passed resolutions (which operate not as statutes but as administrative direction to the executive) in 1891 and 1909 to this effect, in the latter demanding that contractors observe standards "commonly recognised by employers and trade societies" in the relevant district. The present resolution drafted after agreement between the T.U.C. and Employers' Confederation and was passed in 1946. It applies to all conditions of employment, to *all* employees at workplaces occupied or used for the execution of the contract; and to the employees of subcontractors (in respect of whose observance of the "fair" conditions the contractor is made guarantor). The resolution reads:

1. (a)   The contractor shall pay rates of wages and observe hours and conditions of labour not less favourable than those established for the trade or industry in the district where the work is carried out by machinery of negotiation or arbitration to which the parties are organisations of employers and trade unions representative respectively of substantial proportions of the employers and workers engaged in the trade or industry in the district.

(b)   In the absence of any rates of wages, hours or conditions of labour so established the contractor shall pay rates of wages and observe hours and conditions of labour which are not less favourable than the general level of wages, hours and conditions observed by other employers whose general circumstances in the trade or industry in which the contractor is engaged are similar.

2.   The contractor shall in respect of all persons employed by him (whether in execution of the contract or otherwise) in every factory, workshop or place occupied or used by him for the execution of the contract comply with the general conditions required by this Resolution. Before a contractor is placed upon a department's list of firms to be invited to tender, the department shall obtain from him an assurance that to the best of his knowledge and belief he has complied with the general conditions required by this Resolution for at least the previous three months.

3.   In the event of any question arising as to whether the requirements of this Resolution are being observed, the question shall, if not otherwise disposed of, be referred by the Minister of Labour to an independent Tribunal for decision.

4.   The contractor shall recognise the freedom of his workpeople to be members of Trade Unions.

5.   The contractor shall at all times during the continuance of a contract display, for the information of his workpeople, in every factory, workshop or place occupied or used by him for the execution of the contract a copy of this Resolution.

6.   The contractor shall be responsible for the observance of this Resolution by sub-contractors employed in the execution of the contract, and shall if required notify the department of the names and addresses of all such sub-contractors.

Thus it will be seen that the measure of "fairness" is, whenever possible, taken to be that of voluntary collective bargaining between organizations of employers and trade unions representing substantial proportions of employers and workers (clause 1(a)). But the obligation to observe such "fair" standards is not in Britain given the force of law, as it is in other countries such as France and the United States.

The sanction here is removal from the list of firms with whom the government department will contract (a three months' "clean bill of health" is required under clause 2) or, in a particular case, the rescision of the contract by the department in question. The "independent tribunal" to which the minister refers "questions" arising is always the Industrial Court, but that body sits in rather an unusual capacity in such cases. In 1964, the High Court decided that the court was acting not in any of its capacities under the Industrial Courts Act, 1919, or any other statute, but as a voluntary arbitral tribunal.[31] The Minister of Labour had on the application of a trade union (A.S.S.E.T.) referred to the Industrial Court an allegation that a firm contracting with the Ministry of Health was not permitting the required trade union freedom for its workpeople, and had not displayed the necessary notices (the second allegation being ultimately upheld by the Industrial Court but not the first). The employers objected to the reference to the Industrial Court on the ground that it might not be an independent body as the clause required, especially in view of the fact that it rested with its own president to decide who actually sat. The court rejected these contentions saying:

> It seems to me that this practice of the Minister of Labour is justifiable in this way: that, as Cl. 3 of the fair wages condition says that the matter shall be referred by the Minister of Labour to an independent tribunal for decision, there is really an implied term or contractual term between the parties to the effect that, if the Ministry of Labour refers the matter to an existing tribunal which, ex hypothesi, is not a tribunal specially set up with statutory powers for the purpose, the arbitration tribunal will be constituted in a way that the tribunal in question would be constituted if it was undertaking one of its statutory functions. If one looks on it as a matter of implied contract, it seems to me that this can well be justified. It is really no different from the many cases that occur in the City of contracts providing for arbitration in regard to wheat, or some other produce, with an appeal to an appeal committee of the trade association in accordance with their rules, and in such a case, although the appeal committee may consist of twenty-five or more persons, one of the rules will be to allow a certain number to be chosen, maybe five, under the rules, and those five, though not named and though selected by somebody else, are a perfectly good arbitral appeal tribunal. So, here, although there is no reference to "subject to the rules of," it seems to me an implied term that the parties agree to the actual numbers being chosen according to the normal practice of the Industrial Court, and, indeed, maybe also, although it is unnecssary to decide it,

---

[31] R. v. *Industrial Court ex parte ASSET* [1965] I. Q. B. 377; *Cases,* p. 333.

that the reference shall be conducted according to the procedural rules of the court. Accordingly, I have come to the conclusion in the present case that the Industrial Court, which has undertaken the reference and only stayed its hand because of these objections, has full jurisdiction to continue and decide the question.

On the other hand, because the Industrial Court was not exercising any of its statutory jurisdictions the court refused to grant the union the remedy they sought, an order of mandamus, directing the Industrial Court to hear the case. Such a remedy is appropriate only to bodies with a legal duty to determine an issue. That was not so here:

> The remedy of the parties in such a case, if there is thought to be an excess of jurisdiction, is, I think, to proceed in an appropriate case for an injunction, or to get a declaration of the court that he has no jurisdiction, or to await the award and have it set aside, or, indeed, still further, when sued on the award, to set up lack of jurisdiction as a defence. It has been urged on us that really this arbitral tribunal is not a private arbitral tribunal, but that, in effect, it is undertaking a public duty or a quasi-public duty and, as such, is amenable to an order of mandamus. For my part, I am quite unable to come to that conclusion. It is abundantly clear that they had no duty to undertake the reference. If they refused to undertake the reference they could not be compelled to do so. I do not think that the position is in any way different once they have undertaken the reference. They are clearly doing something which they were not under any public duty to do, and, in those circumstances, I see no jurisdiction in this court to issue an order of mandamus to the Industrial Court.

In a later action[32] the court refused to grant the remedy of a declaration where the matters in dispute turned essentially on the *interpretation* of the Fair Wages Resolution. Such points did not go, the High Court thought, necessarily to the jurisdiction of the Industrial Court, and an injunction or declaration would be issued only where there was a case which prima facie disclosed lack of jurisdiction. Such strict decisions may be regarded as exceptional illustrations of a continuation of the philosophy of "absention" by the ordinary courts into the 1960's.

On the other hand the minister is under a duty by the terms of the resolution to refer the question to the court. But once again, the circumvention of voluntary procedures and of conciliation is protected by the phrase "if not otherwise disposed of." The minister will try to

---

[32] *B.B.C.* v. *A.C.T.T.*, *The Times*, November 30, 1966; described in *Cases*, p. 337 n.

see whether an accommodation can be reached between the parties before reference to the court.

The form of the awards of the Industrial Court on these questions follows the normal pattern, without reasons. Thus it is very hard to know what is the predominant view of the court on certain issues arising. For example, in determining whether terms and conditions are not less favorable than the established terms, does one look only to the terms about which complaint has been made (holidays, for example), or is one entitled to balance an inferiority in those particular terms against a superiority in other conditions of the employment? Both in decisions under the Fair Wages Resolution and under section 8 of the Act of 1959 (below, p. 204), we found examples that could be interpreted as possibly supporting either answer, or sometimes even both at once. But since reasons are not given, further analysis was impossible. An examination of the twelve most recent available awards under this heading (November 1957 to December 1965)[33] revealed that ten cases raised issues concerning clause 1; six, issues concerning clause 4; and only two other issues were raised.

Out of the 18 heads of complaint, the court found that there had been no breach of the employer's obligation in 15 of them. In regard to the complaints under clause 4, freedom to join trade unions, the court has undoubtedly taken a narrow view of its terms. For example, in Case 3009,[34] some 90 of 670 toolmakers at an employer's plant had resigned from the A.E.U. and joined a breakaway union (whose total membership was little more than 1,000) and claimed to negotiate separately. The employer sought to dissuade them from so doing and eventually, when the A.E.U. shop stewards told him that the recognition of the small union would "prejudice the negotiating rights on behalf of toolmakers accorded by domestic agreement, custom and practice to the A.E.U.," and that there would be a withdrawal of labor by A.E.U. members, suspended and dismissed those of the 90 who persisted in this demand. The union claimed that as the employers were on government contracts, this suspension was a breach of clause 4. But the Industrial Court rejected the claim, giving the clause thereby its narrowest meaning but one that would support the established collective bargaining machinery.

It cannot be sufficiently emphasized that an award under this heading does not affect the legal position of the employee. The contract in

---

[33] Before 1958 the distribution of questions raised here might be a misleading guide to the present position because of the existence of the compulsory arbitration provisions under Order 1376; see below, p. 210.

[34] See *Cases*, pp. 330 to 344, for this and other Awards concerning Fair Wages.

issue is not even his contract of employment; it is the commercial contract between the government department and the employer-contractor. On the other hand, there seems in theory to be no limit to the ambit of possible complainants. For example, the employers in the A.S.S.E.T. case objected that A.S.S.E.T. had no locus standi, being mere third parties to the contracts in issue. But Lord Parker, C. J., replied:

> It seems to me that, on a fair reading of that clause, it is not a simple arbitration clause providing for reference by one of the parties to the contract to an independent tribunal, or, indeed, to a tribunal appointed by the Minister of Labour. It does not take that form; the clause is making it a term of the contract that, if the Minister of Labour is satisfied that a question has arisen whether the contractor is observing the contract in relation to the fair wages resolution, he, the Minister of Labour, shall have the right, and I venture to think the duty, to refer the matter as there set out. Looked at in that way, it matters not whether the suggestion that there has been non-observance is made by the other contracting party or by a third party; it is not a question of the third party having any rights, but of the Minister of Labour being satisfied that there is a question whether the contractor is observing his obligations, and, for the purpose of satisfying himself as to that, the Minister of Labour can consider, and, indeed, should consider, representations by third parties, in this case representations by A.S.S.E.T. Indeed, I venture to think that, approached in that way, there is nothing inapt in the wording of the reference itself, because the reference itself is: whether, in the execution of contracts placed by the Ministry of Health, the Fair Wages Resolution, that is, the obligations of the contractor, are being observed by the company; that is the question raised. It is true that it begins by saying that the question has arisen on a complaint; all that that meant is that the question has arisen as the result of a representation made by A.S.S.E.T.

Of the twelve cases analyzed in recent years, we found that nine had been initiated by complaints from trade unions. Two had originated from complaints sent to the ministry formally by individual employees (though these were union members) and one had come from another firm in the industry. In another case before the Industrial Court which involved a similar (standard) clause in a contract between a firm and a department of a local authority, the complaint had come from the department itself.

This jurisdiction of the Industrial Court is, then, in theory, consensual—contractual on the part of the parties, and even "voluntary" on the part of the court itself as it is under no legal obligation to accept the cases. Furthermore, its awards have no effect on the employment contract. But in practice, since acceptance of the resolution and of this jurisdiction is the price of being allowed to tender for public contracts, it constitutes a protection for the employee and a method of processing his grievance that he is receiving less than the "fair" (i.e., collectively established) conditions of employment in the industry.

"Statutory" Fair Wages

Since 1925, a few statutes have in exceptional situations gone further. The "fair wages" principle has been enshrined in a number of statutes "which provide assistance to industries or public authorities by way of grant, loan, subsidy, guarantee or license."[35] Not every such statute has adapted the device as the price of government aid; and those statutes that have display a variety of structures. In outline, four main types can be distinguished of which the last three have recently given rise to all the cases brought before the Industrial Court (Table 23, p. 193).

Various Statutes

First, there is a group of statutes which demand that an employer or employers in an industry shall comply with "fair wages" standards of a similar kind to that set out in clause 1 (a) of the resolution. Examples are the Films Act, 1960, section 42; the Television Act, 1964, section 16,[36] and the Sugar Act, 1956, section 24, which typically provides in regard to the Sugar Corporation:

> (1)   The wages to be paid by the Corporation to persons employed by them, and the conditions of employment of persons so employed, shall, unless agreed upon by the Corporation and by organisations representative of the persons employed, be no less favorable to the persons employed than the wages which would be payable, and the conditions which would have to be observed, under a contract which complies with the requirements of any resolution of the House of Commons for the time being in force applicable to contracts of Government departments and if any dispute arises as to what wages ought to be paid, or what conditions ought to be observed, in accordance with this section, it shall, if not otherwise disposed of, be referred by the Minister of Labour and National Service to the Industrial Court for settlement.

It is here noteworthy that the problem can arise only where the parties have not settled the matter *themselves* by collective bargaining. Whatever is agreed between the corporation and "representative"

---

[35] Ministry of Labour Evidence, p. 106.
[36] Replacing the Act of 1954, section 17, governing the "commercial" companies on "Independent" television, not the B.B.C.

trade unions takes precedence over the section—yet another reinforcement of voluntary methods. In this instance, however, the end product of the process is quite different from that of the Fair Wages Resolution standing alone, for the section continues:

> (2) Where any award has been made by the industrial court upon a dispute referred to that court under this section, then, as from the date of the award or from such other date, not being earlier than the date on which the dispute to which the award relates first arose, as the court may direct, it shall be an implied term of the contract between the Corporation and workers to whom the award applies that the rate of wages to be paid, or the conditions of employment to be observed, under the contract shall, until varied in accordance with the provisions of this section, be in accordance with the award.

Thus *after* the process has been exhausted the workers involved obtain a legal right to the "fair" wage *via* their contract of employment —for what that is worth. Before that stage, however, they have no such rights. In a case of 1948, for example, a worker covered by a statute preceding the Films Act, 1960, tried to establish that, if he could show what he was receiving was less favorable than the established terms in the cinematograph industry, he could sue his employer directly by relying on the statute. The court rejected the argument saying that the statute established a procedure for disputes through which he had not gone. His express employment contract prevailed, and "there is no right of action other than that which arises on the original contract between the parties, until some implication has been established that some different rate of wage prevails."[37] As Table 23 shows, disputes under these statutes do not seem to be taken up frequently by the unions before the Industrial Court. But it must be of importance to trade unionists in negotiation to have at their elbow the lever of such action where these statutes apply.

Civil Aviation   Under the Civil Aviation Act, 1946, section 41, and (later) 1949, section 15, the independent airline companies are placed under an obligation to observe terms and conditions not less favorable than those observed by the public airways corporations. Thus, the measure of "fairness" here is what is determined by collective bargaining in the public sector of the industry, except that once again, an agreement at Joint Industrial Council level or with representative trade unions can oust the section's requirements. Here too, an award

---

[37] *Simpson* v. *Kodak, Ltd.* [1948] 2 K.B. 184; *Cases*, p. 331.

of the Industrial Court takes effect as an implied term of the employee's contract of employment.

Road Traffic A sophisticated structure was established by the Road Traffic Acts, 1930 and 1933, now replaced by the Act of 1960, section 152. This scheme applies to those bodies requiring a license to provide road passenger services, a condition of a license being that wages and conditions of employment must comply with the principles applicable to contracts falling within the Fair Wages Resolution. If the employing body fails to do so, a complaint may be made to the Traffic Commissioners. But this statute is different: the complaint cannot be made by an individual employee. The right to complain is expressly reserved in this case to "any organization representative of the persons engaged in the road transport industry." If the matter cannot be "otherwise disposed of," it must go to the Minister of Labour who "shall" refer it to the Industrial Court in the usual way "for settlement." The Industrial Court in judging the "fairness" of conditions is directed to have "regard" to decisions of any "joint industrial council, conciliation board or other similar body or in any agreement between organizations representative of employers and workpeople." Such decisions or agreements do not here oust the section altogether. But it is not the job of the court to determine what the proper wage should be; its award will merely pronounce whether or not there has been a breach of the section. Even more important, an award against the employer by the Industrial Court does not, in this instance, become an implied term of the relevant employment contracts. Instead a person in breach of the fair wages section in passenger road transport is "liable to be dealt with in all respects as if he had failed to comply with a condition attached to his road service license. This means that the licensing authority may direct that the license be revoked, suspended or curtailed (sec. 178, Road Traffic Act, 1960). Thus, in these cases, the trade union is pursuing a complaint, in a sense, about workers' existing "rights," which can give rise to an administrative, but nevertheless effective, remedy. It is interesting that the postwar figures disclose such a falling off in the use of the procedure (Table 23, p. 193).

Road Haulage Road haulage enterprises now fall under the minimum wage legislation via the Road Haulage Wages Council set up under the Wage Councils Act, 1959 (above, p. 11); but employees who drive road haulage vehicles used by firms for their own purposes (other than with the carriage of goods for reward) still fall within the provisions of Part II of the Road Haulage Act, 1938,[38] under which a number of cases are regularly taken to the Industrial Court (above, p. 193) and even more are disposed of by negotiations conducted through the Ministry of Labour's local industrial relations officers. The act deals only with "remuneration" and "holiday remuneration"; but in other respects its structure is much wider than the statutes discussed above. First, it allows the Industrial Court to determine whether the wages of a road haulage worker are "unfair" but it does not spell out the meaning of "fairness" in this context. Instead, it provides that remuneration is not to be "deemed to be unfair" if it complies with certain standards; i.e. (1) is equivalent to that payable to the worker under the Minimum Wage Order; (2) is in accordance with a collective agreement with a union made by the employer or his association; (3) is equivalent to remuneration of other similar workers in the district under a collective agreement made by an association representing a substantial number of employers; (4) is equivalent to the district rate made by a Joint Industrial Council, conciliation board, or other similar body; (5) is equivalent to what was awarded under previous decisions of the Industrial Court. The nineteen cases between 1946 and 1965 were mainly concerned with these problems about "fairness"; and in seven of them the employer relied on the argument outlined in (1). In deciding the question of "fairness," however, the Industrial Court is obliged to have regard not merely to all these factors, but also to any collective agreements governing remuneration in trades or industries which, in the opinion of the court, are comparable to the trade or industry in which the worker is employed, to the general level of remuneration paid to workers in the trade or industry other than road haulage workers, and to such further circumstances as the Court considers relevant. If, having done all that, the court regards the wage as unfair, it must *fix* the new fair wage in its award (sec. 5(1) and (3)).

However, two points must be stressed before considering the sanctions applicable to such an award. First, the avenue to the remedy is open to all workers, since any *individual* may complain, as may a trade union of which the worker is a member, or any trade union representing, in the opinion of the minister, a substantial number of workers employed in road haulage work. In the sample of nineteen cases, we found that twelve had been begun on the complaints of individual employees. It is clear that individual workers have made use of this procedure, probably as an alternative to having their union take up the matter, where there is no strong union or procedure. Where cases

---

[38] On the details of this act see O. Kahn-Freund (1948) 11 M.L.R. pp. 437–443.

are brought by individual employees, however, any organization of employers or any trade union "appearing to the Court to have an interest in the question" has a right to attend and be heard (sec. 5(7)); and this right has been exercised in such cases. The minister must refer complaints, unless satisfied they are vexations or frivolous, to the Industrial Court *except* in one circumstance. When, there is collective bargaining procedure in the industry concerned which the Minister finds has parties representative of substantial proportions of employers and employees, then, unless the employee is not himself a member of an organization party to the procedure, the minister is obliged to refer the dispute to the voluntary procedures. He may not refer it to the Industrial Court except where requested so to do by *both* parties to that agreement after a failure by them to settle within procedure (sec. 4(4)).

If an award is made by the court, however, a battery of sanctions becomes available. First, the award becomes a legally implied term in all the contracts of employment of workers by whom or on whose behalf the complaint was brought. That term is given six months retrospective effect with regard to those who brought the claim and is compulsory for three years for all the workers covered by the award unless varied by the court. Second, noncompliance with the award is a criminal offense; and the employer falls under the surveillance of the ministry's wages inspectorate whose job it is to enforce the provisions of minimum wage legislation either by persuasion or, if necessary, legal action (sec. 7). Third, if the employer is convicted of such an offense, he becomes liable to have his vehicle license revoked or suspended.[39]

Thus, the Road Haulage Wage Act, 1938, in this small sector of employment has introduced a complicated system of what Professor Kahn-Freund called "legislation through adjudication." The Industrial Court is utilized as a body perfectly suited to process a grievance that is ultimately one (in this case) of "interest," but that, by being fed through the stages of the statutory fair wages machinery, can be given the flavor of "rights," and ends with an award enforceable by a variety of methods. It must, however, be remembered that we are dealing with a dispersed group of workers where union organization has, at times, not been strong, and it seems doubtful whether the 1938 statute will ever be a precedent for other similar plans.

---

[39] Section 178 (i) (c) seems to have introduced this as a new sanction in the Act of 1960.

The "Extension" Procedure: Terms and Conditions of Employment Act, 1959, Section 8

Compulsory arbitration existed in Britain from 1940 to 1951 (under Order 1305) and from 1951 to 1958 (Order 1376) in the form described below (p. 210). Even after the repeal of Order 1376, however, it was thought necessary to have some machinery to deal with the problem of a black-sheep employer in an otherwise well organized industry who observed employment conditions less favorable than those established in the industry. The Terms and Conditions of Employment Act, 1959, section 8 (the only remaining section of the act) was the result.

Under the act a "claim" may be reported to the minister in writing stating:

> (a)   that terms or conditions of employment are established in any trade or industry, or section of a trade or industry, either generally or in any district, which have been settled by an agreement or award, and
> (b)   that the parties to the agreement, or to the proceedings in which the award was made, are or represent organisations of employers and organisations of workers or associations of such organisations, and represent (generally or in the district in question, as the case may be) a substantial proportion of the employers and of the workers in the trade, industry or section, being workers of the description (hereinafter referred to as "the relevant description") to which the agreement or award relates, and
> (c)   that as respects any worker of the relevant description an employer engaged in the trade, industry or section (or, where the operation of the agreement or award is limited to a district, an employer so engaged in that district), whether represented as aforesaid or not, is not observing the terms or conditions (hereinafter referred to as "the recognised terms or conditions") [sec. 8 (1)].

No claim may be made where terms and conditions are fixed by other statutes (as in the case of minimum wage enactments or the Road Haulage Wages Act, 1938). Also, a claim may be made only by an organization or association falling within the terms of section 8 (1) (b) above. Thus, the right to complain is reserved for workers trade unions, on the one hand, and employers' *federations or associations*, on the other. Where a claim is made,

> the Minister may take any steps which seem to him expedient to settle, or to secure the use of appropriate machinery to settle, the claim and shall, if the claim is not otherwise settled, refer it to the Industrial Court constituted under Part I of the Industrial Courts Act, 1919.

In practice this means that the minister attempts to use his conciliation machinery (below, p. 214); but if he fails there he must refer to
the Industrial Court. If the court is satisfied that the claim is substantiated that the employer in question is not observing the industry-
wide or district collective agreement:

(3) . . . then *unless* the Court is satisfied that the terms or conditions
which the employer is observing are not less favourable than the recognised terms or conditions the Court shall make an award requiring the
employer to observe the recognised terms or conditions as respects all
workers of the relevant description from time to time employed by him.

(4) An award under this section shall have effect as an *implied
term* of the contract of employment, and shall have effect from such
date as the Industrial Court may determine, being a date not earlier
than the date on which, in the opinion of the Court, the employer was
first informed of the claim giving rise to the award by the organisation
or association which reported the claim to the Minister; and an award
under this section shall cease to have effect on the coming into operation
of an agreement or award varying or abrogating the recognised terms
or conditions. [Italics supplied.]

The final words of section 8 (4) are a little ambiguous. If "agreement" is read, as it was in one County Court case,[40] to include a contract of employment, the whole point of the section (which is to protect vulnerable workers employed by bad employers) would be cir-
cumvented. The Industrial Court itself in one recent award (3006)
seemed to take the other view, namely that "agreement" here could
only mean *collective* agreement establishing new recognized terms,
since it ordered the employer to observe "the recognized terms and
conditions of employment (and any subsequently agreed amendments
thereto) as respects all employees from time to time employed by
him." Even so the sanction for enforcement is weak, resting as it does
entirely upon a civil action by the employee for breach of his employment contract. This remedy he is not likely to pursue until after termination of his employment. No criminal sanctions or administrative
machineries are provided in this case. Once again the real importance
of the 1959 Act, which at first glance seems such a big legal incursion
into the voluntary system, may in practice lie in the increased power
of argument given to the trade union armed with an award of the
Industrial Court.

There is no doubt that unions have used the machinery provided by

---

40 *Fox* v. *Pianoforte Supplies* (1963) 114 L. Jo. 140.

the 1959 Act, often to attack employers who effectively refused to nego-tiate with them. Usually, but not always, these are the nonfederated firms of smaller size. Between 1946 and 1966, 108 awards were made under the act, of which two were interpretations of previous awards. Of the remaining 106, trade unions were the claimants in all except one (where the claimant was the British Medical Association). The indus-tries concerned covered a wide range, a fact that is not surprising when one sees that section 8 enacts: "(5) for the purposes of this section the carrying on of the activities of public or local authorities shall be treated as the carrying on of a trade or industry." Twenty-five of the cases came from the engineering industry and 12 from building. Forty differ-ent unions were involved. The 82 cases in which it was possible to make the calculation disclosed widely different numbers of employees in dispute, the average being 104; but 55 cases involved 25 or fewer employees, and only 11, more than 100.

Of the 106, the union was successful in 59, failed to establish its claim in 36, and withdrew the claim in 11 cases. The employers were not represented in 16 of the cases, and in 4 of those, did not even send written representations. The court sat outside London on 11 occasions. Delay could be more precisely calculated in these cases than in the Industrial Court's voluntary arbitrations because the published awards give more dates in the section 8 cases.

A section 8 case seems to take about ten weeks on average from the time of reference by the minister. The average time to the hearing was six weeks, 72 cases being heard within this period but only 9 in less than three weeks; and from hearing to the award, the average time was four weeks and only 30 took longer. Having regard to what has gone before, the procedure is not a speedy one.

The issues actually argued in these cases are of some interest. In many respects they resemble the arguments that arise from the court's hearings on the Fair Wages Resolution (above, p. 193). Excluding the 11 withdrawals and 4 cases where the employers did not appear at all even on paper, we found that in the remaining 91 cases we could identify some 109 "main arguments put forward by employers." They are listed in Table 24.

As in the Fair Wages cases, it is not entirely clear whether the court judges argument (2) ("not less favorable" conditions) according to the particular terms in issues or the whole range of employment con-ditions. In many cases it does the former. For example, in Award 3086 the Draughtsmen's Association (D.A.T.A.) claimed that Tubewrights, Ltd., a subsidiary of Stewarts and Lloyd, Ltd., were not observing the 1965 Engineering Agreement which had reduced the working week

TABLE 24

Employers' Main Arguments in 91 Cases under Act of 1959

Argument	Number of cases in which it appeared
1. Complying with the relevant agreement..................	36
2. Terms and conditions not less favorable than those "recognized".......................................	33
3. Not engaged in the "industry" to which the agreement related	21
4. Party to the agreement not a *representative* organization of either employers or employees	8
5. No established terms and conditions	7
6. Clauses not "terms and conditions of employment" (e.g., procedure clauses)	3
7. Workers not "employees" but self-employed	1

SOURCE: Published Industrial Court awards.

for draughtsmen. The agreement was "reached on an informal basis and its provisions are not specifically set out in any formal document," except a letter. The company admitted being within the "engineering industry," though, being the subsidiary in a group of steel firms, they were not in the Engineering Employers' Federation and wished to observe the policies of this group. They also submitted that they were observing in respect of the employees concerned terms and conditions of employment which were in general not less favorable than those laid down in the national agreements in the engineering industry, in that they provided four additional days of statutory holiday, making a total of ten days a year.

> Those additional four days were granted at the Company's convenience, but one day was normally added to each of the Bank Holidays at Easter, Whitsun, August and Christmas. They were the equivalent of 30 hours a year, and represented a greater concession than would be given by the reduction of half-an-hour in the normal working week which the Union were claiming.

The court's award read:

> Having given careful consideration to the evidence and submissions of the Parties the Court find and Award as follows: (1) The recognised terms and conditions of employment in relation to the normal working week which are applicable to the workers concerned in the claim (hereinafter referred to as the recognised terms and conditions) are those laid down in the 1965 Agreement. . . . (2) The Company are not observing the recognised terms and conditions, or terms and conditions not less

favourable. (3) The Court accordingly require the Company to observe the recognised terms and conditions."

In cases of this sort it is perhaps a pity that the Industrial Court adheres to its normal practice of not specifying reasons. The dispute is, in fact, one which is clearly amenable to a judicial process of reasoning, at least as much as many other disputes that find their way into ordinary courts; and it would be more helpful, perhaps, if the Industrial Court went a little further toward a reasoned judgment in the ordinary section 8 case.

The extent to which the court is prepared to go in enforcing recognized terms is indicated in Award 3056 brought by a union against Ripley Urban District Council (a small local authority), where the findings include:

(1) The recognised terms and conditions applicable to the worker concerned in the claim (hereinafter referred to as the recognised terms and conditions) are those laid down in the National Agreement. (2) The Council are not observing the recognised terms and conditions in that they are not paying to the worker concerned overtime calculated on the basis provided for under those terms and conditions. (3) *It is not known what would be the appropriate rate of pay for the worker concerned under the recognised terms and conditions, since this is a matter for agreement between the Parties or, failing such agreement, for determination by the Conciliation Committee. It follows that it cannot at present be shown whether the terms and conditions which the Council are observing are more or less favourable* than the recognised terms and conditions, and that the Council have not satisfied the Court that the terms and conditions which they are observing are not less favourable. (4) The Court accordingly require the Council to observe the recognised terms and conditions. [Italics supplied.]

The vagueness of the ordinary British collective agreement where procedural rules predominate here meant that the employers could not show whether or not they were doing better than the agreement, since the substantive terms of the agreement could only be settled via the procedures.

On the other hand, we have already noted that the court has recently been very firm in *excluding* from the province of recognized terms and conditions those clauses of the collective agreement which establish machinery for recognition of the union and its shop stewards or other officials, and procedures whereby grievances are processed. After appearing in 1964 to go the other way, the court quickly corrected a misleading award by "reinterpreting" it to this effect (National Society of Metal Mechanics against Newton Polish, Ltd., No. 2, Award 3069), having already reached the same conclusion in Award 3059 (National Union of Vehicle Builders against Fairview Caravans).[41] In the former case they spelled out their reasons for the reinterpretation, saying:

> The Court's view was and is that none of the provisions of the Procedure Agreement referred to at (a) in the said paragraph 2, which provisions consist of a short Section headed "General Principles" and a longer Section headed "Procedure for Dealing with Questions Arising," constitute terms or conditions of employment or, consequently, recognised terms or conditions within the meaning of S.8 of the Terms and Conditions of Employment Act, 1959.

One vexing question is what the court understands to be an "industry" for the purposes of the section. In Award 3064, for instance, it rejected an argument by employers that their firm making "pallets" (which is neither a box nor a case) did not fall within the national agreement for the Packing Case Industry. Such a question is one of fact. But in other cases it seems to have been accepted that, even though the majority of workers in a plant do not fall under an agreement for an "industry," a minority may do so. This was so in Awards 2808 (where draughtsmen in a rubber factory were brought within the National Engineering Agreement) and 2924 (where a group of upholstery workers in a general engineering plant were brought within the recognized terms not of the engineering but of the furniture manufacturing agreement). Once again reasoned decisions would help here to clear away obscurities as to just what interpretation is being put upon a statutory section. The arguments for not giving reasons, powerful in their proper province, are not applicable to such a problem.

Sometimes the court indicates its view more clearly. In Award 2994, for example, the Variety Artistes Federation claimed that the B.B.C. should observe the terms of an agreement reached with the Independent Television Companies' Committee. The B.B.C. argued that it was "unique" and there was no "industry" into which it fell; and also that the committee was not a representative organization within section 8(1)(b). The court expressly accepted this latter argument by finding that the agreement with the committee did not satisfy either section 8(1)(a) or section 8(1)(b) of the act. Also, on the one occasion on which the court were presented with the argument that ordinary building workers were not "employees" who could fall within the act, but were "self-employed" independent contractors in respect of whom the com-

---

[41] These and other awards are described in *Cases,* pp. 345–366, *Appendix.*

pany need not observe the National Joint Council conditions, it broke through the surface of the apparent "self-employment" relationship and boldly stated:

> that the expression "self-employed" is a misdescription of the true position of the said workers in relation to the Company; and that the Company are employers and the workers concerned are employees within the meaning of Section 8 of the Act.

In this same case, the Industrial Court added a recommendation to the parties to reconsider certain aspects of the N.J.C. Working Rules, "although it is no part of their functions in this reference to do so" (Award 3107, Creighton, Ltd., against Amalgamated Slaters, Tiles and Roofing Operatives Soc., 1966).

The Industrial Disputes Tribunal, 1951–1958

There are two reasons for assessing briefly the British experience of the years 1951 to 1958 under the Industrial Disputes Order (No. 1376) then in force. First, certain trade unions have called on the Royal Commission to reintroduce the forms of compulsory arbitration which it continued, and have been supported in this by the T.U.C. Evidence.[42] Second, the experience is of comparative interest in disclosing what happens in fact when legal strictures *are* introduced into the British system.

The 1951 Order established a three-man Industrial Disputes Tribunal, with a chairman and the two habitual wingmen representing employers and employees. Its awards became compulsory implied terms of relevant employment contracts. The minister referred to it "disputes" or "issues" that were not settled by reference to ordinary negotiation or arbitration machineries (to which he first referred them and where, if a settlement was reached, it was as final as an award of the tribunal). Strikes and lockouts were not prohibited by the order (as they had been from 1940 to 1951). A "dispute" could be reported to the minister by a trade union, an employer, or an employers' organization. It was defined as *not* including a dispute about employment or nonemployment of a person, or whether he should be a member of a trade union, but otherwise it included any dispute between an employer and *his* own workmen connected with their terms and conditions. An "issue" could be reported by an *organization* of employers or a trade union which "habitually" took part in settling recognized

---

[42] "Trade Unionism," para. 324–327. And see Oral Evidence, R.C.M.E. vol. 65, para. 10359.

terms and conditions for the trade, and the term covered the question "whether an employer in [a] District should observe the recognized terms and conditions." In effect, the "issue" procedure was one for extending collective agreements to employers not party to them[43] (like the 1959 Act which followed).

In 1954 the Court of Appeal still tried to maintain the distinction between "issues" in article 2 of the order and "disputes" under article 1.[44] But by 1955, in a case where a local authority had dismissed an employee and reengaged him on terms different from the recognized terms that the I.D.T. had said applied to him, the court was hard put to it to maintain the distinction.[45] Birkett, L.J., said:

> It is clear, I think, that while there can be "issues" which can only be "issues" within the meaning of this Order, and "disputes" which can only be "disputes" within the meaning of the Order, there can be controversies which partake of the nature of a "dispute" and an "issue" at the same time; and in any such case it would seem that it might be reported as a "dispute" or an "issue."

And commenting on the earlier case of 1952, Denning, L.J., said:

> There are many matters which can properly be described either as a "dispute" or as an "issue." The Technaloy case is, I think, a good instance. It raised an "issue" whether the employers would pay their men the recognized rates. That is how the Divisional Court looked at that case. It also raised a "dispute" between an employer and some of his workmen connected with the terms of their employment. That is how this court looked at it. So also with the present case. . . . In these cases . . . it seems to me that the choice lies with the persons who report it to the Minister and the Minister must deal with it as reported.

This problem about the distinction between a "dispute" and an "issue" under the order, together with others, had not been finally settled when the order was repealed in 1958. But what is clear is that there was no simple analysis to be made of cases arising under the 1951 Order by equating "issues" with questions of "rights" and "disputes" with questions of "interests," though this approach seems to have been the one adopted by the man who made the only previous analysis of I.D.T. awards.[46] We analyzed the substance of each award and only

---

43 Goddard, L.C.J., in *R. v. I.D.T. ex parte Practical Banking, Ltd.* [1952] 1 All E.R. 1370.

44 *R. v. I.D.T. ex parte Technaloy, Ltd.* [1954] 2 Q.B. 46.

45 *R. v. I.D.T. ex parte Portland U.D.C.* [1955] 1 W.L.R. 949.

46 For one year (1953) by Dr. W. F. Frank, in XIX *Louisiana Law Review*, at p. 636. Our results are very different from those there produced.

TABLE 25

Analysis of Content of All Industrial Disputes Tribunal Awards, 1951-1959

Year	Disputes*						Issues		
	Economic Claims				Miscellaneous claims	Claims for regrading ("interest" disputes)	Regrading disputes with a "rights" element	Other interpretation of agreements	"Recognized terms and conditions"
	National	District	Firm level	Individual					
1951	12	10	36 (10)	—	2	—	1	20	—
1952	47 (2)	17 (1)	65 (21)	14 (11)	9 (1)	14	2	28	17
1953	40	24	49 (15)	3 (1)	4	3	14	21	24
1954	37	20	40 (6)	1	8	31	4	8	29
1955	27	15	41 (14)	1 (1)	3	35	—	17	32
1956	20	6 (1)	32	2 (1)	1	20	—	2	25
1957	27	7	32 (5)	1	7	15	1	4	22
1958	28	11 (2)	35 (7)	1	5	11	3	5	35
1959	14	6 (1)	37 (21)	4 (2)	2	6	1	3	17
Total	252	116 (5)	367 (99)	27 (16)	41 (1)	135	26	108	201 (121)

*Figures in parentheses show the number of disputes which could probably have been regarded as issues.

SOURCE: Awards of Industrial Disputes Tribunal, Nos. 1-1270.

subsequently considered its status as a "dispute" or "issue" under the order. The results are produced in Table 25. Whatever else that table shows, it illustrates simply that the 1951 Order was not based upon a neat division between "rights" and "interest" claims. In one sense the last three columns may be regarded as the total number of cases raising questions over "rights"; but a third of these were reported as "disputes." The figures in brackets, on the other hand, show the number of reported "disputes" which might well have been reported as "issues" on our analysis of the awards. (Such an analysis is not, of course, assisted by the practice adopted by the I.D.T. of not giving a *reasoned* award; in most cases the award is in the same curt form as an Industrial Court award. Such is the force of tradition.) In truth, even in this period of compulsory arbitration, the legal system did not introduce the distinction, familiar in other systems of law, between disputes as to "rights" and disputes as to "interests," but a distinction based upon a more pragmatic approach. Even that distinction could not be sustained. The pressures from the courts on the one side, and from the realities of British labor relations on the other, had by 1958 obscured and nearly destroyed the boundary between "disputes" and "issues." Order 1376 bequeathed to us only the better drafting of section 8 of the 1959 Act, where even the word "issue" was avoided and replaced by the more general word "claim."[47]

---

[47] [Since this subsection was written, an account of the work of the Industrial Disputes Tribunal has been written by W. E. J. McCarthy as Part 2 of Research Paper No. 8 for the Royal Commission on Trade Unions and Employers' Associations, "Three Studies in Collective Bargaining." That account concentrates on other questions than those raised in this subsection, but is now the fullest description of the work of the I.D.T.]

10.
CONCILIATION

We have already seen that the Minister of Labour has power to appoint conciliators under the Act of 1896. In respect of any "difference" existing or apprehended between employers and workmen he may:

    (b)   take such steps as may seem expedient [to him] for the purpose of enabling the parties to the difference to meet together, by themselves or their representatives, under the presidency of a chairman mutually agreed upon or nominated by the [Minister] or by some other person or body, with a view to the amicable settlement of the difference;

    (c)   on the application of employers or workmen interested, and after taking into consideration the existence and adequacy of means available for conciliation in the district or trade and the circumstances of the case, appoint a person or persons to act as conciliator or as a board of conciliation:

This act does not define "difference" so that the minister is not limited in this respect. But if he acts under (c), the minister is requested to "take into consideration" the parties' own procedure for conciliation. The 1896 Act also included some provisions no longer relevant. For example, it provided for the registration of conciliation boards and the formal signing of conciliation settlements. Neither provision now operates in practice.

There are also powers that would allow for both conciliation and mediation in the Industrial Courts Act, 1919, which in section 2(1) empowers the minister to "take such steps as seem to him to be expedient for promoting a settlement" of any existing or apprehended trade dispute reported to him. But it will be recalled that here there is a definition of "trade dispute" which limits the opportunities for action under this statute. On the other hand, the limitations in section 2(4)—that the minister must not *refer* a dispute for settlement or advice without the "consent of both parties," and "until there has been a failure to obtain a settlement" by the ordinary procedure—do not seem to attach to his powers under section 2(1).

In practice, the 1896 Act is normally regarded as the basis of the ministry's extensive conciliation activities. The Ministry of Labour Evidence speaks of the "flexibility of its provisions" as giving "a practical advantage"; and adds generally: "The present legislation allows the Minister to exercise his discretion in deciding at what stage in a dispute it would be appropriate for conciliation to take place."[1]

The Statute of 1896 also envisages conciliations by outsiders brought in for the purpose. This still happens, but rarely. Since 1918 the ministry has provided an extensive service for conciliation both at headquarters level (where there is a Chief Conciliation Office) and at regional levels where there are Industrial Relations Officers (I.R.O.'s). The I.R.O. service was integrated into the regional organization of the ministry in the early 1940's; and in 1962 the conciliation work of the service was combined for the first time with advisory work to industry on personnel management, with results that, in the ministry's view, are "likely to prove beneficial."

None of the powers used by this service include anything in the nature of compulsory conciliation or mediation. On the other hand, they can cover all types of disputes. Despite the wide discretion given to the minister, however, the intervention of an I.R.O. is meant to be no more than a means to the parties achieving their own settlement—one more illustration of the primacy of voluntary methods. As the ministry put it:

> Government policy regarding the practice of conciliation has for many years been closely related to Government policy regarding voluntary collective bargaining. . . . Notwithstanding the discretion which the legislation gives to the Minister, it has been the general policy to avoid intervening in a dispute until the agreed procedure in the industry has been exhausted. Even if in a particular instance there is no agreed procedure the parties are generally expected to try and settle the difference themselves before seeking conciliation.
>
> When conciliation does take place it is in effect a continuation of the process of collective bargaining with outside assistance. The intention of

---

[1] Ministry of Labour Written Evidence, p. 94. Other quotations in this section also come from this valuable memorandum on conciliation, if not otherwise cited. We are grateful to the ministry for additional information. See, too, the concluding appendix, p. 419.

TABLE 26

Conciliation Action by Cause, 1962-1966

(i) Percentage of total; (ii) Percentage of (i) settled; (iii) Percentage of (i) involving stoppages

Cause	1962			1963			1964			1965			1966		
	(i)	(ii)	(iii)	(i)	(ii)	(iii)	(i)	(ii)	(iii)	(i)	(ii)	(iii)	(i)	(ii)	(iii)
Pay	45	67	17	40	67	17	46	74	21	46	75	22	35	74	16
Demarcation	1	33	67	1	50	50	2	88	50	3	62	23	2	100	45
Redundancy and dismissal	17	59	50	13	60	47	10	67	48	12	78	26	11	73	39
Other personnel matters (e.g., manning)	3	77	33	5	44	22	3	57	36	3	64	36	4	94	29
Trade union recognition	27	39	10	32	46	15	29	61	13	21	57	9	30	61	11
Closed shop or 100 percent membership	1	67	67	2	57	43	2	57	57	2	50	75	2	50	–
Other	7	67	17	8	59	14	7	73	30	14	26	19	16	64	12
Total	100	58	22	100	58	21	100	69	24	100*	71	23	100	69	17

*Total does not agree because figures have been rounded off.

SOURCE: Ministry of Labour unpublished figures.

conciliation is to help the parties concerned to find a mutually acceptable basis for the settlement of the difference which has arisen between them. (Failing settlement an attempt will usually be made to secure agreement to arbitration.) If possible it is also hoped to bring about a permanent improvement in the relations between the parties which will enable them more easily to settle future differences without outside assistance.

An essential feature of conciliation has been the independence and impartiality of the conciliator. It is on this basis that a relationship of trust has been built up between the Ministry's conciliators and employers and trade unions. In their position of neutrality the Ministry's conciliators cannot be identified with either one side or the other. Their aim is to help both sides reach a settlement for which the parties are then responsible.[2]

There are certainly variations in different industries in the practice of initiating conciliation action. In engineering, for example, where the employers' sense of their prerogatives is very strong, no such action will be taken until procedure is clearly exhausted or has broken down. In other industries with joint bodies rather than "employers' conciliation" procedures, the resistance to an earlier intervention in the face of an apparent deadlock might not be so great.

The number of occasions on which official action by way of conciliation is recorded has been increasing over the years. From 1919 to 1938 the total number of *settlements* achieved by conciliation was 1,199, an average of about 60 a year.[3] From 1961 to 1966 the total number of settlements was 1,682, over 260 a year. Table 26 shows the total number of conciliation actions rising from 339 in 1961 to 447 in 1966. The success rate in settlements seems to have jumped upward in 1964; we cannot determine whether or not this was the result of the new structure brought about by the amalgamation of personnel advisory and conciliatory functions in the I.R.O. service. It must be said at once that a "settlement" can mean different things in these figures. It may mean a final agreement between the parties. Or it may mean an agreement to take a dispute back into ordinary procedures once more, or to arbitration. Or, in a recognition dispute, a settlement may mean merely that the parties have agreed to talk together over substantive issues of bargaining. There is at present no formal method of following up cases after they leave the hands of the ministry's conciliation offices. As will be seen, most references come from trade unions, and the proportion is increasing. Table 26 also reveals the small number of occasions on which an I.R.O. will intervene without request; only 7 of 447

---

[2] Ministry of Labour Evidence, p. 95.
[3] Sharp, *Industrial Conciliation and Arbitration in Great Britain*, p. 366.

TABLE 27

Conciliation Action, 1961-1966
Numbers of cases, settlement, and type of initiation

Year	Total	Settled	Percent	Trade union approaches	Employer's approaches	Joint approaches	Intervention by Ministry Industrial Relations Office
					Initiated by		
1961	339	200	(59)				
1962	335	195	(58)	———— NOT KNOWN ————			
1963	358	206	(58)				
1964	408	281	(69)	290	72	37	9
1965	406	288	(71)	282	66	45	13
1966	447	310	(69)	351	61	28	7

SOURCE: Ministry of Labour records.

actions so originated in 1966. The different causes that prompted the initiation of conciliation action are analyzed in Table 27.

Although there are fluctuations, the relative weight of the causes does not vary too much, the two most important being regularly pay questions and trade union recognition. The latter problem gives rise to conciliation action, especially in respect of small nonfederated firms which refuse to recognize a trade union. It is on this problem of recognition, in particular, that the figures seem to disclose the most marked increase in the so-called "success rate" for settlements after 1963 (a fact that may have been overlooked in the recent demand for new legal machinery to deal with recognition disputes). Table 27 also gives the percentage of conciliation action in which stoppages of work took place despite the effort of the conciliator. Most of these stoppages were "unofficial." The I.R.O.'s do in fact record whether a stoppage is "official" or not, but the figures compiled were not available. To some extent the line is very difficult to draw since trade union officials may tacitly approve "unofficial" action, and sometimes union approval is given retrospectively. In any case, stoppages occur in less than one quarter of the cases recorded. All industries contribute a share of disputes to conciliation figures, but engineering regularly heads the list. Between 1962 and 1966 disputes in "engineering and electrical goods" (excluding vehicle manufacture) gave rise to an average of 20 percent of the conciliation actions (falling from 25 percent in 1962 to 14 percent in 1966). The next largest totals were distribution trades and transport (each averaging 8 percent of the total actions). One sector for which the conciliation service is *not* available is the civil service, industrial or nonindustrial. The view has been taken that one government department cannot conciliate disputes in another. But the service is, of course, available for disputes in the public corporations running nationalized industries.

The increase in the number of conciliations over the past five years has not come about through any change in ministry policies. There has, however, probably been an increase in the readiness of the parties (especially, as we have seen, the unions) to turn to ministry I.R.O.'s. This may have been partly caused by the new roles played by the ministry under legislation such as the Industrial Training Act, 1964, and Redundancy Payments Act, 1965. Whatever the explanation, the increase is paradoxical since it has come at a time when government policies have inevitably created new tensions for the ministry. For example, it has responsibilities in trying informally to restrain wage demands in the light of criteria set out in government "white papers." This responsibility might be thought to have made unions less, rather than more, ready to approach their officers, and the opposite tendency must speak to the qualities of the I.R.O.'s themselves. One illustration of the tension has been in regard to cases going to the Industrial Court under its "special" jurisdiction (above, p. 192). It has long been the practice for the ministry to use its conciliation machinery in cases arising under the Terms and Conditions of Employment Act, 1959; Road Haulage Wages Act, 1938, Part II; or Fair Wages Resolution before reference to the court. The figures in Tables 26 and 27 include such conciliations. But after the Prices and Incomes Act, 1966, and its accompanying white papers calling for voluntary restraint, for a period at least, the conciliation process appeared not to work. Cases came to the court in which employers, for example, were quite ready to abide by the "recognized terms" of pay for their industry but preferred to have an award from the court directing them to do so in order not to be defenseless if accused of breaking the rules of "voluntary" wage restraint.[4] It is believed, however, that the conciliation stage has in 1967 been reinstated and allowed to operate again in such cases.

The methods of conciliation are not laid down by statute. Usually they include only conciliation properly so-called, that is, bringing the parties together. But sometimes it is clear that an element of "mediation" may creep in (i.e., the recommendation to the parties of certain terms of settlement). Sometimes the ministry's offices will bring the

---

[4] See for example Awards 3137 (Keighley Grinders, Ltd., against D.A.T.A.) and 3145 (Buckwell Industries, Ltd., against T.G.W.U.), both in 1967.

conciliation services to the attention of parties to an actual or threatened dispute, but usually this is unnecessary as the services are widely known. The ministry describes its role as follows in its evidence:

> The officers concerned satisfy themselves that any agreed procedure has been fully used by the parties, and only in exceptional circumstances will they consider it appropriate to conciliate when these conditions are not fulfilled.
>
> The first task of the conciliator is to ascertain the facts of the dispute, usually by separate discussions with the parties. Occasionally separate talks of this kind will bring about a change in the situation as a result of which the parties are able to resume direct negotiations of their own. More commonly, however, a conciliator will invite the two sides to meet under his chairmanship. Occasionally one party may refuse this invitation but usually it is accepted. Joint meetings of this character are conducted on informal lines and their object is to enable the conciliator to explore fully the attitudes of the two sides and to find out, as a result, whether an acceptable basis can be found for bridging the gap between their two points of view.

Where a trade union reports a pay claim, for example, the conciliation officer will frequently see the trade union officials and then the employer before arranging a joint meeting. At such a meeting there will, if possible, be a side room. After each party has presented its point of view and no agreement has been reached, a frequent practice is to separate the parties by use of the side room, the conciliation officer adopting a peripatetic role until agreement at a joint meeting can be reached or, at second best, until the parties can agree on arbitration or some other procedure for settling the disputes. The officer would not necessarily refrain from comment, such as that an offer of one side seemed to him generous or conciliatory, in which case his role approaches that of mediation. If the issue were not a pay claim but a dispute over the interpretation of an agreement, the I.R.O. might adopt an even more active role in suggesting interpretations to the parties in the separate talks. His aim here is undoubtedly always to find an interpretation to which the parties will adhere in the future rather than to concern himself with what was the original "intention of the parties." In recognition disputes, of course, there is less room for maneuver. The strain on the conciliation service is indicated in the Ministry's Evidence where it says:

> The typical situation is that a union has organised a proportion of the workers at a particular firm; sometimes they have a majority and sometimes considerably less than this. The union then approach the employer for negotiating rights on behalf of their members. The employer in

answer to the claim may say that he does not consider that the union is sufficiently representative of the workers, or that even if a claim to majority membership can be substantiated he does not wish to recognise them. More exceptionally, he may say that he already recognises another union and cannot, therefore, recognise a second union for the same group of people. The union seeks assistance from the Ministry of Labour whose officers then approach the employer and, as it may appear to him, argue the union's case to him. . . . It is . . . appropriate to mention here that conciliation is in certain respects not a satisfactory method of attempting to settle differences between employers and unions on this subject. There may be no common ground as to the facts about trade union membership which can, therefore, only be ascertained by thorough and independent investigation. Also, on a recognition issue a conciliator who is seeking a basis for settlement cannot in practice take up a neutral position between the parties. He is bound to appear to the employer as an agent for the trade union. On general grounds this is undesirable.

Even so, as we have seen, recognition cases happen to be the category where the officers score a very high percentage of successs in settlements.

Where there has been a stoppage of work, employers will normally demand that there be a resumption before engaging in a conciliation process, especially where they claim that the stoppage is unconstitutional in breach of procedure. In such cases the trade union is called on to get its members back to work and the I.R.O. has to be careful not to become embroiled in issues that may arise between union and members. Exceptionally, conciliation does begin while a strike is in progress, although the Ministry's Evidence states that it "never deals with unofficial strike leaders but only with authorized officers of the trade unions concerned." In this respect the Motor Industry Joint Labour Council may have an advantage in that, being a voluntary body, it can talk with local "unofficial" leaders without any risk of giving to them any kind of "official" approval or status. In general the ministry reported:

> It is not often that the conciliation is prevented by the refusal of one or other of the parties to take part in joint discussions. Occasionally, however, an employer does refuse to meet a union under the auspices of the Ministry of Labour, for example because the union has not been recognised or because, in the employer's view, the union is supporting unconstitutional action. It also sometimes happens that union officials, although not actually refusing to attend a joint meeting, may prove in practice not readily available and this may make it difficult to arrange a joint meeting. In general, however, the refusal or evasion of conciliation is comparatively rare.

CONCILIATION

It may be said that the statutory machinery of conciliation generally, like arbitration, is not a significant factor in the processing of employ- ment disputes because the figures are so low. In 1966 there were only 447 officially recorded conciliation actions in which 78 stoppages of work took place; whereas in the same year the national total of work stoppages recorded was 1,930, and the total number of differences or disputes must have been many times that figure. Such a comparison can, however, be misleading. Often the I.R.O. will take "informal" steps to get parties talking again after a deadlock in procedure. Many cases of this kind may not appear in the records. We have heard of cases where a regional I.R.O. spent most of the day on the telephone between two sides but ended with no formal "conciliation action" to report. Sharp records that for a year as long ago as 1928, when official conciliation action was running at a rate of about 50 cases a year, the ministry estimated the number of unofficial discussions in which offi- cers were actively engaged as 500.[5] It would not be unreasonable to think of officials today being actively engaged in many times more than 400 differences every year, probably ten times as many. Indeed, the Ministry's Evidence speaks eloquently of the opportunity for "preven- tive work" which arises for the I.R.O. at local level, saying:

> At both Headquarters and in the Regions, officers engaged on con- ciliation work endeavour to keep in close touch with leading represen- tatives of employers and trade unions. It is desirable that these officers should be personally known to representatives of both sides of industry and in a number of industries formal contacts are maintained through the appointment of a Ministry of Labour liaison officer to the industry's Joint Industrial Council. Such appointments, which are made on request from the joint negotiating body concerned, exist in about 60 industries. The liaison officer attends meetings of the J.I.C.; he takes no active part in the proceedings but is always ready to assist by supplying any infor- mation which may be required. There would be advantage if more of these appointments could be made.
>
> As a result of the close contact which exists between the Department's officers and industry, it is quite common for representatives of employers or trade unions to approach the Department informally for advice about a difference which they think may arise in the future. It is well known that this facility for informal consultation is readily available and some- times advice given in this way has a preventive value.

This short survey of conciliation in Britain scarcely does justice to its importance in the practice of industrial relations. It oils the wheels

---

[5] Ministry of Labour Annual Report (CMD. 3333; 1928), quoted in Sharp, op. cit., p. 368, n. 1.

of voluntary procedure far more than the statistics tell. Few legal problems arise. Indeed, the Acts of 1896 and 1919 are so widely drawn that they seem able to accommodate even more new experiments in the future. The ministry reported, for example, to the Royal Commission that compulsory conciliation did "not appear to offer a solution to the problem of unofficial and unconstitutional strikes," going on to say,

> The exercise of compulsory powers of intervention to investigate and find facts about a strike by a procedure less formal than the Court of Inquiry or Committee of Investigation does however merit consideration. As regards mediation, which involves recommending a basis for settlement to the parties, it would appear that this form of intervention can take place now through the existing powers of inquiry under the Conciliation Act and the Industrial Courts Act. It is doubtful whether additional powers to this end are needed.

II.

INQUIRY AND INVESTIGATION

The Minister of Labour possesses powers to set up bodies to inquire into or investigate employment problems without the consent of the parties. Such inquiries can take a variety of forms; but their findings have a common characteristic: they have no binding legal effect. Their force lies solely in the persuasiveness of the report and its standing in the light of general public opinion. The inquiries may be appointed either as (1) Courts of Inquiry or as (2) Committees of Investigation or Inquiry.

COURTS OF INQUIRY

The power to appoint such a "court" (which is here not even an arbitral tribunal, but an investigating body) stems from the Industrial Courts Act, 1919, which provides in section 4:

> (1) Where any trade dispute exists or is apprehended, the Minister may, whether or not the dispute is reported to him under Part I of this Act, inquire into the causes and circumstances of the dispute, and, if he thinks fit, refer any matters appearing to him to be connected with or relevant to the dispute to a court of inquiry appointed by him for the purpose of such reference, and the court shall, either in public or in private, at their discretion, inquire into the matters referred to them and report thereon to the Minister.
>
> (2) A court of inquiry for the purposes of this Part of this Act (in this Act referred to as "a court of inquiry") shall consist of a chairman and such other persons as the Minister thinks fit to appoint, or may, if the Minister thinks fit, consist of one person appointed by the Minister.

It is true, therefore, that no consent of, or report from, the parties to

224

a dispute is formally required. But McCarthy and Clifford[1] in their authoritative review of the 75 Courts of Inquiry appointed between 1919 and September 1965 point out that the minister does not normally appoint where both sides would object. On the other hand, even if both sides request a court, as in the London busmen's dispute of 1958, the minister may still refuse.

The Court of Inquiry is meant to be a very formal means of establishing the facts about a dispute. As the Ministry of Labour put it:

> Courts of Inquiry are primarily a means of informing Parliament and the public of the facts and underlying causes of dispute. A Court is generally appointed only as a last resort when no agreed settlement of a dispute seems possible, and when an unbiased and independent examination of the facts is considered to be in the public interest. The power to set up a Court of Inquiry is used sparingly and is reserved for matters of major importance affecting the public interest.[2]

As we shall see, however, the function of the courts may have changed from that originally conceived of for them.

Since it is formally established to inform Parliament and the public about important "trade disputes," the Court of Inquiry is required by section 5 to lay its report (including "any minority report," of which there has been but one instance) before Parliament. Further, the minister may—and invariably does—publish the report as an official publication. The act gives to the minister the right to confer upon the court powers for the exercise of this function (section 4):

> (4) The Minister may make rules regulating the procedure of any court of inquiry, including rules as to summoning of witnesses, quorum, and the appointment of committees and enabling the court to call for such documents as the court may determine to be relevant to the subject-matter of the inquiry.
> (5) A court of inquiry may, if and to such extent as may be authorised by rules made under this section, by order require any person who appears to the court to have any knowledge of the subject-matter of the inquiry to furnish, in writing or otherwise, such particulars in relation thereto as the court may require, and, where necessary, to attend before the court and give evidence on oath, and the court may administer or authorise any person to administer an oath for that purpose.

The penalties for refusal are not specified; but this problem has

---

[1] W. E. J. McCarthy and B. A. Clifford, "The Work of Industrial Courts of Inquiry" (1966) IV *British Journal of Industrial Relations* 39, which overtakes all previous studies of the courts.

[2] Ministry of Labour Written Evidence to Royal Commission, p. 106.

never been put to the test because, with a few exceptions, the parties have cooperated with Courts of Inquiry. Trade unions have on six occasions refused to appear before courts; but proceedings have never followed. McCarthy and Clifford described the general position in the following terms, which contain an important formulation of the function of Courts of Inquiry today:

> The reasons why disputants generally agree to give evidence are not absolutely clear. It is often said that the main reason is that "the court has official standing and draws considerable publicity so that a refusal is likely to be construed as weakness and to alienate sympathy." In fact it seems more likely that, in recent years at least, a much more important factor has been the attitude which the Ministry has come to adopt towards the Court of Inquiry machinery. Essentially they view it as one more technique for facilitating voluntary settlements, after the exhaustion of customary procedures—much as they regard the other facilities they provide for this purpose, such as the conciliation service. This being so they are concerned to find out all they can about the attitudes of the parties, and their likely reactions to the establishment of a court, before taking any action. Effectively they are unlikely to set the machinery in motion if they have any reason to believe that either party would regard this as unhelpful.[3]

None of the courts appointed in 1966 or the first half of 1967 disprove the thesis that they are now but "one more technique for facilitating voluntary settlements"; on the contrary, all support it, so long as it is remembered that this is a weapon of last resort.

The usual membership of a Court of Inquiry is three, an independent chairman and appointees from both sides of industry. McCarthy and Clifford found that 59 of their 75 courts had consisted of three such persons. Eight had had five members; and the very first court had nine (but that was the only one with a minority report!). In recent years the chairman has usually been either an academic professor or a practicing lawyer (but never an academic lawyer); and persons with previous experience of such courts tend to be appointed again. There has perhaps been an increased tendency within the last two years to appoint one person to sit alone. This happened only twice before 1965; but occurred at least once in 1966 (Professor H. A. Clegg inquiring into a dispute concerning the use of forklift trucks at some docks)[4] and in 1967 (Professor Robertson on the dispute over guards' duties and wages on British Railways).[5] The Court of Inquiry normally

---

[3] McCarthy and Clifford, op. cit., p. 42.
[4] Report (CMND. 3061; July, 1966).
[5] Report (CMND. 3426; October, 1967).

sits in public and conducts what are meant to be quasijudicial hearings. Representation by lawyers is frequent, though it lies within the discretion of the court itself.

It might be thought that the sledgehammer of a Court of Inquiry would not be used to crack nuts that could come under the heading of employment "grievances." Such a view would be misguided. Mc-Carthy and Clifford analyzed their 75 disputes and found 49 concerned with wages, hours, and conditions; 9 with trade union recognition; 5 with demarcation; 5 with alleged victimization; and 7 with "other" considerations. We analyzed the 41 Courts of Inquiry between 1946 and 1966 and found comparable figures to be: 28, 5, 1, 3, and 4. The last 4 contained 1 concerned with the interpretation of an agreement, and 3 were general industrial relations inquiries (which must, however, be precipitated by a particular dispute existing or apprehended).

McCarthy and Clifford[6] identified four case categories into which most courts could be placed. First, where the bulk of workers in an industry were concerned and a national strike threatened. (It may be said that the Court does not always solve such a problem, as we proved in 1967 when the union rejected Professor Robertson's findings and a national strike was averted only by reason of strong governmental pressures and threats to use emergency powers.)[7] Second, when a potential strike would have a disruptive effect on a wide section of the public (and this explains why about a third of all the disputes concerned transport, one of them being the national shipping strike in Britain in 1966). Third, disputes in apparently isolated conflicts where the secondary effects were feared (as in a bitter battle over dismissals at the Savoy Hotel in 1947 which was seen as a threat to the tourist industry). Fourth, the investigation of "notorious trouble spots" where unofficial strike action had caused public concern (such as the inquiries into Briggs Motors, 1957; Ford Motors, 1963; and the London building sites in 1967).[8] It must be added that some of these disputes are not, on inspection, found to be at all different from the kind of problems which end up in front of the Industrial Court or other arbitrators, and the reports effectively play the role of an arbitration. This is true, for example, of the report on a dispute between the sides of the National Joint Council for the Port Transport Industry in 1958.[9]

Similarly, a court may be used where no further arbitration or nego-

---

[6] McCarthy and Clifford, *op. cit.*, p. 43.

[7] Under the Emergency Powers Act, 1920. This act allows for direct running of essential public services but prohibits industrial conscription of the strikers.

[8] Respectively, CMND. 131, 1999, and 3396.

[9] Report (CMND. 510; 1958).

tiation machinery is left (as in the case of the withdrawal of the British Air Line Pilots Association from the National Joint Council for Civil Air Transport in 1967).[10]

This study is, however, not concerned with economic claims. The Court of Inquiry is, therefore, a rare instrument in the processing of those employment disputes which fall within its province. Nevertheless, it is useful to assess the approach taken by courts to employment disputes which are not mere economic claims. For example, it is clear that in all the reports, but especially those dealing with "notorious trouble spots," a legalistic approach is taken to any breach of procedure by the workers concerned. This "constitutionalism" is shown by McCarthy and Clifford to dominate the reports and all decades; and they cite two examples:

> In 1957 Lord Cameron, reporting on the situation at Briggs, while admitting that some of the complaints and grievances of the workers "raised fairly serious questions of practice of policy" concluded
>> None, however, appeared to be of such a character as to justify wholesale resort to methods of unofficial stoppage instead of following agreed and legitimate channels.
> Six years later Professor Jack, after condemning the continued inability of the unions to "re-establish their authority among their members" concluded that it was
>> . . . intolerable that production should be interrupted or brought to a halt by Shop Stewards acting irresponsibly or as a result of "spontaneous" resolutions adopted at unconstitutional meetings of employees.
> These are a few examples of the uncompromisingly hostile attitude adopted to unconstitutional action of any kind. It is, of course, always conceivable that future courts might take a less inflexible view—but this would represent an unprecedented departure from past attitudes.[11]

In 1967 Lord Cameron maintained the tradition by roundly condemning a series of unofficial strikes on certain London building sites in parallel terms, though he reserved strictures also for a company who "deliberately created a situation designed to produce a strike" by dismissing shop stewards on "contrived and flimsy" grounds.[12] In the cases that have involved dismissals, McCarthy and Clifford also pointed out that, although some courts had favored unions' negotiating rights, none had ever suggested the reinstatement of a dismissed workman. Professor Jack in the Ford Report, quoted above, even doubted whether it was his task to pass judgment on the dismissal of twenty-

---

[10] Report (CMND. 3428; 1967).
[11] McCarthy and Clifford, op. cit., p. 46.
[12] CMND. 3396, para. 193.

seven men the company said it would not reengage. They cite a Report of 1941 in which the court did not take up the question of re-instatement or any other remedy despite finding that the "real cause" of an employee's dismissal was her activity as a trade unionist.[13] It is not surprising that in militant trade union circles Courts of Inquiry are felt to be a weapon aimed at them: for "abuse and invective against militants," as it has been put.[14]

Whether or not this is so, it remains true that the appointment of a court has frequently taken the steam out of situations that might other-wise have boiled over into a strike, or helped to solve a serious strike after it had begun. Furthermore, it is the general view that the find-ings of such courts are frequently made the basis of a settlement by the parties. McCarthy and Clifford set out to discover how often in practice this happened. They found that this was so in two-thirds of the cases where they could follow up in detail:

> It appears that the assessment of Ministry officials and academics is broadly correct, although it must be stressed that the courts have been much more successful in influencing the course of wages and hours issues than they have been in affecting other kinds of disputes. Take, for example, four recent disputes in engineering, shipbuilding, and printing, where on each occasion the parties broadly accepted the suggestions about wages or hours, while ignoring proposals aimed at overhauling al-legedly defective procedure. Or consider the two disputes where the published reports can be demonstrated to have had virtually no influence on the parties; it is notable that both of these turn exclusively on issues other than wages and hours.

And they give an illustration of the proposition that:

> even where there is evidence that courts have had some influence on disputes other than those involving wages and hours, it is arguable that they often do not attempt to deal with the really controversial issues. An example of this was the report on a dispute at D. C. Thomson's. Here a group of unionists was dismissed for organizing an undercover branch in a firm which insisted on a written undertaking that workers would not join a union. It is true that the court suggested that the firm should "reconsider" its insistence on such an undertaking, and that eventually this was revoked. But their report did not attempt to deal with the crucial issue of the reinstatement, or compensation, of the workers dismissed. Consequently the unions offered to submit the matter

---

[13] *Report on Dispute between Trent Guns and Cartridges and N.U.G.M.W.* (CMD. 6300; 1941).

[14] Paul Foot, *The Anti-Cameron Report* (1967), a pamphlet answering the building site report.

to arbitration and, when Thomson's refused, sought the intervention of the Prime Minister. During the following year the matter was raised in the House of Commons but it was never settled. Eventually, most of the men involved found new positions.[15]

Nevertheless, despite these limitations the device of the Court of Inquiry has recently been put to new uses. One may be a slightly greater flexibility on the part of those conducting some of the recent inquiries. We have seen already that in certain instances it was found useful to appoint Mr. Scamp, Chairman of the Motor Industry Joint Labour Council, as a Court of Inquiry, sometimes because the firm to be investigated fell outside the strict boundaries of that council's voluntary jurisdiction. So it was with his second and third reports;[16] in each case Scamp sat with two "wingmen" members of the Council as "assessors," a useful device which it is always possible to adopt in the court. More important, however, is his twelfth report in 1966 on a dispute at Birmingham Aluminium Castings, Ltd. This report is interesting for its terms of reference alone. Such terms normally require the court to "inquire into the causes and circumstances" of a dispute and to report. On this occasion the national "prices and incomes" policy was worked into the reference to inquire into a dispute concerning a claim for higher wages by maintenance workers. It read:

> to inquire into the causes and circumstances of the dispute at Birmingham Aluminium Castings Limited involving members of the Transport and General Workers' Union and the National Society of Metal Mechanics, taking into account all the relevant considerations including those set out in the White Paper—Prices and Incomes Standstill: Period of Severe Restraint (Cmnd. 3150), and to report.[17]

More important, however, to the present purpose is the procedure and character of the inquiry. It is still the orthodox proposition in the words of the Ministry of Labour's Evidence that:

> It is not the function of a Court of Inquiry to act as an instrument of conciliation or arbitration, and it has no power to enforce a settlement or make an award, but Courts may, and generally do, make recommendations upon which a reasonable settlement of the dispute can be based. As a rule, the report of a Court of Inquiry will not only deal exhaustively with the causes and circumstances of the dispute but will also, in the

---

15 McCarthy and Clifford, *op. cit.*, pp. 53–54.
16 Published as CMND. 2905 and 2935.
17 (CMND. 3201; 1966).

framework of its conclusions and recommendations, comment freely on the arguments and actions of the disputants.

But in the Birmingham Aluminium inquiry, Scamp found that he was faced by a union refusal to negotiate about mobility of labor. He induced management to write down clearly (for the first time) what it meant by mobility of labor. The unions at once gave up their objections of "principle" and accepted the written classification as a basis of negotiation. The employers met their proposals with an offer, to which the unions made a counter offer. At this point Scamp's report to the minister reads as follows:

> 18. At this stage I concluded my hearing.
> 19. I was informed later, however, by the parties concerned that immediately following the hearing, they had met and agreement had been reached on the basis of an increase of 1s an hour to all the maintenance workers mentioned in paragraph 6 in exchange for their acceptance of full mobility of labour as defined in paragraphs 15 and 16. The proposals for regrading had been dropped. I informed the parties that I would report this settlement to you, and stressed that it would need to be examined in the light of the requirements of the Government's incomes policy.

Although it may still count officially as heresy to say so, it is surely clear that Scamp had here adopted the role of conciliator and mediator during the course of the inquiry. He "concluded the hearing" without more in order that the parties could come together informally; and it is hard to believe that he played no role in the events that occurred after paragraph 18 and before 19 which begins so disingeneously, "I was informed later, however . . . ."

Such a discovery in 1966 should, in fact, cause us no surprise. McCarthy and Clifford reported that, although in 1924 a court had interpreted its terms of reference to mean that it had to find the facts and not even "express an opinion upon the relative claims of employers and the workpeople," such an attitude was by 1965 "quite exceptional." They stated that since the war, courts had regularly felt impelled to make recommendations to the parties; and on five occasions had adjourned *in order to mediate* with a view to persuading the parties to accept the proposals. Four of the five efforts to mediate were successful and the court then adjourned sine die. Although these occasions, like the Birmingham Aluminium case, seem to have involved economic claims, there is no reason to doubt that a Court of Inquiry would today use the same methods when faced with other types of disputes if it seemed right to do so. In fact, McCarthy and Clifford go so far as to describe the Court of Inquiry in these terms:[18]

> On examination, then, the court of inquiry emerges as an unusual device for facilitating dispute settlement which is without an exact parallel elsewhere in the British system of industrial relations. Its special characteristics can best be defined by describing it as a form of *public* conciliation and mediation, which begins with a quasi-judicial examination of the parties, and ends with the publication of specific conclusions and suggestions.

In a footnote to this passage they contrast the "methods adopted by arbitrators—who do not give their reasons." Since they made that description, the flexibility of the Court of Inquiry has been further proved by the use to which it has been put by Mr. Scamp and the Motor Industry Joint Labour Council in cooperation with the Minister of Labour. It may well be that future developments for the processing of employment disputes in Britain lie along the path of less formal inquiry procedures which can, like the council, be inserted into the thick of a trouble spot as soon as it is seen that ordinary procedures have broken down. In that case it would be well if the investigating bodies could be better equipped with research and expert assistance. As McCarthy and Clifford said:

> Would it not be better if it were to be recognized that courts undertaking the investigation of problems of this kind would normally be expected to arm themselves with some form of qualified assistance? It might also be thought advantageous, in cases of this sort to have at least one expert in the study of industrial relations serving on the court.

As far as informality is concerned, however, there is already an alternative weapon at hand, the Committee of Investigation or Inquiry.

COMMITTEES OF INVESTIGATION OR INQUIRY

The minister has power to appoint a committee under the Conciliation Act, 1896, in "inquire into the causes and circumstances of the difference" between employers and workmen that has arisen. We have previously noted that there is no definition of "difference" so that his power is a wide one. Such committees are usually called "Committees

---

[18] McCarthy and Clifford, *op. cit.*, p. 51.

of Investigation." The committee is less formal than a Court of Inquiry, and its report does not have to be laid before Parliament. But the minister has also on occasion appointed "Committees of Inquiry." This he may do under his "general powers" as a minister. The Ministry of Labour Evidence gives three reasons this may be a preferable procedure:

(1) The minister may wish to act jointly with another minister (which is not provided for by the 1896 Act);

(2) The minister may wish to inquire into matters not currently in dispute between the parties; and

(3) The terms of reference under "general powers" may specifically include some aspect of "national interest" (same as the government's incomes policy).

It must not, however, be assumed that every Committee of Inquiry is appointed under these powers. We have analyzed the 19 Committees of Inquiry which delivered 21 reports between 1946 and 1966 and found that 7 of them were expressly appointed under the Conciliation Act, 1896. We, therefore, have three categories: Committees of Investigation, Committees of Inquiry under the 1896 Act, and Committees of Inquiry under "general powers."

Of the Committees of Investigation between 1946 and 1966 (also 19 in all), all except two consisted of three persons, the usual triumvirate of independent chairmen and wingmen from each side of industry. In one case the committee was a one-man affair (a report by Allan Flanders in 1965 on a dispute in Bristol Docks that had given rise to an unofficial strike over piecework rates and manning). Another in 1951 which tackled the vexing problem of the "retain and transfer" system and wages for football players was felt to need five members. In two, assessors were called in.

The picture in Committees of Inquiry is rather different, reflecting, as we shall see, the rather different range of subject matter. Ten took the usual three-man form (in one of which the chairman died and the two wingmen completed the inquiry). One man sat alone in six cases, but in one of these, three assessors were appointed (the "banks inquiry" of 1963 described later). One committee had four members, and the other two, five. Lawyers are in a marked minority among those presiding over the committees; but academics appear as chairmen in a large number, once again mainly economists and social scientists. The proceedings before most of these committees were informal, and lawyers are recorded as representing the parties in only two (including the "banks inquiry"). Normally the parties presented their own cases.

An analysis of 20 Committees of Investigation between 1946 and early 1967 showed that (excluding one exceptional case which took five months from appointment to report and was heard seven times) the average time from appointment to hearing was seven days, and from hearing to report was eleven days. Ten cases needed only one hearing; five involved two; the four others needed three. Apart from the bigger investigations into "general industrial relations" or the like, the picture for Committees of Inquiry appeared, where the details were available, to be broadly similar.

The Ministry of Labour describes the place of a Committee of Investigation (to which the inquiry is an alternative for the three reasons mentioned) in this way:

> A Commitee constituted in this way is normally used in cases where the public interest is not so wide and general as to call for a Court of Inquiry. Its procedure is therefore less formal, and its report is not laid before Parliament. Just as in the case of a Court of Inquiry, however, the report made by the Committee to the Minister may lead to an agreed settlement of the dispute.[19]

The increasing significance of the reports of committees may be indicated by the fact that, despite the lack of obligation to do so, more reports are now being published. The football investigation of 1952 and four other such reports between 1964 and early 1967 were published; while since 1958 twelve reports stemming from ten Committees of Inquiry have been published.[20] A study of the latter in particular shows that in a number of cases it must have been almost fortuitous whether the inquiry took the form that it did or (in the big cases) a Court of Inquiry or (in the others) a Committee of Investigation.

A study of the subject matter of the reports reveals that a majority of them were basically about economic claims (for pay, better conditions, etc.); but in our analysis, which produced Table 28 we tried to isolate those claims that were fundamentally questions of interpreting existing agreements or arrangements. (Many of the cases listed as "claims" *also* involved such questions in the course of argument; but that, of course, is the usual British experience.)

Two points stand out from this table. First, the usual form for an inquiry into a "general industrial relations" problem is the "general powers" inquiry. This was used, for example, for the elaborate study of the problems of the Port Transport Industry under Lord Devlin in

---

19 Ministry of Labour Evidence, p. 107.
20 We are very grateful to the Ministry of Labour for information they provided concerning the unpublished reports of the two types of committee, without which it would not have been possible to make our analysis.

TABLE 28

Subject Matter	20 reports* of committees of investigation	21 reports of 19 committees of inquiry	
		Under 1896 Act	Under "General Powers"
Claims (wages, hours, etc.)	9	2	6
Interpretation of agreements......	4	1	1
Demarcation and interunion problems	1	3	1
Trade union recognition problems..	3	—	1
Closed shop claim	1	—	—
Claim to remove foreman	1	—	—
Dismissal cases	—	1	—
Recruitment problems	—	—	1
"General industrial relations" inquiries	1	—	4
Total	20	7	14

*The total includes one report published early in 1967, not included in Table 21, p. 159.

SOURCE: Published reports of committees and information supplied by Ministry of Labour.

1965,[21] a report on which all subsequent discussion of the industry's difficulties has been based, and famous for such wise comments as "a trade union leader is not a policeman who can be called in by employers to enforce the law"; or "an industrial agreement is not a contract which can be enforced by an action for damages for non-delivery." The same format was adopted for the Banks Inquiry (which we have classified as a "recognition" problem). The trade union organizing bank employees complained to the International Labour Organization Freedom of Association Committee of the refusal of the banks to recognize it; the committee referred the matter to the British government; and the government (having no other machinery on recognition problems) set up a Committee of Inquiry under a Scottish judge, Lord Cameron.[22] But an inquiry into what may fairly be called "general industrial relations" at the Port of Glasgow in 1947 took the form of a Committee of Investigation, there being a "difference" concerning the size of the labor force sufficient to invoke the 1896 Act. In truth the

[21] Interim report (CMND. 2523; 1964); final report (CMND. 2734; 1965).
[22] Report (CMND. 2202; 1963). At the time of writing (November 1967), Britain was experiencing its first major strike threat of bank employees, whose union was still not recognized by most big banks.

analysis revealed that the exact form taken by any particular committee must have depended on factors that were known to the ministry at the time of appointment but cannot be clearly discerned from the reports. The differentiation does not, on the face of those reports, accord exactly with the three reasons advanced for "general powers" inquiries; and one is inclined to agree with the ministry's comment, in its evidence, on

> the question of whether the Minister should seek statutory authority for setting up the sort of inquiries which he has recently appointed under general powers. If such inquiries are to become more frequent, there may be some cases on general grounds for the Minister to seek specific statutory authority for his actions.

There seems to be even less correlation between subject matter and any distinction between those committees under the 1896 Act called "investigation" and those called "inquiries"; but once again there is maximum flexibility.

Second, an inspection of the committees—and especially of those appointed under the 1896 Act—reveals that they often deal with problems that might well have come before some other body, such as a Single Arbitrator or the Industrial Court. An example is the dismissal case heard in 1947. Here the union was claiming that the dismissal of a laborer who was their branch secretary was unjustified and sought his reinstatement. Amid various disputes at the factory, he had been suspended for his part in an unofficial stoppage of work. The inquiry (conducted by one man) concentrated upon his conduct on the specific occasions in issue (and not on previous conduct put in evidence by the employers); but the dismissal was found to be justified, though the inquiry also commented upon certain interunion squabbles which had been a factor in the troubles. The parallel with what might have been the award of a Single Arbitrator is striking, except that the form of the reasoned report is different. Again the published report of a three-man "general powers" inquiry into certain London markets, including Spitalfields, in 1964 concerned a dispute that arose from a union claim for a five-day 40-hour week in all fruit and vegetable markets. A resumption of work was arranged during the hearings. The committee heard evidence from all sides and said:

> Our terms of reference do not require us to make specific recommendations in regard to the negotiations of a settlement of the dispute. Nonetheless we think it right to do so in the hope that such accommodations, coming from an independent source, may help break the deadlock. . . .

Appointed on June 11, 1964, the triumvirate made its report on July 22. In all respects, although the language and form of the award would have differed, one could easily find a parallel to the dispute, the arguments, the tribunal hearing them, the time taken, and the outcome in an Industrial Court award.

Various Committees of Investigation suggest the same parallel. For example, in 1950 a three-man investigation reported on a long dispute arising out of trade unions' claims for a bonus for tugboat crews in the port of London which had given rise to stoppages of work. The committee made detailed recommendations concerning various aspects of the employment terms, very like an arbitration award. The same is true of the football report published in 1952; and of another committee on lightermen's wages in 1951. Similarly, a Committee of Inquiry in 1950 had to deal with the interpretation of the Civil Engineering Conciliation Board's working rules and the situation created by the withdrawal of unions from a Joint Demarcation Agreement made with the employers in 1934. The report had to interpret the scope of the "industry" but also made a number of suggestions for future action, suggestions that might well have been added to an arbitration award. A Committee of Investigation in 1952 dealt with a complaint against a foreman who had allegedly adopted overbearing ways in his workplace, and a shop steward's claim to have him removed. The claim was rejected. Without difficulty one can imagine the parties might have agreed not to a committee but to a Single Arbitrator for the settlement of this grievance. Instead, no doubt because of the preferences of the employer and of the four unions concerned in the case, a three-man Committee of Investigation made what can only be called an "award" in the case.

In other respects the postwar reports of the committees bear strong similarities to those of the Courts of Inquiry. For example, in many of them the conflict had led to a stoppage of work in breach of agreed procedures. The committees uphold the "constitutional" approach which McCarthy and Clifford found dominant in the courts' reports. A Committee of Inquiry report in 1957, for example, refused to regard as justified, stoppages on the union side in breach of procedure in a dispute concerning holiday pay merely because the employer had also and antecedently acted in breach of the agreements: "Two wrongs do not make a right." Similarly, in the Investigation into the Bristol Docks dispute, the report, published in 1966, criticizes both the workers' acting "impetuously and irresponsibly" in breach of the procedures and also the employers for their "policy of delay" in the face of an "explosive situation," before going on to make positive recommendations for the future. This latter report marks a trend in the committees of 1965 and 1966 to balance an indictment of unconstitutional action with an investigation of the real function and causes of unofficial strikes—a determination to get beneath the surface of what McCarthy and Clifford called the "naive and legalistic" approach of certain earlier Courts of Inquiry.

Two Committees of Inquiry may be cited as evidence pointing in the same direction and as evidence of the flexible utility of the method. In the first, Mr. Flanders was appointed in 1964 under the 1896 Act to "inquire into the causes and circumstances of the difference over the appointment of dock foremen at Southampton Docks." The appointment was made on August 25; the hearing held on September 14; and report made on October 19. The dispute centered around the promotion of men to docks' foreman, a post traditionally reserved for dock workers in the T.G.W.U. An agreement had been made in 1955 concerning the advertising of such posts, and the National Union of Railwaymen alleged that their men on the docks were now equally eligible for such posts. The T.G.W.U. resisted the claim, saying that the traditional custom had survived the agreement which said nothing explicitly about extending the range of possible applicants. The report carefully studied the complicated history of the dispute, essentially one between the unions with the British Transport Docks Board caught in the middle. The board had tried to get the unions to agree, but "should have adopted a more positive role" in trying to meet the difficulties. Although the Advertising Agreement of 1955 said nothing explicitly:

> Nevertheless in the absence of any provision restricting particular vacancies to particular categories of applicants, the Unions signing the Agreement were entitled to assume that all applicants for any advertised vacancy would be considered fairly on their merits.

For the lawyer this might seem to be the end of the problem; and if the matter had been approached merely as a "rights" dispute concerning the interpretation of the 1955 Agreement, to which all three sides were parties, it must have been so. Such was not the approach, however, of an industrial relations expert conducting an inquiry. Having made that interpretation of the agreement, he wrote, some ten paragraphs later:

> I come now to the underlying causes of this dispute. Clearly it was based on a conflict between the implied provisions of the Advertising Agreement of 24 August 1955 and an established practice at Southampton Docks which reserved dock foremen's positions exclusively to dockers.

What made the dispute particularly difficult to resolve was that it involved a *conflict of rights: rights taken to be established by a collective agreement were being opposed by other rights derived from custom and practice.* [Italics supplied.]

No passage could better convey the spirit of British industrials relations or the approach of most of those conducting modern inquiries into them. The report naturally proceeds to a careful examination of the best way out of the dilemma. A procedure for selection was recommended in which representatives of both unions would participate as observers; and the British Transport Docks Board was kind enough to inform us in 1967 that this procedure had been successfully followed thereafter.

The value of an inquiry under the 1869 Act, rather than a quasi-judicial hearing *inter partes*, was also illustrated by the report of Mr. Picton published in 1965 on the difference between the National Association of Colliery Overmen Deputies and Shotfirers and the National Coal Board (appointed June 8; hearings, June 24 and 25; and report, August 12—in this case on a dispute that had begun on April 21). An incident had occurred in a coal mine in which a miner and deputy exchanged swear words. The miner was sent out of the pit, and all the miners stopped work. Various inconclusive meetings and resumptions of work followed. The National Coal Board eventually decided to hold an inquiry. The result of that inquiry was a decision to move both the miner and the deputy to different workplaces. Thereupon, deputies in the association in the district went on strike. The association alleged that there had been victimization of the deputy and that the N.C.B. had failed to honor conciliation arrangements at the pit. The N.C.B. rejected these contentions. There was a troubled history of over thirty disputes at this particular colliery during the two years preceding these incidents, and in many respects the dispute had taken on the overtones of an interunion conflict. Mr. Picton felt that his terms of reference did "not involve a full-scale inquiry into all the surrounding circumstances" but required an investigation "directed in a reasonably concentrated way upon the stoppage itself." Thus he places the alleged victimization of the individual deputy in the context of the collective problems. The association alleged that "the Board's inquiry was a farce because it was confined to the swearing scene." Any adjudication between the parties which tried to adjudge the individual parties' "rights" without taking account of the collective realities would have been equally farcical. This approach was not the one an inquiry under the 1896 Act had to take. The report ended by holding that the board had "acted reasonably throughout" and the "complaints of the Association are not well founded." Mr. Picton added a number of proposals for future action, prefacing them with the paragraph:

> I have been at pains to analyse a complex situation in such a way as to illuminate the anxieties of the Association, and I invite their consideration of the following views which I offer with every sympathy for their difficulties and with the hope that I can avoid the appearance of pompous moralising. At the same time, I commend these reflections to the Union and to the Board.

This short review of the postwar use of various types of committees prompts two reflections in conclusion. First, the variety and flexibility of the weapons at the disposal of the Minister of Labour is very great. While it is true that none of the recommendations made is binding, the increasing number of committee reports which have recently been published probably indicates an attempt to harness the pressure of public opinion to ensure their implementation. We can expect to see a development and extension of the use of such powers of inquiry. Within the spectrum of procedures for processing employment disputes in Britain, the committees may be seen as another form of that "public conciliation" (with the public element more in the discretion of the minister), of which McCarthy and Clifford spoke in connection with Courts of Inquiry.

Second, such a development points in the same direction as various tendencies already noticed. We may recall, for example, the growth of the Motor Industry Joint Labour Council, armed sometimes with the powers of a Court of Inquiry. In another context, the 1967 N.J.A.C. Report on "Dismissals Procedures" said that if (which it did not recommend) statutory tribunals were introduced for "unjust dismissal" cases, then two factors would be particularly significant: "the need for flexibility and the importance of conciliation"—the latter especially being "more likely to produce an all round satisfactory settlement than (for example) a quasi-judicial hearing alone." All these tendencies are in the direction of informal inquiry and conciliation rather than legalistic hearing and adjudication.

Part Four
NEW TRIBUNALS

12.

THE PRACTICE OF THE
INDUSTRIAL TRIBUNALS

A development that has within the last four years caused British labor law and practice to take strides in an opposite direction—toward, rather than away from, the judicial method in employment disputes—has been the institution and growth in jurisdiction of the Industrial Tribunals. These three-man tribunals have already been mentioned (above, p. 24). The object of Part IV is threefold: first, to explain the origin and growth of the tribunals; second, to give the results of a statistical analysis we were able to carry out (with the generous assistance of the president of the tribunals for England and Wales and his officials)[1] on a structured sample of tribunal decisions; and third, to describe very briefly how the more important legal issues have fared before the tribunals and on appeal from them. There is a need to look carefully at the work of these tribunals, for it has already been suggested that "the nucleus of a system of labour courts exists potentially in these tribunals."[2]

The jurisdiction of the tribunals comprises a hodge-podge of questions under modern statutes. The tribunals sprang to life, like Athene from the head of Zeus, under the Industrial Training Act, 1964. Their task here is largely to determine appeals by employers against levies which can be imposed on them by boards to finance the training of workers. But subsequently, other questions of greater importance were

---

[1] We are most grateful to the president, the chairmen, and the secretary and officials of the central office of the tribunals, as well as to officials of the Ministry of Labour, for their cooperation in providing information and new material which have made possible the writing of chapter 12.

[2] Ministry of Labour Evidence, p. 92.

added, so that in 1967 the main jurisdiction of the tribunals could be listed as follows:

(1) Employers' appeals against levies under Industrial Training Act, 1964.[3]

(2) Questions arising under the Redundancy Payments Act, 1965, as to the employees' right to payment or the amount of the payment, or the employers' right to a rebate from the national fund.[4] This jurisdiction came into effect on December 6, 1965.

(3) Disputes concerning payments similar to redundancy payments, for example, to civil servants, or under previous isolated legislation where the 1965 Act transferred juridiction.[5]

(4) Disputes and questions concerning the written particulars an employer is bound to give his employee under the Contracts of Employment Act, 1963. We have already noted that the opportunity was taken in 1965 to replace the cumbersome sanction of criminal prosecution with that of reference to the tribunals.[6]

(5) Questions as to whether a business is an establishment within the terms of the Selective Employment Payments Act, 1966, and as to the refund to which an employer may be entitled under the act.[7] The details of this statute do not concern us; it was a tax statute imposing a tax per worker, graduated according to sex and age, on employers, but allowing refunds in certain sectors of the economy.

(6) The determination of a dispute whether work is "dock work" within a statute of 1966.[8] The act aims to regulate the employment of dock workers; it also is the current basis of licensing of employers in the docks and regulates various other matters relating to docks and harbors.

Thus it can be seen that the tribunals have become maids-of-all-work. When a modern statute creates a justiciable issue that has the flavor of an employment problem, it seems to be given (even on tax questions) to these tribunals. In their actual work, however, one statute dominates all others, and it is the most relevant to our study, the

---

[3] Industrial Training Act, 1964, sec. 12.

[4] Redundancy Payments Act, 1965, sec. 9, sec. 34, and sec. 44. Similarly under section 11 the tribunals would have jurisdiction over disputes arising under any collective agreements providing for redundancy payments which had been "exempted" from the act by the Minister. It is thought that no such exemption orders have been made at the time of writing.

[5] Secions 41 and 42; and schedule 7 which transfer proceedings under 23 statutes to the tribunals, largely concerning payments to persons employed by nationalized industries.

[6] Section 4A of the 1963 Act, added by section 38 of the 1965 Act.

[7] Selective Employment Act, 1966, sec. 7(5).

[8] Docks and Harbours Act, 1966, sec. 59.

Redundancy Payments Act, 1965. In their report for 1966, the Council on Tribunals stated that the tribunals had sat in London and thirteen provincial centers in England and Wales; and of the 4,779 cases heard in that period, 3,733 were concerned with redundancy payments (although it should be noted that these figures relate to a period during most of which the Selective Employment Payments Act was not in operation).[9]

Part IV concentrates upon the redundancy payments hearings before the tribunals because they are both the most numerous and the most relevant. It is remarkable that this statute was passed into law with so little controversy. Not only, as we noted in Part I, did it extend in a major way a new process begun in 1963—the statutory regulation of minimum rights in what had previously been thought of as the preserve of collective bargaining—but many authoritative voices were raised early in 1965 arguing for other ways of meeting the problem of redundancy. For example, some time before the bill, both the Confederation of British Industry and the Trades Union Congress seemed to favor the method of increased regular unemployment benefits rather than lump-sum payments to long-service employees dismissed by reason of a statutorily defined "redundancy." In the midst of this debate about substance, scant attention was paid to the procedural question of where disputes should go. The debates took place while the ordinary courts were under criticism for their decisions in such cases as *Rookes* v. *Barnard* and *Stratford* v. *Lindley*, and many such critics were only too ready to turn to the easy answer of a tripartite tribunal "representing both sides of industry" with an "independent" chairman. There was little hardheaded debate—at least, in public outside the Ministry—and the jurisdiction of the tribunals, like Topsy, "just growed."

The tribunals consequently extended their work considerably and steadily. The figures given by the council for 1966 stood in need of some amendment by early 1967. The Ministry of Labour in April 1967 stated that tribunals had "sat at eighteen centres in England and Wales and at seven in Scotland"; and gave the total number of cases registered in England and Wales from December 1965 up to March 31, 1967, as 12,872 of which 7,097 had been disposed of at hearings and 2,646 disposed of without hearings. In Scotland the total was 1,594 (950 hearings).[10] Of the English total, the bulk were, again, on redundancy payments—8,455, of which 5,114 had been determined at hear-

---

[9] Report of Council on Tribunals (1966), Appendix C, p. 32. The Council on Tribunals exercises general guidance over administrative tribunals under the Tribunals and Inquiries Act, 1958.

[10] *Ministry of Labour Gazette*, April 1967, pp. 291–292.

ings. As is explained later, we discovered that 3,934 cases on redundancy were registered between April 18, 1966 and November 22, 1966. The ministry's figures indicate that the rate has increased. The same report in April stated that the tribunals were "hearing and adjudicating on average 250 cases a week," and that "applications or appeals are reaching the central office in London at the rate of about 200 to 250 a week," most of them being redundancy cases. The eighteen centers in England and Wales mentioned are in fact eighteen towns, and the number of tribunals may be expected to increase; but until they sit in very many more towns, they can hardly be called "local" tribunals.

The regulations governing the work of the tribunals allow for the appointment of a president (who must, like the other chairmen of the tribunals, be a barrister or solicitor of not less than seven years' standing) in each of the two jurisdictions, in England and Wales (by the Lord Chancellor), and in Scotland (by the Lord President of the Court of Session). The account in Part IV concentrates on the former "jurisdiction."[11] (The English President is Sir Diarmaid Conroy, Q.C., an ex-Chief Justice of Northern Rhodesia.) From 1965 the president determined the number of tribunals and the places at which they sat. The pressure of work became so great in 1967 that the regulations were amended to provide for regional centers and the delegation of these powers of the president to permanent chairmen who may be appointed in London and in those centers.[12] Appointments were made in 1967 to regional centers in Manchester, Leeds, Newcastle, and Birmingham; and two permanent chairmen now assist the president in London. These permanent chairmen are all members of the local bar, an intentional feature of the appointments, in order that they should become acquainted with the requirements and problems of their regions. The permanent chairmen are paid not, as the other chairmen are, on a fee basis, but, like the president, are on salary and will, in the manner of County Court judges, be eligible for "judicial pensions" under the Superannuation (Miscellaneous Provisions) Act, 1967.

The new regulations also provide for the appointment of regional assistant secretaries. One objective of the new arrangements is to have the regional offices take over certain of the administrative functions, previously concentrated in London. A center, it may be noted, may have a number of different tribunals sitting in the town in any one

---

[11] Industrial Tribunals (England and Wales) Regulations (1965) S.I. 1101, amended by S.I. 301, 1967. The regulations for Scotland are here, and below, equivalent to those cited for England and Wales.

[12] Regulations, S.I. 301, 1967, regs. 3 and 4.

day. In the first three and a half months of 1967, we found a wide variation in distribution of "hearing days," (i.e., the number of days on which hearings took place, multiplied by the number of tribunals for any day where more than one tribunal sat). In this period when the number of days on which sittings could occur was 71, London (with 6 tribunals) totaled 306 "hearing days" (under 11 different chairmen); Birmingham, 135 (14 chairmen); Manchester, 119 (6 chairmen); Newcastle, 53 (4 chairmen); Leeds, 58 (2 chairmen); and the number in other centers declined down to Carlisle, 5 (1 chairman).

PERSONNEL

The composition of tribunals merits special attention. The Lord Chancellor nominates a panel of lawyers of at least seven years' standing from whom the president (or now a regional chairman) selects a chairman for a sitting of a tribunal. Similarly, panels of persons have been appointed by the Minister of Labour "after consultation with any organization or association of organizations respresentative of employers" and of "employed persons"; and from each of these panels the president (or permanent chairman) appoints a wingman to each tribunal to make up the triumvirate. In practice, the Confederation of British Industry and the Trades Union Congress have been consulted in respect of the wingmen. The T.U.C. reported on its nominations to the minister in 1967, showing that it had passed on 130 of the 342 nominations received from 52 affiliated unions.[13] The number of persons on the wingmen panels in March 1967 is given in Table 29.

TABLE 29

Jurisdiction	Employers			Employed Persons		
	Part time	Full time	Total	Part time	Full time	Total
England and Wales........	204	27	231	156	31	187
Scotland	23	0	23	18	0	18
Total	227	27	254	174	31	205

SOURCE: Ministry of Labour.

The part-time nominees on the employees side appear mainly to be district or other officers of trade unions. A considerable number of

---

[13] T.U.C. General Council Report, 1967, para. 70. The total given for serving trade union wingmen (219) does not tally with the ministry's figure given above.

those on the panels have not in fact been used often or, indeed, at all. The "full-time" members of the tribunals are almost all, of necessity, retired persons, in particular retired trade union officials. They are paid on a fee basis. There is clearly a tension in the structure which has not so far been resolved. On the one hand, the tribunals need to have young active wingmen, in close touch with the problems of industry, though it is the practice not to appoint a wingman from the particular industry involved in the case. But this means the appointment of many different wingmen; no particular tribunal can build up continuity; and the power of the legal chairman is bound to increase. On the other hand, the appointment of full-time wingmen from retired persons suffers from obvious demerits.

This problem of personnel is even more marked in regard to the chairmen. There is, it will be noted, no requirement in the regulations for the Lord Chancellor (or Lord President in Scotland) to consult any representative bodies before nominating the legal chairman. Nor does the British law require, in the manner of German law, any industrial or similar experience, but only seven years' legal practice. The Ministry of Labour's publications stated that in April 1967 there were 39 chairmen.[14] We identified 36 actually sitting at that time from the lists of the central office (including the president), and these chairmen all answered a small questionnaire we compiled. From their answers we found that they included 31 barristers and 5 solicitors. Two

TABLE 30

Careers of 36 Chairmen of Industrial Tribunals, April 1967

(a) Straightforward British legal practice $\begin{cases} \text{Barrister} & 13 \\ \text{Solicitor} & 2 \end{cases}$ 15	
(b) British "judicial" experience of any kind	11 (6 as County Court judges)
(c) Experience on administrative tribunals	14
(d) Period in the civil service	5
(e) Legal practice mainly abroad...................	9
(f) Judicial experience abroad....................	8 (6 as judges)
(g) Commercial or industrial experience?	
Definitely not......................	17
Apparently not	7
Probably not	4
Commercial experience	4

SOURCE: Correspondence with chairmen of Industrial Tribunals.

---

[14] *Ministry of Labour Gazette*, April 1967, p. 292. It seems clear that this figure failed to take account of retirements; our list of 36 was obtained from the central office.

were under 40 years of age; 27 were over 50 (of whom 14 were over 60). Table 30 is an analysis of their careers in very broad terms. It will be seen that few had had experience outside legal practice; and that a high proportion had had legal and even judicial experience abroad (all of it in British colonial or similar territories, these judges or magistrates having retired, like the president himself, at a relatively young age). The only appointee with experience of academic or research work was an expert on international law and the law of war.

We took this analysis a little further. Of the 801 total "hearing days" in all the centers in the seventy-one day period mentioned above, 505 were presided over by only ten of the chairmen (including the president). These "top ten" represent the first division of tribunal chairmen in 1967. Such chairmen were appointed (even before the regional system was introduced) for a week at a time, whereas other chairmen were, and are, brought in only when pressure of work in a district requires them. Their regular appearance on tribunals with a large turnover of wingmen, especially of the part-time wingmen, must have ensured that they played a major role in developing the law in the tribunals. They include four of the six permanent chairmen appointed in London and regional centers. We found that all ten were barristers over 50 years of age (six over 60). Five had had a career abroad, four ending as judges. None of the home-based lawyers had had judicial experience; only in one case was there evidence of commercial experience and, in two, of civil service experience; otherwise, the careers had been strictly legal.

PROCEDURES AND DECISIONS

Much depends upon the way in which the legal chairman conducts the tribunal's procedure. The decision to which it leads "may be taken by a majority" of the tribunal.[15] No provision is made for formal dissenting opinions; but in some of the reported decisions (a series of Industrial Tribunal Reports having begun in 1966), it is indicated that one wingman or the other took a different view from the majority. For example, in one case, at the end of the decision it is recorded that one

---

[15] Industrial Tribunals (Redundancy Payments) Regulations 1967, S.I. 359 (replacing previous regulations S.I. 2019, 1965). Equivalent regulations govern the procedure and decisions in other jurisdictions, e.g., the Contracts of Employment Act jurisdiction, S.I. 361, 1967; selective employment tax, S.I. 1231, 1966; dock work, S.I. 313, 1967.

of the wingmen "while not dissenting, doubted the soundness of the majority view and desired to reserve his opinion on the question"; and the decision states that it was taken "by a majority."[16] One of the very earliest decisions reported states simply that the chairman and one wingman took one view, the third member, another.[17] Another unusual case revealed that the "legally qualified chairman was in a minority" on the question whether the employee's employment was "continuous" and whether the employer had rebutted the presumption under the 1965 Act that a dismissal was caused by redundancy—a rare example of a chairman being outvoted by his wingmen on issues that involved legal inferences to be drawn from the facts.[18]

The decision must be recorded in a document that "shall contain the reasons for the decisions," and must be entered on a central register open to public inspection (unless the tribunal otherwise directs, under the new regulations, on the ground that disclosure would prejudice the interests of a party, in which case the written decision is sent only to the parties and the minister). Redundancy payments or rebates payable under awards of the tribunals are enforceable by execution through the ordinary County Courts "as if payable under an order of that court."[19] It is worthy of note that the tribunal is directed *not* to award costs against a losing party except where he has acted "frivolously or vexatiously," in which case he may have to pay part or all of the costs of other parties. Otherwise, not only does a party not pay costs; he may, in a redundancy case, be paid his expenses for the "day in court," including travel costs; an overnight allowance where the stay was unavoidable; an hourly expense allowance; and a sum for loss of earnings up to £3 5s 0d a day ($7.80). Furthermore, the same allowances are payable to his witnesses, and to any person who comes to present his case other than a lawyer or a full-time trade union official.

The procedure itself begins with an originating application to the secretary of the tribunals. One problem that arose under the old regulations was the large number of obviously bad applications often outside the range of the jurisdiction, which no one had power to strike out and which wasted the time of tribunals. Under the 1967 regulations[20] the secretary has power, where he is of the opinion that the

---

16 *Sneddon* v. *Ivorycrete, Ltd.* (1967) 2 I.T.R. 538, at p. 540.

17 *Bainbridge* v. *Westinghouse, Ltd.* (1966) 1 I.T.R. 55.

18 A Scots decision reported on the appeal to Court of Session: *Rencoule Ltd.* v. *Hunt* (1967) 2 I.T.R. 475.

19 Redundancy Payments Act, 1965, sec. 46 (3).

20 S.I. 359, 1967, schedule para. 1(2), which is the basis of what follows.

originating application does not set out a case which it is within the power of a tribunal to remedy, to state this opinion to the applicant and ask him whether he agrees to withdraw; if there is no reply from the applicant, the case is dropped. Where a case goes forward, a party may obtain from a tribunal an order compelling the other party to furnish written particulars of grounds and contentions, or to discover relevant documents, or compelling any person to attend as a witness. Such persons may themselves petition the tribunal to vary or set aside the order. The hearing itself takes place in public unless the tribunal otherwise directs. The tribunal has power to administer an oath or affirmation to witnesses. Plainly this procedure can be made to work informally or legalistically. In attending various tribunals, we found both tendencies, on one occasion hearing a chairman actually ask an applicant appearing in person whether she wished to "amend" her "pleadings." On the whole, however, our impression is that the majority of tribunals are probably conducted in an informal manner; that is certainly the intention of the president.

Whether or not he is a party (as in an employer's claim for a rebate), the minister always has the right to appear and be heard in a redundancy case. The minister is usually represented by a lay official from the ministry and only in exceptional cases by someone from the legal department. The other parties may appear in person "or be represented by counsel or solicitor or by a representative of a trade union or of an employers' association or with the leave of the tribunal by any other person."[21] If a party does not appear at all, the tribunal may either adjourn the case or dispose of it there and then.

A SAMPLE OF TRIBUNAL CASES

The Minister of Labour in introducing the Redundancy Payments Bill in 1965 stressed that the tribunals in handling the cases would be "easy of access to workers and employers" and would "provide a speedy means of settling disputes with less formality and expense than might be entailed if disputes were to go to the courts."[22] We were able to test certain aspects of what has ensued on a sample of early cases. The central office kindly made available the records of 3,934 redundancy cases registered between April 18 and November 22, 1966. Since the earlier cases almost certainly exhibited different features from the

---

[21] Ibid., sched. para. 7(1).
[22] 1965, Vol. 711 H.C. Deb. col. 46.

later ones (the act having been in force less than five months by April 1966), we examined the first and last 400 cases, and a random sample of the cases between them, a total of 1,697 cases. (This is referred to below as "the sample of cases.") Of these, 344 were ultimately withdrawn, but some withdrawals were at the hearing so that certain details were available about its conduct. The analysis of the withdrawn cases was itself interesting, showing the following reasons:

Settled by a payment (from employer or ministry)[23]   252
Applicant decided he had no case   39
Tactical reasons (e.g., fear of publicity, or
   acceptance of alternative job)   13
No reason given or ascertainable   40

The character of the conduct of proceedings before labor courts is frequently as much determined by whether lawyers argue the case as whether a lawyer judges them. This important question led us to make the analyses presented in Table 31 (where the totals represent the number of cases in which the information was available). It will be seen that only some 14 percent of employees' cases and 26 percent of employers' cases were presented by lawyers. The same picture appeared from an inspection of 187 cases registered as being brought

TABLE 31

Representation before Industrial Tribunals

| Claimant | Represented by | | | | | | Total cases giving such infor- mation |
| | Self (including managers, etc., for companies) | Trade union or Em- ployers' asso- ciation official | Lawyer | | Not present or repre- sented | Other repre- sentative* | |
			Solicitor	Barrister			
Employees	615	342	130	54	140	43	1324
Employers[†]	574	108	268	89	331	1	1371

*Viz.: Husband, 16; fellow workman, 7; friend, 6; father, 3; wife, son, brother, each 2; nephew, step-brother, alderman, and office of British Legion, each 1.

†Usually as respondent to a claim; but sometimes as claimant, e.g., against the minister claiming a rebate.

SOURCE: Sample of cases registered from April to November 1966.

23 The ministry is obliged to pay when an employer refuses or fails after the employee has taken all reasonable steps or when the employer is "insolvent" (a word defined widely). In these cases the minister is subrogated to the employee's right to claim from the employer: sec. 32, Redundancy Payments Act, 1965.

under the Contracts of Employment Act, 1963, between December 1965 and January 1967. In those (of which only 30 were successful) only 9 percent of employees' and 17 percent of employers' cases were so presented. The great majority were argued personally by the worker and by a nonlegal representative of the employing company, as in the case of the redundancy claim. A further calculation was made in all the redundancy cases *reported* in the Industrial Tribunal Reports. These are cases notified by the chairmen of tribunals as of special interest, and chosen by the editor of the reports (a barrister). Since these were selected as cases of particular legal interest, they might have been expected to show a dramatic rise in the incidence of legal representation. In cases for 1966 this was not so. Legal representation was found for employees in 14 percent of 175 cases, and for employers in 23 percent of 176 cases—an even lower figure than in our sample. But in the cases reported in Parts 1 to 9 of the 1967 Reports (January to October), there is an increase. Employees used lawyers in 23 percent of 139 cases, and employers, in 35 percent of 140 of the reported cases. (The minister it may be noted appeared—always by way of a lawyer—in 13 reported cases as a third party in 1966 and the first three quarters of 1967.) By 1967 the points litigated are no doubt becoming more complex, and the parties are probably beginning to use lawyers more often (even on the employees' side). There is no reason to think that the reported cases for 1967 are less representative than those for 1966. On the other hand, it is perhaps remarkable to see that the trade union official appeared for fewer than half the employees in our sample. He also figures in fewer than half of the reported cases in 1966 and 1967. Many of the workers who presented their own cases were not members of trade unions at all. In that sense (bearing in mind the payment of expenses) the tribunals were "easy of access." The high proportion of employees presenting their own cases (46 percent in our sample; and in the reported cases, 49 percent in 1966 and 32 percent in the first three quarters of 1967) is not surprising where there are statutory rights available to an individual worker whether he is organized or not.

Various estimates have been given of the time taken to determine redundancy cases. One commentator, for example, suggested in March 1967, that between " a redundancy occurring" and the settlement at a tribunal there was a delay of "six to eight weeks."[24] Our sample showed a slightly longer period. It is true, of course, that the work of

---

[24] R. Winsbury, "The Road from Redundancy," *Management Today* (March 1967), 96, at p. 99.

the tribunals may have been speeded up by the institution of the regional centers and permanent chairmen from April 1967 onward; but the indications are that these reforms will not alter the picture greatly unless the number of redundancy claims falls away sharply (an unlikely eventuality in years of less than full employment). Indeed there is a point beyond which the hearing of cases cannot be speeded up since the regulations require the central office to give at least two weeks' notice of a hearing and permit the respondent two weeks within which to enter an appearance. Where this point lies is no doubt disputable, but with regard to the length of time actually taken, our sample, at least, provides an answer for 1966 which we believe to be the first piece of hard information on the subject. We were able in 1,200 cases to establish the time passing between receipt of Form I (the originating application) and the hearing at the tribunal. The former date is not, of course, the same as the date of the "redundancy occurring" but usually seems to be a number of weeks afterward. The average time between the two dates was nine and a half weeks. The actual distribution is shown in Table 32.

TABLE 32

Redundancy Cases, 1966

Length of time from receipt of Form I by Central Office to hearing by tribunal	Number of cases
4 weeks or under	1
5 weeks or under	20
6 weeks or under	74
7 weeks or under	138
8 weeks or under	194
9 weeks or under	222
10 weeks or under	168
11 weeks or under	105
12 weeks or under	108
13 weeks or under	37
14 weeks or under	29
15 weeks or under	32
16 weeks or under	31
Over 16 weeks	41
Total	1,200
Average	9 to 10 weeks

SOURCE: Sample of cases registered from April to November 1966.

The tribunal very often comes to a decision on the day of the hearing, but not always. In quite a few cases, the decision will be made known then to the parties, but the exact reasons will not be made available until the written decision is promulgated. We were able to determine the delay that occurred between the hearing and formal promulgation of the written decision in 1,235 cases. The average delay was 23 days and the distribution showed it was 1 week or under in 118 cases; 2 weeks or under in 250; 3 weeks or under in 319; 4 weeks or under in 246; 5 or under in 155; and over 5 weeks in 147. But it would be unfair to add the delay until formal promulgation to the previous time because the decision will often be known to a claimant before the formal document is received. Nevertheless, it seems clear that a three or four months delay between a *dismissal* and a decision from a tribunal on a redundancy claim was in no way exceptional in 1966; and there is no reason to believe that the period is markedly less in 1967.

One further source of information is once again the reported decisions. The dates given in reported decisions of the tribunals broadly confirmed the results of our sample. Another group of cases, however, comprises those that are taken on appeal to the High Court in London or the Court of Session in Edinburgh. These are the "difficult" cases, and the delays would be expected to be rather longer. An inspection of the 16 appeals reported in the first nine parts of the 1967 Industrial Tribunal Reports showed just that. First, in ten cases the delay between the *dismissal* and the tribunal's promulgated decision could be established. This varied between 3 and 7 months (the average being 5). Second, the delay in 13 cases between the *tribunal's decision* and the appellate decision of the High Court or Court of Session ranged between 4 and 10 months (the average being 6). Third, the 11 cases in which the time lag between the *dismissal* and final appellate decision could be established showed a variation between 7 and 14 months (average 11). Late in 1967 it seemed that about 150 appeals in redundancy matters were awaiting hearing before the High Court.[25] Plainly in cases where appeals on points of law are taken to the ordinary courts, a delay of nearly a year causes little surprise. Indeed, most practitioners would regard the procedures adopted in these cases as

---

[25] In April 1968 the central office was kind enough to give us the figure of 147 cases filed in the Divisional Court in England (at which date the number of cases heard by the tribunals was around 15,000) with a smaller but unknown figure for cases filed with the Court of Session in Scotland. By July 1968 the central office gave the rate of appeals as 163 (51 outstanding) out of a total of 17,200 tribunal decisions. The rate of appeals seems, therefore, to be fairly constant at just under 1 percent of the total tribunal decisions. The judges have been insistent on maintaining a wide meaning for "a question of law," on which alone an appeal can be taken: see *O'Brien, Pritchard & Browning* v. *Associated Fire Alarms* (1968) 3 I.T.R. 182 (Court of Appeal).

speedy. But against the background of industrial life, it cannot be regarded as established that the industrial tribunals have, even in cases where no such appeal is taken, so far established a claim to the "speed" of which the minister spoke. Contrary to general belief, there is reason to doubt whether a decision is reached in an ordinary dispute very much more quickly here than in (say) engineering negotiating procedure (above, p. 90). Moreover, many of the cases to which a negotiated settlement might be found in such a procedure, or in a procedure that utilized some form of arbitration, would be just those redundancy cases taken on into the longer delay by means of an appeal to the High Court on a point of law. To these cases we return below (p. 266). Although it is not possible to give any figures on the question, it is also interesting to ask whether the delays—or even the character of the decisions—would have been materially different had this jurisdiction been given not to the tribunals but to (an increased number of) County Court judges, exercising the ordinary local civil jurisdiction. Delays in the County Courts are not, in simple cases, greater than the periods discussed. On the other hand, there is a greater formality in these courts, and it would no doubt have been more difficulty for workers to present their cases in person.

Figures issued by the ministry give a general picture for redundancy payment cases in 1966 and 1967, as follows:

	1966	1967
Claims taken to Tribunals:		
England and Wales	5,929	9,436
(Scotland)	(806)	(1,082)
Cases outstanding at end of the period:		
England and Wales	1,843	2,730
(Scotland)	(293)	(276)

The increase in the number of cases and the parallel increase in the number outstanding suggests that, despite the reorganization of the tribunals, and valiant efforts by the president and others, the delay in hearing cases is unlikely to be significantly smaller at the beginning of 1968 than in the cases that formed our sample. The rise in absolute numbers reflects, of course, the increasing rate of unemployment in Britain during 1967. It should be remembered finally, that the disputes taken to tribunals represent only a small fraction of the number of payments actually made under the Act of 1965. The number made in 1966 was 137,208, and in 1967, 241,581. The total amount of money paid out in 1966 was £26.5 million (of which about £20 million was borne by the National Fund, the rest by employers themselves) and in 1967 just over £50 million (of which the fund bore £38 million in rebates). The figures for 1968 are likely to be as high or even higher in all respects.[26]

---

[26] The figures for the first two quarters of 1968 were: Cases taken, 4,220 (549); cases outstanding, 2,190 (339). Payments in this period amounted to nearly £30 million to 134,000 persons.

13.
THE INDUSTRIAL TRIBUNALS
AND THE LAW

I t is not possible here to attempt a full review of the three hundred or more reported decisions of the tribunals up to the autumn of 1967. The aim of this chapter is to present some illustrations of general themes that emerge from reading those reports, themes that are of particular relevance to any plan to turn the Industrial Tribunals into labor courts. The general points may be put in a threefold manner. First, the 1965 Act is a highly complex and intricate statute of 59 sections and 9 schedules.[1]

The tribunals frequently, therefore, find themselves driven by its precise wording to technical decisions, usually against a claimant. (The tribunals also find themselves sometimes called upon to decide questions of common law.) Second, where they have a choice, the tribunals have in many cases shown a tendency to construe the statute liberally, often with a view to allowing a claim for a redundancy payment. Third, however, an appeal may be taken from a tribunal's decision to the High Court (or Court of Session in Scotland) on any point of law.[2] The judges have adopted a generous interpretation of what is a point of "law";[3] and in many of the appeals they have curbed the liberal spirit of the tribunals, imposing both a strict adherence to the

---

[1] For a more detailed analysis of the act, see (1966) 29 M.L.R. 55.

[2] By virtue of Tribunals and Inquiries Act, 1958, sec. 9, applied by the Tribunals and Inquiries (Industrial Tribunals) Order 1958, S.I. 1403.

[3] O'Brien, Pritchard & Browning v. Associated Fire Alarms (1968) 3 I.T.R. 182 (Court of Appeal). But for an example where a more legalistic narrow interpretation of "point of law" was taken, contrary to the interests of an employee: see Wagstaff v. Trade and Industrial Press, Ltd. (1968) 3 I.T.R. 1 (High Court).

black letter of the statute and, as we shall see, to more general legal doctrines.

The first point is easily illustrated throughout the reports. These are the cases, where, without doubt, the wingmen are kept in check by the legal chairman. For example, the act permits an employee who is not dismissed but who is laid off for four consecutive weeks to claim a payment, so long as he "terminates his contract of employment by a week's notice at least when claiming a payment" (sec. 6 (3)(a)). Where an employee gave notice in writing on a Monday to take effect on a Saturday the tribunal rejected the claim. The "application fails on this single point of technicality based on the length of his notice.[4] Similarly, it is often important for workers to establish continuity of employment. Two years of continuous service are needed to qualify for a payment; and payments vary with service (half a week's normal pay for each year between 18 and 21 years; one week's pay per year between 21 and 40; one and a half week's pay per year from 40 to 65, with a maximum of 20 years' service and £40 a week [$96]). "Continuity" was defined in the Act of 1963, and provision is made for preserving it where a "trade or business or an undertaking . . . is transferred from one person to another," and the employee goes on working there (Contracts of Employment Act, 1963, Schedule 1, para 10 (2)) and section 13 of the 1965 Act makes similar provision for a change of "ownership of a business." In *Dallow Industrial Properties Ltd.* v. *Else*[5] the workers were employed by JI, Ltd., at a factory in Luton. In 1962 the manufacturing business of JI, Ltd., was transferred to Bristol and the factory premises put up for sale. Pending the sale the company used the premises for storage, and the respondents were employed there, one as a maintenance worker and the other as a security officer. In 1964 the factory premises were sold to the appellants. The respondents entered their employ but after 101 weeks were dismissed. An Industrial Tribunal awarded each of the respondents a redundancy payment, having decided that their employment with JI, Ltd., and the appellants was to be regarded as continuous. The appellants appealed. The High Court decided that the tribunal had erred. There had been no transfer of an undertaking, because that required a transfer of at

---

[4] *Homson* v. *F.M.S. (Farm Projects), Ltd.* (1967) 2 I.T.R. 326.

[5] (1967) 2 I.T.R. 304 (High Court). See too *Ault* v. *Gregory* (1967) 2 I.T.R. 302 (a separate part of the business sold) and *Rencoule* v. *Hunt* (1967) A I.T.R. (Court of Session: transfer of whole business). [The same approach is subsequently to be found in *Bandey* v. *Penn* [1968] 1 All E.R. 1187; *Kenmir* v. *Frizzell* (1968) 3 I.T.R. 159; *Chapman* v. *Wilkinson* (1968) 3 I.T.R. 39; *Lloyd* v. *Brassey* [1968] 2 All E.R. 1228 (all High Court).]

least "a separate and self-contained part" of an enterprise. All the sellers did, said the court,

> was to sell to Dallow some real property which had been used for the purposes of their trade and which Dallows were using for the purposes of an entirely different business, namely the management and disposition of factory premises. . . .
>
> In order to come within Section 13(1) there must be a change of ownership, not merely in an asset of a business as in this case, but a change of ownership in the combination of operations carried on by the trader or by the non-trading body of persons, and there can only be a change of ownership in a business or part of a business, including business activity in the sense which I have construed it, if what is transferred is a separate and self-contained part of the operations of the transferor in which assets, stock in trade and the like are engaged.

This is our first example of the High Court restricting, in an appeal on a point of law, the liberal tendencies of the tribunal at first instance. It will be noticed that, as soon as a problem of interpretation of the statutes is in issue, the High Court is seized of a point of "law."

Common-law questions can come before the tribunals in a variety of ways. For example, under section 2(2) of the 1965 Act, an employee is not entitled to a redundancy payment if his employer dismisses him "being entitled to terminate his contract of employment without notice," that is, where the worker's breach merits summary dismissal at common law.[6] Thus, where a skilled engraver undertook work for competitors of his employers during working time, he was held to be rightly dismissed for misconduct. The case was argued by a barrister and a solicitor; and the decision must have been largely that of the legal chairman, for it turned (apart from a conflict of evidence on the facts) on common-law notions of misconduct.[7] The same result occurs if the employee is dismissed for regular bad timekeeping.[8] But here the High Court has restrained the tribunals in a more general manner. Where, for example, the union and the men objected to an employer, who reduced hours of work from 40 to 32½ per week, on the grounds that he was in breach of the collective agreement, negotiations failed

---

[6] But if the employer gives notice here, he must then specify in writing that he is entitled to dismiss summarily: sec. 2(2)(c).

[7] *Crowe* v. *Lewden Metal Products, Ltd.* (1967) 2 I.T.R. 68.

[8] *Essen* v. *Vanden Plas, Ltd.* (1966) 1 I.T.R. 186; *Cases*, p. 220, where the tribunal pointed out that section 2(2) is otiose because in such a case the employee is not dismissed "by reason of redundancy" within section 1 (discussed below). [See too *Hindle* v. *Percival Boats, Ltd.* (1968) 3 I.T.R. 192 (High Court: employees dismissed in a redundancy situation, but for the reason that they were too slow at their work.)]

to solve the problem, and the employer finally dismissed the men. The tribunal gave only a very short decision saying merely that the men were not redundant but the dispute arose by reason of the alleged breach of the collective agreement "which is not within the jurisdiction of the tribunal." The High Court remitted the case to the tribunal for fuller reasons, the present decision being "short, very unilluminating and certainly not the full reasons which a tribunal of the sort was supposed to give." Probably the tribunal had meant to find that the dismissal was for misconduct; but they had not even found the exact terms of the employment contracts, and "it had been assumed that the trade agreement formed some part of them."[9] Thus the High Court enforces strictly the rule that tribunals must give reasoned decisions.

A problem touching on the common law can arise in connection with "continuity." A firm in 1966 wished to "lay off" temporarily an employee who had worked continuously for them since 1964. The union official pointed out that the collective agreement made no provision for suspension. After this conversation, the employers dismissed the man but three weeks later offered him work again, which he refused because he had found a better job nearer home. The tribunal, by a majority, upheld the claim for a payment, holding that this was truly a "dismissal" within the act.[10] They remarked:

> Layoff is a common feature of employment in certain industries but seems to be almost unknown to the common law. . . . The right to lay off an employee may arise by usage of trade; or as an implied condition of the contract of employment and modifying it to meet conditions not foreseen by either party.

These are plainly the tones of the legal chairman; and indeed at one point he refers to the authority of a common-law case (which would not have been presented *to* him in argument, since the case was argued by a union official and the company manager). The same strict interpretation can sometimes work to the disadvantage of an employee; as in the case of a skilled polisher dismissed in 1959, whose employment had been continuous since 1935. He was told to come back in a fortnight, when he was reengaged, shortly afterward getting his old job as a polisher back again. In 1966 he was dismissed for redundancy. The tribunal felt compelled to hold that nothing in the schedule of the 1963 Act could avoid treating the 1959 dismissal as a rupture of his

---

[9] *Hanson* v. *Wood, The Times,* November 2, 1967 (1968) 3 I.T.R. 46.
[10] *Sneddon* v. *Ivorycrete, Ltd.* (1967) 2 I.T.R. 538.

continuity, so that the calculation of his redundancy payment was based on only four years of service.[11]

Many of the cases in which the wingmen's influence may be detected have concerned not the right to a redundancy payment but this computation of the exact sum to be paid. Of these a number have turned on the interpretation of what is the amount of a "week's pay" on which the computation is to be based. One ingredient in the calculation is often the "normal working hours." The effect of the Act of 1963 (schedule 2, para. 1) is that if there are fixed hours of work and voluntary overtime, then the only hours of work that are to be considered are the fixed hours. On the other hand, if the contract provides for compulsory overtime on top of the fixed period, then the total period for which the workman is contractually bound to work, whether at ordinary rates of pay or at overtime, is to be taken as the normal working hours. In some cases the tribunals have been quick to regard overtime as "compulsory," thereby increasing the amounts due;[12] but in 1967 the High Court checked this tendency in a case where the collective agreement in the building industry, referred to in the written particulars of employment, established "normal weekly working hours" as 40.[13] A Joint Shop Stewards Negotiating Committee negotiated site agreements with the employers on various matters, including overtime which the employers wanted to encourage to combat absenteeism. After one such agreement, a notice went up on the site stating:

> Following agreement with the stewards representing our operatives, and as approved by the resident engineer, the following working hours will be introduced on Monday, 22nd March, 1965, the overtime being calculated on the basis of a five day week in accordance with the work-

---

[11] *Lane* v. *Wolverhampton Die Casting, Ltd.* (1967) 2 I.T.R. 120. [But subsequently a rather more liberal approach was evinced by the High Court in *Hunter* v. *Smith's Dock* [1968] 2 All E.R. 81 (above chap, 2 n. 34).]

[12] See *Pioli* v. *B.T.R., Ltd.* (1966) 1 I.T.R. 255; *O'Connor* v. *Montrose Canned Foods, Ltd.* (1966) 1 I.T.R. 171. [See too *Country Bake, Ltd.,* v. *Ministry of Labour* (1968) 3 I.T.R. 166.]

[13] *Turriff Construction, Ltd.,* v. *Bryant* (1967) 2 I.T.R. 292. See too the High Court in *B.T.R., Ltd.,* v. *Spicknell* (1967) 2 I.T.R. 298, and *Pearson and Workman* v. *William Jones, Ltd.* (1967) 2 I.T.R. 471 (interpreting the agreements in the engineering industry to mean that overtime was not compulsory and not part of "normal working hours" for redundancy calculations). A remarkable decision was given by the High Court in *Loman & Henderson* v. *Merseyside Transport* (1968) 3 I.T.R. 108, where a local agreement referred to a working week of some 68 hours but the national agreement established a basic 40 hour week. The court incorporated the latter into the worker's contract, calling the first a "gentleman's agreement" which could have no legal effect at all. For criticism of this in the light of the *Donovan Report's* recommendations, see (1969) 32 M.L.R., p. 99.

ing rule agreement. . . . The average working week will total 51 hours, the average pay, under civil engineering rules, being 58½ hours.

The tribunal had concluded that this meant the calculation had to be based upon a 51-hour week; but the High Court allowed an appeal against their decision. The Lord Chief Juctice said of the notices:

> I myself find it impossible to say that they can be construed, because it is partly a question of construction, as a variation of the contract of employment so as to compel any of these men to work for 51 hours. It seems to me that the only way in which these documents can be construed is on the basis that the employers, who were behind with their programme, were suffering from absenteeism, were eager to get the men to work longer hours; equally the shop stewards, who were being very cooperative in the matter, were expressing their willingness to persuade the men to co-operate and to work longer, but it was to be on the basis of co-operation and not as a matter of contract.
>
> One asks oneself what would be the reaction of any of these respondents if they were told when they had not worked for 51 hours in any week that they were in breach of their contract, particularly when one realises that not one of these seven respondents ever did work 51 hours a week every week. . . .
>
> For my part I think that any one of these respondents would have been staggered if they had been told that they were in breach of contract because they had only done that amount of work. . . . At the most, the trade unions were co-operating and were in effect saying: we will not complain as guardians of the workmen if you seek to get them to work for 51 hours.

There is no doubt, however, that three questions dominate the work of the tribunals. In our analysis of the sample of decisions mentioned earlier, we took a subsample of 989 decisions to test the frequency of the issues arising. Out of a total of 1,082 issues argued in those cases during 1966, we found that 803 (or over 75 percent) fell under only three heads:

(1) Whether there had been a "dismissal" within the meaning of section 3 (1) of the act (165 issues);

(2) Whether a dismissal had occurred "by reason of redundancy" within the meaning of section 1 (1) and (2) (405 issues); and

(3) Whether an offer of another job had been made within the terms of section 2 (4), especially whether it was "suitable employment in relation to the employee" and he had "unreasonably refused that offer" (233 issues).

No other single issue arose more than 40 times in the 989 decisions. It seems proper, therefore, to conclude this chapter by concentrating upon the decisions that relate to the three dominant issues. It is thought that they also illustrate the tendencies listed earlier (on p. 258). In addition, they highlight the difficulty sometimes felt in finding any coherence in the decisions of tribunals as a whole. Concern over this matter led to a Parliamentary question on May 1, 1967, asking the Minister of Labour what action he proposed to take to ensure that the tribunals adhered to common principles and criteria, to which the reply ran:

> The Industrial Tribunals are independent judicial bodies and it would not be proper . . . to attempt to influence their decisions. Published reports of selected decisions, with the reasons, are available to all chairmen and members of the tribunals. The selection is made by the Presidents of the Tribunals in conjunction with a legal editor, and the reports include all decisions of the High Court and Court of Session on appeal on a point of law. I understand that the Presidents of the Tribunals also hold discussions with the chairmen which are helpful in achieving consistency.

If we examine the three issues listed above, the first two go very closely with one another and may be discussed together. Dismissal is defined by section 3 to include situations in which

(1) the contract under which he is employed by the employer is terminated by the employer, whether it is so terminated by notice or without notice, or

(2) where under that contract he is employed for a fixed term, that term expires without being renewed under the same contract, or

(3) the employee terminates that contract without notice in circumstances (not falling within section 10 (4) of this act) such that he is entitled so to terminate it by reason of the employer's conduct.[14]

To qualify for a payment the employee must have been continuously employed for the 104-week period and then "dismissed by his employer by reason of redundancy" (or else laid off or put on short time for certain stated periods). Section 1 (2) provides:

> For the purposes of this Act an employee who is dismissed shall be taken to be dismissed by reason of redundancy if the dismissal is attributable wholly or mainly to
> (a) the fact that his employer has ceased, or intends to cease, to carry on the business for the purposes of which the employee was employed by him, or has ceased, or intends to cease, to carry on that business in the place where the employee was so employed, or
> (b) the fact that the requirements of that business for employees to carry out work of a particular kind, or for employees to carry out work

---

[14] Section 10(4) excludes a lockout from this definition.

of a particular kind in the place where he was so employed, have ceased or diminished or are expected to cease or diminish. . . .

Furthermore, section 9 (2) establishes:

(a) a person's employment during any period shall, unless the contrary is proved, be presumed to have been continuous;
(b) an employee who has been dismissed by his employer shall, unless the contrary is proved, be presumed to have been so dismissed by reason of redundancy. . . .

This presumption places the burden on the employer of proving that a dismissal did *not* take place by reason of redundancy. Thus, one finds employers leading evidence to show that an employee was dismissed because of illness and advancing age; or, in the case of a secretary, because of her relationship with a director which led to her knowing too much about aspects of the business; or because of personal differences which had arisen between the employee and his employers; or because it was shown that the employers wanted to repossess a flat that went with the job.[15] In all these cases, the tribunals accepted the employers' evidence, and, therefore, (whether or not the *situation* was one of redundancy) had to hold that the dismissal had not arisen by *reason* of redundancy, so that the employers had a good reason for not paying. The statute places this odd task of judging motivation on the tribunal. On the other hand, the tribunals have not felt able to escape from the interpretation of the act which places the burden of proving a dismissal in the first place on the *employee*.[16] Thus, where an applicant left the employment because he was unwilling to perform extra duties, although the tribunal was satisfied that a situation of redundancy had arisen because the need for work of that kind had diminished, they were not satisfied that he had been forced to leave and therefore "dismissed."[17] Similarly, we have already noted the importance

---

[15] *Ross* v. *Alex. Campbell Ltd.* (1966) 1 I.T.R. 189; *Howarth* v. *Delta Bureau* (1966) 1 I.T.R. 568; *Morrison* v. *Rowen Engineering, Ltd.* (1967) 2 I.T.R. 211; and *Arnold* v. *Thomas Harrington, Ltd.* (1967) 2 I.T.R. 467 (the last on appeal to High Court). [See too for a technical decision defeating the burden of proof placed upon the employer: *Styles & Son, Ltd.*, v. *Saunders* (1968) 3 I.T.R. 126 (High Court). In this case, a one-eyed carpenter refused to move to more dusty place of work. The High Court, reversing the tribunal, held that there was no evidence of redundancy; the notion of a "particular kind of work" was again given a meaning inimical to liberal awards of redundancy payments; the employee was held to have refused to transfer to the new site for "personal reasons of his own," despite the increased risk to his eye.]
[16] *Connop* v. *Unit Metal, Ltd.* (1966) 1 I.T.R. 486.
[17] *Cummings* v. *Jas. Shepherd & Son* (1967) 2 I.T.R. 401.

of an order to the employee to work in a different place. Various decisions have had to interpret whether this was proved to be a dismissal, or whether it was only a reasonable lawful order within the terms of an employment contract under which the worker was engaged and could be required to move his place of work.[18]

The tribunals have found themselves constricted by sundry other technicalities in the act on such questions. To mention only one, section 4 provides that where an employer gives notice of dismissal, an employee who wishes to leave to go to another job before the end of that notice will still be entitled to a redundancy payment if he gives due notice to terminate on his side (which may be a shorter period than the employer has to give, e.g., under the Act of 1963, above, p. 23). But this section only operates if the worker gives his notice in writing within the "obligatory" period of the employer's notice, that is, the period the employer is bound by law to give. Therefore, in one case where the employer was bound to give only four weeks' notice but actually gave two months, an employee who gave his week's notice to leave early lost his payment because he gave it before the "obligatory" four weeks had begun to run.[19] In another case an employee similarly placed lost his payment for the further reason that he had given a *verbal* notice, which fell outside section 4.[20] In such cases the tribunals are given no discretion by the act and have to reach technical decisions which must leave the applicants disgruntled.

The signs of stress felt by tribunals placed in such a legal straitjacket—especially, one suspects, felt by the wingmen—can be seen in liberal decisions which go beyond the strict words of the act. Here it has been, and will be, the unhappy but inevitable function of the High Court to curb the enthusiasm of the tribunals and reverse their decisions. Two illustrations suffice. In *Morton Sundour Fabrics, Ltd.,* v. *Shaw*,[21] the respondent was employed by the appellants as a foreman in their velvet department. He was entitled to 28 days' notice if they

---

[18] See *Noquet* v. *Essex Publishing, Ltd.* (1966) 1 I.T.R. 160; and other decisions mentioned in *Cases*, p. 224. See too, however, *McCulloch Ltd.* v. *Moore* (1967) 2 I.T.R. 289, discussed above, p. 26. [See now: *Bective Electrical, Ltd.,* v. *Warren* (1968) 3 I.T.R. 119: decision of tribunal overturned by High Court where electrician had refused to take work at alternative site, the court holding that the employers had by "custom" power to require the employee "within reason to go where he was sent."]

[19] *Phillips* v. *Morganite Carbon, Ltd.* (1967) 2 I.T.R. 53.

[20] *Armit* v. *McLaughlan* (1966) 1 I.T.R. 280.

[21] (1967) 2 I.T.R. 84. [See too *Saunders* v. *Paladin Coachworks, Ltd.* (1968) 3 I.T.R. 51 (High Court): employee who was ill entitled to treat wrongful act of employer as dismissal, but he returned to work on recovering and then gave one week's notice; *held* he was not "dismissed" within the Act of 1965.]

wished to dismiss him. In March 1966, the appellants decided to close down the velvet department and told the respondent of this and that his employment would cease, but they did not specify when that would occur. With their help, the respondent made arrangements to move to other employment and he gave the appellants notice on March 24, terminating his employment on April 22. On that date he left and subsequently made an application to an Industrial Tribunal for a redundancy payment. The tribunal awarded him a payment, finding that the appellants had dismissed him when they informed him of the intended closure of the velvet department. The tribunal said:

> We are satisfied that the respondent was definitely told that his services would not be required when his department closed, which it definitely would do at some date not then fixed and that no alternative employment would be available to him.

This decision was plainly sound in policy. Good industrial relations make it desirable that employers should give long warnings of redundancy dismissal; and an employee should not be penalized for having both a good employer and the initiative to look for another job after warning of impending dismissal. Nevertheless, the High Court felt compelled to allow an appeal in law against the tribunal's decision. There had been no "dismissal" (though there clearly was a redundancy situation). Widgery, J., said for the court:

> This is not solely a matter of fact; it involves questions of law as well. It is the law, as I understand it, that just as a tenancy determined by notice to quit requires a certain amount of particularity in the notice, so are there certain formalities about the type of notice necessary to determine a contract of employment. The notice may be a peremptory notice, sometimes referred to as a dismissal without notice, but if it is to operate on a future day the notice must specify that date, or at least contain facts from which that date is ascertainable.
>
> As a matter of law an employer cannot dismiss his employee by saying "I intend to dispense with your services at some time in the coming months." In order to terminate the contract of employment the notice must either specify the date or contain material from which that date is positively ascertainable. It is, I think, evident from what the Tribunal has found that nothing which the employers in this case said to Mr. Shaw in the early days of March could possibly be interpreted as specifying a date upon which he was to go, or as giving material upon which such a date might be ascertained. It was on its face not inappropriately described by Mr. Henry in his argument to us as a warning of what was to come. If that is the true position, then nothing done by the employers at the beginning of March operated to terminate the contract of employment, and it would follow that the actual terminating event was the

notice given by Mr. Shaw later that month and not any action taken by the employers. That is a result achieved by applying the strict principles of law to this case, as in my judgment they clearly must be applied.

A similar reversal of the tribunal took place in *North Riding Garages, Ltd.*, v. *Butterwick*[22] where a worker was employed as workshop manager at a garage that was the subject of a "take-over" by the appellant employers in 1965. He had worked at the garage for 30 years and had slowly achieved his present position. On January 15, 1966, he was given notice terminating his employment and after his dismissal he claimed a redundancy payment. At the hearing before the tribunal, the appellants contended that they had dismissed the respondent because he was inefficient and did not measure up to the standards they required of him, but the tribunal found that the appellants' requirements for a workshop manager with the duties the respondent had previously undertaken had ceased when they reorganized the garage and a redundancy payment was awarded to the respondent. The High Court reversed the decision, saying that the tribunal had misunderstood the meaning of section 1(2)(b). The court declared:

> For the purpose of this Act an employee who remains in the same kind of work is expected to adapt himself to new methods and techniques and cannot complain if his employer insists on higher standards of efficiency than those previously required; but if new methods alter the nature of the work required to be done it may follow that no requirement remains for employees to do work of the particular kind which has been superseded and that they are truly redundant. . . .
>
> If one looks at the primary facts disclosed by the evidence in this case it is difficult to see what is the particular kind of work in which a requirement for employees has ceased or diminished. The vehicle workshop remained, as did the requirement for a workshop manager, and we do not understand the Tribunal to have found that the volume of repair work had diminished to such an extent as to make the respondent's dismissal wholly or mainly attributable to that fact. The only possible conclusion which appears to us to have been open to the Tribunal on the evidence was that the respondent was dismissed because he could not do his job in accordance with the new methods and new standards required by the appellants.
>
> The Tribunal seems to base its decision on the fact that a requirement for a workshop manager "of the old type" had ceased. . . .

---

[22] (1967) 2 I.T.R. 229. [The restrictive approach apparent in the Butterwick case has been confirmed by *Arnold* v. *Thos. Harrington, Ltd.* [1967] 2 All E.R. 866; *Styles & Son, Ltd.*, v. *Saunders* (1968) 3 I.T.R. 126; and *Stride* v. *Moore (Metal Spinners), Ltd.* (1968) 3 I.T.R. 117 (High Court): employee dismissed for inefficiency, and replaced by worker previously made redundant, not entitled to payment.]

We think that the Tribunal has fallen into error by applying the wrong test in that they have not looked at the overall requirements of the business but at the allocation of duties between individuals. It is irrelevant that the duties of the new manager are not identical with the duties formerly undertaken by the respondent if the overall requirements of the business are unchanged.

Here the High Court can only be said to have replaced the tribunal's policy with its own; for neither interpretation is demanded by section 1(2)(b)—and both are possible. The act certainly says nothing about the obligation of an employee to "adapt himself to new methods and techniques" or the "overall requirements of the business." In the Butterwick case, English labor law had its first encounter with a problem that has beset some other systems with labor courts, the subjection of those courts to the jurisdiction and policies of the ordinary judiciary by way of appeal. The Butterwick decision has had a most restricting effect upon the act. For example, in the case where the employer dismissed a motor fitter employee because he wished to repossess the flat occupied by him, he also decided to close down an emergency breakdown service which he could run only because the fitter lived in the flat over the garage. The tribunal and the High Court held that this was not the cessation of "work of a particular kind." The general work was that of motor fitter, and the emergency work was no more than a part of that; the requirements of the overall business for fitters had not declined.

A similar set of problems can be seen in the cases surrounding the other major issue to come before the tribunals. This issue concerns section 2(4) which provides:

> An employee shall not be entitled to a redundancy payment by reason of dismissal if before the relevant date (the dismissal) the employer has made to him an offer in writing to renew his contract of employment or to re-engage him under a new contract, so that . . . the provisions . . . as to the capacity and place in which he would be employed, and as to the other terms and conditions of his employment, would differ (wholly or in part) from the corresponding provisions of the contract as in force immediately before his dismissal, but
> (a) the offer constitutes an offer of suitable employment in relation to the employee, and
> (b) the renewal or re-engagement would take effect on or before the relevant date or not later than four weeks after that date, and the employee has unreasonably refused that offer.

The tribunals have had no alternative but to say that the burden of providing unsuitability of the employment or the reasonableness of the refusal is on the employee.[23] On the other hand, the restrictions of the technicalities of the section do not here always work to the disadvantage of the employee. Thus an allied section (section 3(2)(b)) provides that in the case of such an offer as is described by section 2(4) the employee shall not be taken to be dismissed if he is actually reengaged; but an employee is able to continue in the employment and still claim his redundancy payment in such a case if the employer has failed to take the precaution of making the offer *in writing*.[24]

On the questions of "reasonableness" and "suitability of employment," the tribunals' decisions are hard to classify. Unlike the statute on unemployment benefit (which establishes certain refusals of suitable employment as a disqualifying event for benefit, but sets out the most elaborate and restricted definition of "suitable" for that purpose),[25] no guidance is given the tribunals by way of definition in the 1965 statute. There has been, perhaps, a tendency in 1967 toward toughness. For example, a building worker in Scotland was held to have refused unreasonably a job at a site that would allow him to return home only one weekend every six weeks when his doctor had advised that he should be able to get home every night;[26] and a coal face worker was held to have unreasonably refused a job at another colliery where he would have started at only 75 percent of his previous earnings.[27] In other cases, the tribunals have been quick to seize on loss of earnings (though not loss of overtime opportunities) or fringe benefits or even loss of status as factors making the alternative job unsuitable or the refusal of the employee not unreasonable.[28] Moreover, in a very large number of cases the tribunals have taken account of family circumstances to judge the suitability of the job for that employee and the reasonableness of the refusal. Thus an employee offered work in the North of England instead of the South East was held to be entitled to a payment when he refused, the tribunal finding:

> The applicant is married, has a rented house in South-East England, a family of two boys aged 16 and 17, the younger still at school. His

---

[23] *Collier* v. *Pollard, Ltd.* (1966) 1 I.T.R. 399.

[24] *Dubiel* v. *William Park, Ltd.* (1967) 2 I.T.R. 268. The offer must give details of the new job: *Marriot* v. *Oxford District Co-op.*, *The Times*, December 7, 1967 (High Court).

[25] Now National Insurance Act, 1965, sec. 22(5); see *Cases*, p. 119; pp. 210–215 give decisions of the insurance commissioner under this provision.

[26] *MacGregor* v. *William Tawse, Ltd.* (1967) 2 I.T.R. 198.

[27] *Duffin* v. *N.C.B.* (1967) 2 I.T.R. 198.

[28] See *Sheppard* v. *N.C.B.* (1966) 1 I.T.R. 177; *Ramage* v. *Harper-Mackay, Ltd.* (1966) 1 I.T.R. 503; *Skillen* v. *Eastwoods Froy, Ltd.* (1967) 2 I.T.R. 112; and *Wedderburn* v. *King* (1967) 2 I.T.R. 325.

wife objected to his going away so far. . . . He wished to accept this employment on Tees-side but had to decide whether to risk breaking up his marriage by domestic upset or whether to forego the job. In this difficult position he made the choice he thought was right, to give up the employment. On all the facts of the case, we are satisfied that it was not an unreasonable refusal of the offer and in relation to him this was not an offer of suitable employment.[29]

Similarly the tribunals have taken account of a desire not to move away from a sick father; a wife's refusal to move which would "break up the marriage"; a wife's need to go home to care for a semi-invalid husband; the children of the employee being at a "crucial stage" of their education and about to take examinations; the absence of a suitable school for the children except at long traveling distance from the new place of work.[30] In a decision in 1967, a tribunal went so far as to say that it would take account, not merely of family matters (the wife's health), which made the job (night-shift work) unsuitable, but would also consider the *reason* for the redundancy itself in judging the attitude and reasonableness of the employee:

> If it is forced on a business by adverse trading conditions . . . it may be that there would be less reason for refusing the work the management were able to offer. On the other hand if it arises from rationalisation or automation or reorganization to promote economy or efficiency it might be thought that the Act was intended to provide for just those situations and perhaps a refusal might be more reasonable.[31]

On the other hand decisions can be found which take a much more hardhearted view of domestic complications. In one, the employment was considered "suitable" despite the fact that it meant a move of some sixty miles, and the wife was so adamant in opposing the move that she found herself a job to support herself and the family (a daughter of 17, working, and a son of 11 at school); but the tribunal did not have to face the reasonableness of a refusal, since the offer had not been made *before* the termination of employment as section 2(4) demands.[32] Furthermore, a wife was held unreasonably to have refused an offer even though the new job would have prevented her from re-

---

[29] *Rawe.* v. *Power Gas Corpn., Ltd.* (1966) 1 I.T.R. 154.

[30] *Silver* v. *J.E.L. Group* (1966) 1 I.T.R. 238; *Dunn* v. *James Jack* (1967) 2 I.T.R. 267; *White* v. *John Boulding, Ltd.* (1966) 1 I.T.R. 446; *Bainbridge* v. *Westinghouse, Ltd.* (1966) 1 I.T.R. 55; and *Storris* v. *Martin Ltd.* (1967) 2 I.T.R. 143.

[31] *Freer* v. *Kayser Bondor, Ltd.* (1967) 2 I.T.R. 4.

[32] *Rose* v. *Shelley & Partners, Ltd.* (1966) 1 I.T.R. 169.

turning home at midday to prepare a meal for her husband who was unwell and on a strict diet.[33]

Few of these cases have so far reached appeal. But in both jurisdictions those that have indicate a similarly strict approach to that taken above. In England, for example, the High Court heard a case in which a toolroom lathe operator had become redundant. The company offered him work (with an associated company) in their toolroom at a higher rate of pay. The respondent refused the offer, and was dismissed. He applied to the Industrial Tribunal for a redundancy payment. The tribunal decided that the respondent had not been unreasonable in refusing the offer because the work offered was in a "contract toolroom" where he would have been under pressure to finish each job in a certain time. This would cause him to worry and, in view of his cerebral thrombiotic condition, would be detrimental to his health. The High Court quashed the award on the ground that the evidence before the tribunal upon which it could hold that the new work place was a "contract toolroom," was insufficient. The court came to this conclusion after a close reading of the affidavits, and even a note of the proceedings made by one of the parties. It might be thought that a tribunal would be the best judge as to the facts presented in evidence before it; but here the court was prepared to say that there was such inadequate evidence before the tribunal that it had erred in *law* by concluding that in *fact* it was a "contract toolroom." Lord Parker, C.J., concluded:

> As it seems to me, this decision could only be justified if this was a contract toolroom in the sense of a room where men worked on a production line. Not only is there no evidence at all of that, but such evidence as there is is to the contrary, namely that it was a contract toolroom in the sense only that work was measured there for the purposes of pay.[34]

An even more technical decision was reached in 1967 by the Court

---

[33] *Cassidy* v. *South Mills, Ltd.* (1967) 2 I.T.R. 272.

[34] *Wolverhampton Die Casting, Ltd.,* v. *Kitson* (1967) 2 I.T.R. 362. [But the High Court seems to be loathe to upset the tribunals' decision on these questions: see *John Laing & Son, Ltd.,* v. *Best* (1968) 3 I.T.R. 3 (employee required to go to another place of work held to be "dismissed" and to have refused reasonably the offer of alternative employment, largely on the ground that the traveling time would be much longer). See, however, *O'Brien, Pritchard & Browning* v. *Associated Fire Alarms* (1968) 3 I.T.R. 182 (Court of Appeal: question whether employment contract included an implied term allowing employer to move workers to new site held to be a question of "law." Court of Appeal reversed the tribunal *and* the High Court in holding that employees were dismissed).

of Session in Scotland in *Carron Company* v. *Robertson*.[35] The worker had been employed for 20 years as a patternmaker at a foundry which was closed in 1966 when he was dismissed. The parent company of the employers offered alternative employment (an "associated" company being adequate for the purposes of section 2(4) by virtue of other sections of the act). He refused, mainly because he would lose "staff" status at the new works and all the advantages that went with it. The tribunal considered the question of reasonableness, decided that he had not been unreasonable in refusing, and awarded him a payment. The employer appealed. The three judges took rather different views. The Lord President considered that the nature of the work and its status were relevant to the suitability of the employment, *not* the reasonableness of refusal. Suitability, in his view, was an "objective matter" concerning the jobs. Reasonableness went to "personal objections." Lord Guthrie and Lord Migdale took rather different views. The former said:

> The problem must be viewed from two stand-points. From the first stand-point, the offer is surveyed (keeping in view the circumstances of the employee). From the second stand-point, the action of the employee is considered (keeping in view the circumstances of the offer). The tribunal must decide whether this particular person acted unreasonably. Now suitability is an imprecise term, but I accept that in deciding as to the suitability of employment in relation to an employee, one must consider not only the nature of the work, hours and pay, the employee's strength, training, experience and ability, but such matters as status in the premises of the employer and benefits flowing from that status. For the present I also assume, as invited to do by counsel for the appellants, that, having had these matters in view, the tribunal reached the conclusion that the emploment offered was suitable in relation to the respondent. But that does not, in my opinion, infer that the tribunal was not entitled to hold that the respondent was unreasonable in refusing the offer. A decision as to the reasonableness or unreasonableness of his refusal depends on a consideration of the whole circumstances in which he would have been placed if he had accepted the offer. These circumstances include such personal matters as the demands upon him of his duties towards his family. They also, in my opinion, include the conditions of the employment offered. These conditions might be such as not to render the employment unsuitable as a job for him, but yet such as to justify a reasonable man in his position in turning down the offer.

Lord Migdale took a middle view, saying:

> In my opinion the Tribunal would be entitled to find that the offer

---

[35] (1967) 2 I.T.R. 484.

was one of suitable employment and then find on the same facts that the refusal was not unreasonable. . . . I see nothing illogical in finding by the Tribunal that the new offer is suitable and at the same time that the workman's refusal is reasonable. The question of suitability is mainly objective while the question of reasonableness is to be viewed subjectively.

The Lord President and Lord Migdale concluded that the tribunal had erred in law because, in the words of the latter: "It looks as if the tribunal had dealt only with the question on the issue of reasonableness. I do not think this is in accordance with the section." Therefore the matter should be remitted to the tribunal for a specific finding on the question of suitability. Lord Guthrie did not think there had been an error of law; but he *agreed* that the tribunal should be asked to make a specific finding on the point and the case remitted for that purpose!

Since the tribunal had already determined the question of unreasonableness, a finding on suitability could not possibly affect the outcome of the case, and the Court of Session's decision can be regarded only as the height of legal technicality. Together with the other decisions that have been cited, however, it serves yet again to point the moral that appeals to ordinary courts (even if restricted to questions of "law") tend to destroy the flexibility and discretion which is one of the reasons for adding wingmen to the chairmen in the tribunals below. It is curious that Britain should have made the mistake of allowing such a broad avenue of appeal to the ordinary courts. A precedent pointed the other way. When in 1946 a new national insurance scheme was set up for social security (including industrial injuries in place of the workmen's compensation legislation), it was enacted that disputes should be decided by commissioners from whom no appeal lies to the ordinary courts. The functions of the latter are restricted to the prerogative orders which ensure that the commissioners do not exceed their jurisdiction. Since the Tribunals and Inquiries Act, 1958, however, the old common-law orthodoxy has crept back into legislation, namely the concept that administrative tribunals must be supervised by the ordinary courts on all questions of "law." This in practice, as we have seen, means not only questions of interpretation and construction but occasionally even the assessment of evidence.

In labor law this is likely to prove an Achilles' heel. Even if the Industrial Tribunals were given new procedures to accommodate them to new tasks (such as a conciliation function, or a conciliation officer to help them, in "unjust dismissal" cases, as the N.J.A.C. report hinted; above, p. 129), the appeal on law to the High Court would severely limit their flexibility. It is perhaps ironic that these new vehicles for the greater use of judicial methods in employment disputes were acceptable to many people (including many trade unionists) in 1965 simply because they were different from those ordinary courts, which at the time were making such unfortunate interventions into labor law via the common law of tort. It is doubtful whether the experience of either employers or trade unionists in the two years that have followed has made them eager to expand their jurisdiction. The tribunals are less legalistic than the courts; but by the complexity of the statutory issues and the character of the decisions on appeal, that gap is being made to narrow. Clearly in these circumstances it will be very difficult for tribunals of this character to acquire the advantages obtained through the methods of inquiry and arbitration described in previous parts. Nor have their teeth yet been tried on any employment disputes which, although individual in form, in reality clothe collective problems. Nor have they been given tasks so far which come into conflict with the older structures of collective bargaining (for it is notorious that bargaining about redundancy was highly underdeveloped in Britain before the 1960's). If Britain is to see a greater use of legal sanction in the handling of those disputes, the tribunals are bound to be utilized in the experiment. But in truth Britain has to choose between an uncertain experiment of that kind and new initiatives pursued with patience and perseverence within the patterns of negotiated procedure, voluntary arbitration, and public inquiry, where legal sanction and lawyers make their greatest contribution to industrial life by being self-effacing rather than obtrusive.

Appendix

THE DONOVAN REPORT

GENERAL

The Report of the Royal Commission set up under the chairmanship of Lord Donovan appeared in June 1968.[1] Its central thesis confirms the work done by its research teams, namely that the formal system of industrywide agreements in Britain dealing with a narrow range of issues by formal procedures is supplemented by, and frequently in conflict with, another informal system of industrial relations (at any rate in private industry) based upon bargaining over a wider range of issues at factory-floor level and using tacit understandings rather than written agreements, the latter even more than the former refusing to distinguish "disputes over interpretation and disputes over new concessions." The commission concluded:

> What is of crucial importance is that the practices of the formal system have become increasingly empty, while the practices of the informal system have come to exert an ever greater influence on the conduct of industrial relations throughout the country; that the two systems conflict; and that the informal system cannot be forced to comply with the formal system. [para. 154]

The problem, then, is how to reform the structures of collective bargaining. On this analysis it is plain that such a reform could not be

---

[1] *Royal Commission on Trade Unions and Employers' Associations 1965–1968: Report* (CMND. 3623; H.M.S.O.).

introduced by the shortcut method merely of introducing legal sanction or legalistic methods (though, as we shall see, some commissioners retreated at one point from that conclusion). Nor could the injection of something equivalent to American "grievance arbitration" solve the problems of a structure where the very disputes procedures themselves are defective:

> The introduction of this kind of arbitration into the existing unsatisfactory procedures of most industries would solve nothing. In other countries a distinction is drawn between "disputes of right" (that is, disputes about the application of an existing collective agreement) and "disputes of interest" (disputes arising out of the negotiation of a new collective agreement or the renewal of an agreement made for a fixed term which has expired). The distinction is not at present important in Britain because most collective agreements lay down minimum standards which are improved and elaborated on by further negotiation at subsidiary levels. Moreover, shopfloor agreements are closely linked with customs and practices which are not set down in any agreement, so that at this level no clear distinction exists between disputes of right and disputes of interest. [para. 456]

After procedures have been reformed, such arbitration of disputes of right might be introduced, as indeed "it could be introduced now in companies which make their own agreements" (para. 457). The results of our study suggest that, even in company or plant agreements, it will be a long time before the distinction becomes of general importance in Britain.

The commission's major proposals for reform involve the establishment of an Industrial Relations Commission and the registration with the Department of Employment and Productivity (as the Ministry of Labour is now called) of collective agreements made by companies above a certain size. This practice would help to change collective bargaining so as to bring about a "more orderly method for workers and their representatives to exercise their influence and for this to be accomplished . . . without destroying the British tradition of keeping industrial relations out of the courts" (para. 190). Thus, although a penalty for failure to register agreements is naturally envisaged, the majority would give the I.R.C. no other major legal powers of intervention. (A minority of commissioners wished to strengthen its hand with a variety of legal powers.) A set of principles to guide the commission is proposed (para. 203); but after that it would "develop its own rules and methods" in promoting the work of reform. The I.R.C. would be involved in reconstructing industrial relations, a job that is "continuous," whereas the administration of an "incomes policy" is concerned with "short-run improvement of the country's economic position" (para. 208). Nevertheless, the commissioners approved of the "incomes policy" and their thinking was, as we shall see, plainly influenced by it.

The theme of voluntary reform prodded by new machinery such as the I.R.C. dominates the report, as does the view that solutions are more likely to be found at company or plant level than in industrywide negotiations. Thus, the report rejects the case for a new tribunal on restrictive labor practices in favor of the proper use by management of more effective factory "productivity" agreements. Similarly, very little *legal* innovation is proposed concerning either the responsibility of management or the place and role of the shop steward; but these two topics recur in the report as points of critical importance where improvement would be sought. The shop steward, for example, should have his role and rights more clearly established under a written plant agreement, and his relationship with his trade union should be made closer and clarified by new trade union rules.

NEW REMEDIES FOR INDIVIDUAL GRIEVANCES

Two proposals for new law are made here by the report. These, it must be remembered, are made in the context of more efficient "disputes procedures" in the registered plant and company agreements. The two proposals form the only amendments suggested in the individual employment relationship (apart from a few proposed changes that are long overdue, such as the prohibition of "yellow dog" clauses in an employment contract whereby the employer forbids membership in a trade union).

Dismissals

Whereas the report of the committee of the N.J.A.C. had favored the extension of voluntary procedures dealing with "unfair" dismissals (discussed above, pp. 129-149), the commission, in chapter ix of the report, preferred (with two dissentients) the early establishment of statutory tribunals. Objections to this course were firmly answered by the commission: foreign experience did not suggest that too great a legalist element would enter into workshop relations or that industrial "discipline" would be undermined; nor was there any reason to limit workers' rights to strike on such questions; nor could the commission discover any good reason to think that a flood of costly appeals would be launched. Voluntary procedures are desirable; but they do not at present provide, the commission thought, for *compensation* to be paid to employees unfairly dismissed. On the other hand, employers and trade unions might well prefer voluntary methods, and within these, the remedy of *reinstatement* could be made more readily available than under legal machinery imposed from without (see above, p. 27). Nevertheless, the commission felt that legal tribunals were necessary and desirable because they would immediately raise the floor of rights for all workers, trade unionists or not; because thereby increased protection for freedom of association could be achieved; and because voluntary procedures are not merely unsatisfactory where they exist, but are unlikely to be introduced in many areas of British industry in the measurable future (paras. 531–541). The evidence clearly supports the last point (above, p. 130).

Nevertheless, the difference between the two reports turns out to be only one of emphasis. Voluntary procedures established by collective agreements could, the commission proposes, be exempted from the new law by the minister (now the Secretary of State of Employment and Productivity) on the recommendation of the I.R.C., provided they met certain tests, including standards of decision-making and the provision of compensation where necessary (to be fixed by a tribunal, if the parties so desired). In such a case, a worker in the exempted plant (union member or not) could not be allowed any access at all to the statutory tribunals. Because, as we shall see, those workers who would have access to tribunals would have further rights of appeal to the High Court, the minister's fiat of exemption might well cause protests among minority groups dissatisfied with the procedure; but this the commission faces with equanimity. The proposal may indeed be pregnant with less injustice than the current arrangements described in chapter 7, especially if the commission is right in believing that the establishment of tribunals would help rather than hinder the evolution of new voluntary procedures.

Dismissal should be deemed to be "unfair" if it is a dismissal by reason of race, color, sex, marital status, religious or political opinion, national extraction, or social origin. These would be explosive introductions into British law (especially as regards that underprivileged group of workers—women). But another ground added to the list is of even greater importance, namely "trade union membership or activity." The employer should be obliged to prove the grounds on which he dismissed a worker, and those grounds should be regarded as "fair" only if related to the capacity or conduct of the worker or the needs of the enterprise. But the worker should be required to prove any of the special grounds listed above. The commission did not consider at length the operation of the Redundancy Payments Act, 1965, in this connection; but our survey in Part IV suggests to us that many employers might, with good advice, easily find valid grounds, such as "inefficiency," in the ordinary case (though that is not, of course, a final objection to such legislation). The report does suggest that a worker should be able to allege that his dismissal was discriminatory even if a good ostensible ground for it exists. In the case of dismissals for breach of disciplinary codes, since "it is the general practice at present for works' rules to be laid down unilaterally by management," the labor tribunal should have power to assess both the reasonableness of the rule and the seriousness of the breach. Rules drawn up after bargaining ought not to be open to such easy challenge. This proposal would, of course, dig deeply into current "managerial prerogatives" in Britain. A majority of seven commissioners go even further. They propose that an employer forced by trade union or workers' pressure in a "closed shop" unfairly to dismiss a nonunionist ought still to be liable, though the worker's reason for not joining the union ought, in certain cases, to be considered by the tribunal. (The minority favored various forms of liability on the trade union in such a case.)

The need for speed in the tribunal is underlined by the proposals that a worker should complain within *five* days of dismissal and that he should have no right merely to be suspended pending the hearing (a point in regard to which the "merits of the voluntary approach" are stressed by the report as it can provide for suspension if the parties wish, though it is our belief that this is not uniformly done at present). To the problem of delay we return below. As to remedies, the tribunals would award compensation, taking account of all the circumstances of the employee. Reinstatement should be available only where both parties agree to it; the maximum compensation should be an amount equal to two years' wages; and no "punitive" element should be included except in cases of clear discrimination.

Labor Tribunals

The report proposes that all individual employment disputes between employer and employee should be heard by labor tribunals. This proposal would exclude from the new jurisdiction collective issues arising under collective agreements (except in so far as these become incorporated into individual contracts, a provisio likely to enhance the problems canvassed (above, p. 50); and all actions for damages arising from accidents at work (currently by far the largest source of employment litigation in County and High Courts in England; see above, p. 38); and all actions between trade unions and members. Solutions for the obvious difficulties of overlapping jurisdiction with the ordinary courts are proposed by the report, frequently by leaving the plaintiff an option to sue in the ordinary court or the labor tribunal. But the latter would have exclusive jurisdiction over certain matters, for example, unfair dismissals and redundancy payments.

The commission was clearly influenced by their investigation of the French "Conseils de prud'hommes" in their proposals for the labor tribunals, although, in our view, more attention might have been paid to the fact that those courts normally have no lawyer as chairman or even as member. Thus, the report insists that each hearing should be preceded by a conciliation session in private; and that *throughout* the proceedings the tribunal should try to promote a settlement rather than adjudicate the strict rights of the parties. "Experience abroad has shown that labour tribunals can settle a very large proportion of all cases before them. There is no reason to believe that a similar result would not follow here" (para. 584). Plainly the commission foresees that, alien though it may be to the common law mind, such a process of conciliation would be essential if labor tribunals are to be accepted by British industry even with this limited jurisdiction. We think that what has gone before in this study supports that view. The proposal, however, differs from those of the N.J.A.C. committee which suggested that, if "fall back" tribunals were established, a special officer should be attached to the courts to promote conciliation. The commission thinks that the labor tribunal itself would conciliate on a "round table" basis. Two points then become critical: speed, and the composition of the tribunal.

The report proposes that the present industrial tribunals should be renamed labor tribunals and "like the present industrial tribunals . . . be established in all the larger industrial centers." We found that the present tribunals sat, at the beginning of 1968, in eighteen centers in England and Wales. The report's proposals for an increased jurisdiction, especially on unjust dismissals, suggests to us that this number would have to be raised. The proceedings, the report goes on, should be "informal and expeditious." No details of current procedure before the industrial tribunals are discussed, even though, as we have seen, specific time limits for complaints about dismissal are suggested. Our own results, presented in chapter 12, suggest that the industrial tribunals are not, at present, as "expeditious" as some commentators think (though that may not be the fault of the tribunals). With the added stage of conciliation, some proceedings might take even longer than the average redundancy payment case before the existing tribunals.

As for composition, the tribunals "would consist of a legally qualified chairman and of two lay judges"—the traditional wingmen, one from a trade union, one from an employers' panel. The report does not discuss the difficulties inherent in obtaining effective wingmen who can establish some continuity on a tribunal, without which power is bound to move centripetally to the legal chairman. It does suggest that "it would be for the chairman to conduct the proceedings," a proposal that would reinforce the same tendency. Our own observation of the existing industrial tribunals has proved to us that interventions during the proceedings by active wingmen can be most valuable. Each judgement, the report proposes, should be of the tribunal without any dissents, a practice the commission wrongly seemed to believe is invariable in the existing tribunals. The report even goes so far as to say: "It might . . . be considered whether decisions on points of law should be left to the exclusive jurisdiction of the chairman." The report discusses neither the function of the wingmen in the present tribunals, nor the role they would be expected to play in the proposed "round table" conciliation sessions.

Two further proposals, however, are made, first that legal aid must be available for the employee, second that an appeal on a "point of law" should always lie to the High Court. The first is essential, especially since the protection of such tribunals will be most often sought by workers who have no trade union assistance. But the second seems to be an unargued genuflection at the altar of legal tradition. The criticisms we would wish to make of it appear clearly in our account of such appeals in chapter 13. Appeals to ordinary courts of appeal seem to be one curse of European labor law from which no easy escape is to be found.

GRIEVANCES AND COLLECTIVE LABOR RELATIONS

We here select the more salient features of the rest of the report which touch upon our subject. They fall under three headings: the choice between legal sanction and legal machinery to promote industrial peace and the reform of collective bargaining; the types of new machinery proposed; and the suggested changes in labor law generally.

Sanction or Machinery?

The analysis made by the report leads the commission constantly back to the thought that: "If employers are seeking increased co-operation from their employees, resort to legal sanctions is not likely to produce it" (para. 315). The basic choice of the commission (sometimes unanimously; at other times, by a majority) is, in fact, always against the use of legal sanction. Thus, the use of compulsory strike ballots or legal "cooling-off" periods is rejected for dealing with the British problem of "unconstitutional" or "unofficial" strikes. Similarly, three main arguments are deployed, and developed in great detail in chapter viii, against the enforcement of collective agreements by legal sanction.

First, it is noted that employers do not now normally use their available legal redress; and for any system of legal sanctions to be useful or effective the employer must want to use it. Second, the introduction of legal sanction would, it is thought, inhibit the development of new and more efficient "disputes procedures." The present failure to preserve peace (which the commission discusses with special reference to the engineering and motor industry and the building industry[2]) are not primarily caused by shop stewards "bent on disruption" (indeed most stewards are "hard working and responsible people who are making a sincere attempt to do a difficult job"), but by an inadequacy of bargaining institutions. Trade union leaders do not view breaches of procedure agreements with indifference. But the improvement of procedures needs new cooperation; and it would be unjust to bind men legally to procedures not adequate to the tasks confronting them. Third, no system of legal sanction proposed to the commission proved to be practicable or likely to improve the structure. Broadly three schemes were discussed: (1) Sanctions against trade unions where members acted improperly. Forcing unions to discipline strikers would not, however, affect the *causes* of strikes which lie deep in the system of collective bargaining; and union "leaders do exercise discipline from time to time, but they cannot be industry's policemen." (2) Sanctions against employees individually. No scheme of either fines or damages was thought satisfactory in British conditions. The famous story of the fruitless fining of over a thousand coal miners in 1941 (above, p. 12, n. 10) was enough to deal with the first idea. We note later, however,

---

[2] The report draws upon many of the sources discussed earlier, and especially, in addition to its own research documents, upon A. Turner, G. Clack, and G. Roberts, *Labour Relations in the Motor Industry* (1967). The analysis of "Strikes and Other Industrial Action" in chapter vii of the report is too long to summarize in this section but should be consulted by those who wish to find confirmation of the analysis presented in Part II of this study. The report's criticisms of the procedures, however, in both the engineering and the building industry may be thought to go rather further than the research results demanded.

that a majority of the commission was not wholly consistent in regard to civil sanctions. (3) "Automatic" sanctions, such as loss of social security benefits or redundancy payment rights. Such sanctions are of little value in that they only "bite" long after the strike has ended; and they can be effective only once, since a worker who has once lost such rights has nothing to lose by striking. In the face of these arguments which dominate chapter viii, it is surprising to find the report later suggesting that a new situation will arise once collective bargaining has been reformed and that some kind of legal sanction (which is described as an action for damages) might then be introduced. Logically one would have thought that either the reform would be successful (in which case legal sanction would not be needed) or it would not succeed in producing new procedures (in which case sanctions would prove even more disastrous on the arguments already adduced in chapter viii).

Finally, the report suggests that section 4(4) of the Act of 1871 be repealed, and it is true to say that in that case the "ordinary" law of contract would apply at collective level to British agreements. However, it does not follow from that, as some commentators appear to have thought, that collective agreements would all become contracts.[3] As the report implies, the presumption would still be that they were not "intended" to be legally binding. It would be open to an employer (as it is today, apart from section 4(4)) to buy legal enforceability by offering a suitable economic price to the trade union. In Britain, however, the union price for this will always be a high one.

New Machinery

The report's positive recommendations concentrate, therefore, upon machinery that can help solve the causes of industrial problems rather than attack their symptoms. In addition to marginal improvements in the existing system of inquiry and arbitration (described in Part III), it proposes that the I.R.C. should be equipped to carry out inquiries into long-term industrial problems. Both in this respect and in widening the Industrial Courts Act, 1919, the commission proposes more extensive means of investigation and inquiry. It is more doubtful, however, about the value of bodies such as the Motor Industry Joint Labour Council (which it describes with what may be thought abrupt

---

[3] See the discussion in *Fair Deal at Work*, Conservative Political Centre, produced in April 1968 as the Conservative Party's approach to industrial relations, chap. 4, pp. 31–35.

brevity in paragraphs 443–446). Instead, at local level the report proposes that the minister should place on Industrial Relations Officers the duty of obtaining facts about work stoppages in an "industry region or undertaking where they are causing particular difficulties"; and the officers should have legal powers to oblige persons to give evidence (para. 448). The report acknowledges that care would be needed not to undermine agreed voluntary procedures or the authority of trade union leaders; but it does not investigate the problems of using the I.R.O.'s for this purpose. We understand that early in 1968 there were only 55 such local officers of the ministry; but that it is the intention to triple that number as soon as possible (a delicate essay in recruitment). Even with 200 I.R.O.'s, however, it may be asked whether they could act both as traditional conciliation officers; and as local midwives of training schemes and "productivity bargains"; and as local filters for informal government approval of agreements within the criteria of the "incomes' policy"; *and*, on top of all that, as "mini-Scamps" for the continuous investigation of trouble spots. It may be recalled that the ministry thought it "doubtful" that new legal powers were needed (above, p. 223).

Second, the report proposes that compulsory unilateral arbitration similar to that which prevailed between 1951 and 1958 be restored, but this time with the jurisdiction vested in the Industrial Court. As we shall see, this would probably be most important in regard to recognition of unions; and its use should, the report says, need to be sanctioned by the minister on the advice of the I.R.C. As for section 8, Terms and Conditions of Employment Act, 1959, the report would remove an obscurity by having the Industrial Court take into account "not only the particular term or condition to which the claim relates but the terms and conditions laid down by collective agreement as a whole." Even more important, the commission proposes that legislation should place "on all arbitrators an obligation to take incomes policy into account when making their awards" (para. 285), a change of fundamental significance. It is, no doubt, with this object of imposing the criteria of "short-run" political policies on all voluntary arbitration that the report goes on to state:

> It is the tradition in Britain for arbitrators to give no reasons for their awards.[4] This practice has a great deal to recommend it so long as the only object of arbitration is to resolve disputes. One or both parties to a dispute might cavil at the reasoning when they would be willing to

---

[4] As we have seen, this is not true of all arbitrators, e.g., Single Arbitrators or the Coal Industry National Reference Tribunal.

accept the award. Nevertheless the practice is incompatible with any attempt to develop a rational incomes policy. . . .

There are disputes in which no reason can be given. . . . But arbitrators should be encouraged to give reasons whenever they can, especially in major decisions on pay which are likely to be significant for the development of incomes policy, and in those cases where they do not feel able to give reasons to state so plainly. There is no need for a change in their terms of reference to enable this to be done. Arbitrators are free to give reasons if they choose. A statement from the Government, backed by the T.U.C. and the C.B.I. should be enough to put an end to the old tradition. [paras. 286–287]

These assertions appear to ignore the arguments advanced by the President of the Industrial Court, among others, for the practice, tempered by the experience of decades, of not giving reasons in most types of arbitration, at least in disputes of "interest."

As for the problem of trade union recognition, which is still a severe problem in the case of some British employers or trade unions (e.g., white-collar unions), the commission proposes that disputes should be referred to the I.R.C. rather than risk "any detailed intervention by the courts in the processes of industrial relations which appears to us to be a consequence of enforcing recognition by law as in the U.S.A." (para. 256). The I.R.C. should have certain powers (e.g., to arrange a ballot of workers if desired), but no power to enforce by legal penalties a recommendation that the employer should recognize or bargain with a trade union. On the other hand, the union would have the power to ask the I.R.C. to recommend to the minister a reference of its claims to compulsory arbitration in the Industrial Court. The commission adds that such arbitration of substantive issues would help solve the procedural problems of recognition:

First, where the employer rejects a recommendation of the Commission to grant recognition, the Commission should be empowered to recommend that the union or unions should have the right of unilaterial arbitration. This will give them at least a foothold and may encourage the employer to change his mind. Second, even where the employer accepts a recommendation to grant recognition he may still be able to evade effective bargaining, for where workers are traditionally reluctant to strike or scattered in small units so that it is difficult to bring their collective strength to bear he may be able to exploit the position to reduce bargaining to a mockery. In these circumstances the Commission should also be empowered to recommend unilateral arbitration as a means of imposing a fair settlement of the union's claims and a means to strengthen its organisation. [para. 273]

APPENDIX

Changes in Labor Law

The commission proposes that employers' associations should be separately defined from trade unions; and that such associations and employees' unions should no longer be allowed to include "temporary" combinations (a feature of the present definition which has significance for both, above, pp. 60-61, 69). It is proposed that trade unions should be under a legal obligation to register and thereby acquire a new *corporate* status, instead of being able, as at present, voluntarily to register.[5] A long chapter of the report (chapter xi) proposes new conditions for the rules and operation of registered unions. Of these the most important legally is the proposal to subject to an external "independent review body" union decisions concerning admission to, or expulsion from, membership. Furthermore, the registrar would be able to demand far more of the rule book before it was registered, for example, specific rules concerning the place of shop stewards. Although not immediately germane to our study, these points are bound to affect the mind of trade unionists in judging the rest of the report, since for the first time in British labor history these proposals would establish "official" trade unions compulsorily registered on state-imposed terms.

The changes proposed for the law of labor disputes (described in Part I) would not disturb the basic pattern. First, despite the dangers inherent in the present law where a strike notice may be often no more than notice of forthcoming breaches of workers' employment contracts, the commission recommends *against* the introduction of a doctrine of "suspension" of employment contracts in trade disputes, listing eight convincing arguments against it.[6] Paradoxically, as we have seen, no sooner was the ink dry upon the pages of the report than Lord Denning. M.R., in *Morgan* v. *Fry* suggested in the Court of Appeal that such a doctrine did, after all, exist in the common law.[7] No better example could be given of the curious mutations that can be produced

---

[5] It is, however, proposed that groups within the *existing* definition of "trade union" (above, p. 42) should continue to receive the protection of the Act of 1871 against doctrines of "restraint of trade" (above, p. 7). Thus there would be *two* types of "trade union," the new, "official" kind, and the old, tolerated species.

[6] Para. 943. Briefly the objections relate to such questions as: How to define "strikes" to which it applies? Whether other actions are included, e.g., overtime bans, go-slows? Must notice be given? Would it apply to gas, water and electricity enterprises? Would it apply in cases of "grave misconduct" by strikers and if so, what does that mean? Could strikers take other jobs? Could suspension be displaced by collective agreements or individual contracts? When would "suspension" end if the strike was never settled?

[7] [1968] 3 W.L.R. 506 (C.A.). See the discussion above, p. 18. The other lord justices in the Court of Appeal did not take this view. As already mentioned, Lord Denning, M.R., answered none of the questions posed in para. 943 of the report.

by a system of "negative" statutes overlaying a common law that is still in the control of judges. The report proposes that British industrial law should be codified under the guidance of a legal committee attached to the I.R.C. Such a proposal is welcome, if only as a way of clarifying once and for all such fundamental legal problems as the legal status of a strike notice, rather than their being left to the hazards of litigation.

Various other changes are proposed. The right to picket should extend to a right to persuade customers not to deal with an employer. The immunity of trade unions to actions in tort (above, p. 10) should not apply to acts done otherwise than in furtherance or contemplation of a trade dispute. The Act of 1965 should be retained, but the possibility of residual liabilities for conspiracy and the like should be set aside by a further statute. The disqualifications of certain workers thrown out of work by a strike from receiving state unemployment benefit should be limited in scope (a proposal of great social significance). The criminal penalties which strikers who cause danger and which gas, water, and electricity workers can, in theory, still encounter (*ante* chapter 1) should be neither extended nor repealed, the latter because repeal "involves the risk that it might be construed as an express license to do that which the criminal law now forbids" (para. 846)—an old conclusion which, in view of the desuetude into which both sections have fallen, may be attributed more to exhaustion than to the main stream of the commissioners' arguments. Again, with three dissentients, the commission would not wish to amend the definition of "trade dispute." The brief argument on this point is convincing in terms of the statutory definition; but it does not deal fully with the recent limited interpretations placed upon it by the judiciary. The proposal to retain the same golden formula for protection is, however, of great moment.

Most important still, however, are the proposals on section 3 of the Trade Disputes Act, 1906 (above, chapter 2). Unanimously the commission, seeing that judicial extensions of liability for inducing breach of commercial contract have now rendered the section only of slender value, proposes that the words "of employment" be repealed, and that all forms of inducing breach[8] of commercial contract should thereby also be protected in trade disputes (para. 893). But a majority of

---

[8] Again, the commission did not even consider liability for "interference" short of inducing *breach;* yet this was imposed by the High Court in *Torquay Hotels, Ltd.,* v. *Cousins* [1968] 3 All E.H. 43, just as the report was being published. [This case has now been taken to the Court of Appeal (1968).]

seven commissioners wish, in return, to limit section 3 to official registered trade unions and to those acting on their behalf, which seems
to mean those "acting in an authorized capacity" for them.[9] Lawyers
will be immediately aware of the problems posed by the "scope of
authority" possessed by, for example, a British shop steward. Furthermore, the majority do not consider the question whether subsequent
"ratification" by a registered union would (as it usually does in law)
"relate back" to the original act and cure its invalidity for the purposes
of section 3. As the minority of five point out (para. 804), this exposure
of nonofficial strike organizers to liability in damages or to injunctions
in tort means that they could be made liable for civil conspiracy (since
section 1 of the Act would not now apply, above, p. 10). Further,
there would be the risk of liability for interfering with commercial
contracts. In effect, therefore, such a proposal would severely curtail
the right to strike of nonunionists and even of union members who
did not enjoy the privilege of being authorized agents of the union.
Moreover, such an amendment would be of serious consequence to the
very fabric of British labor law. The equal protection previously
granted to "any person" who acted in furtherance of a trade dispute
would now be granted only to the functionaries of state-registered associations. The minority commissioners euphemistically remark that
the majority's proposals are "incompatible with the proposals made in
this report for the reform of collective bargaining."

Conclusion

We conclude that the *Donovan Report* proposes developments
broadly in the direction adumbrated by this study, with the exceptions
mainly of its proposals on the giving of reasons for arbitration awards,
and on section 3 of the Act of 1906. The latter is a curiosity against
which we find the minority's arguments overwhelmingly convincing.
The former strangely lacks supporting argumentation in the report,
and was plainly influenced most powerfully by considerations more
germane to incomes policy than to structures of collective bargaining.
The central core of the commission's recommendations are likely to be
more productive. The proposed Industrial Relations Commission, with
its standing committee to review the state of labor law generally, is
the type of organ which might well be planted into the body of British
industrial life without rejection. With its help, reforms in the methods
and structures of collective bargaining, and toward the greater partici-

---

9 Para. 800. The gloss is taken from the Note of Reservation by Lord Tangley
at p. 287, and seems to represent the meaning intended by the majority.

pation of workpeople in decision-making, might well be achieved by the organizations that must make them work in the end, namely the employers and trade unions themselves. In that work, such a commission, together with the new labor tribunals, might offer British lawyers new opportunities to be of assistance. But as the Royal Commission comments:

> The creation of the labour tribunals will inevitably focus on the attention of the legal profession to an increasing extent on questions of labour law. It is desirable that facilities should be provided by the Bar Senate, the Law Society and the universities for the training of lawyers in this subject and for making available to them at least an elementary knowledge of industrial relations. [para. 583]

If more lawyers in Britain were equipped with even that elementary knowledge, one grievance, at least, of those in industry who have dealings with them would have been remedied.

INDEX